Gangs:
A Criminal Justice
Approach

Edited by

J. Mitchell Miller
The University of Tennessee

Jeffrey P. Rush
Jacksonville State University

ACJS Series Editor, Dean J. Champion

Academy of Criminal Justice Sciences
Northern Kentucky University
402 Nunn Hall
Highland Heights, KY 41076

Anderson Publishing Co.
Criminal Justice Division
P.O. Box 1576
Cincinnati, OH 45201-1576

Gangs: A Criminal Justice Approach

ISBN 0-87084-554-3

Library of Congress Catalog Number 95-81325

Gail Eccleston *Editor*   *Managing Editor* Kelly Grondin

Cover photograph credit:
AP/Wide World Photos

Foreword

This volume, edited by Mitch Miller and Jeff Rush, adds a much-needed dimension to the ACJS/Anderson Monograph Series. The rapid escalation of gangs in all major U.S. cities during the past few decades, accompanied by greater technological sophistication and weaponry wielded by gang members in their street warfare with others, has prompted many jurisdictions to re-evaluate their policies relative to gang violence and how gang-related offending should be handled. Commencing in the 1970s, the "get tough" movement has influenced local, state, and federal legislation at both adult and juvenile levels. Currently, laws are being enacted to "beef up" the standards by which juvenile offenders are adjudicated and punished. Indeed, several significant components of the 1994 Crime Bill were directed at street crimes perpetrated by youth gangs.

There is definitely a "gang problem." In Los Angeles, California, for example, there are over 600 gangs. Nearby Long Beach has over 125 gangs. Similar statistics depict gang numbers in other comparable cities. However, it is not always the case that varying *numbers of gangs* in cities or communities translate directly into minor or major gang problems. Many of the smaller cities in the United States have one or two gangs only. There are more than a few examples of communities with one gang where that gang has accounted for most of the criminal activity in any given time interval. Thus, even in one-gang communities, a "gang problem" is recognized as significant in much the same way and to the same degree as Long Beach or Los Angeles might recognize the problems respectively generated by 125 or 600 gangs. The general idea of *gangs*, therefore, is a relevant topic for every person living in communities where one or more gangs exist.

Not all gangs are particularly bad, nor do all of them do bad things. Some gangs exist simply for the purpose of providing companionship. Some groups in some U.S. communities exhibit certain gang characteristics (e.g., they wear certain colors, certain types of clothing, or display certain kinds of insignias), but they may not consider themselves to be gangs in *any* sense. The *Guardian Angels* in New York City, for instance, are a more or less organized group of youths who seek to protect citizens from muggers and also from various gang members who regard pedestrians as targets for victimization. However, we do not ordinarily think of the *Guardian Angels* as a gang.

Regardless of their former conceptualization, today's youth gangs are increasingly typified as crime-oriented and violent. Many gangs in the larger cities are formed along racial or ethnic lines and frequently do battle with one another with sophisticated weaponry. Drive-by shootings are increasingly com-

Intro

monplace, with many innocent victims and non-gang members being killed or seriously wounded in these combative conflicts. The media have done much to give gangs national notoriety and recognition. Simultaneously, law enforcement agencies have devoted greater amounts of time and energy to counter gang offending with different programs and policies. And as mentioned earlier, legislatures and local governmental bodies have initiated ordinances and passed laws to intensify punishments for those belonging to gangs.

Professors Miller and Rush have compiled a wealth of information about gangs. This information explores gang emergence or formation, the persistence element of gangs, and the changing nature of gang activities. Basic questions are raised, such as "Why do gangs form?", "What do gang members derive as benefits from joining gangs?", "Why do gangs persist over time?", and "What are the forces contributing to the transformation of gangs into units with diverse objectives?" Obviously, no one knows the answers to these questions. However, sufficient investigation of gang phenomena has occurred to the extent that we can target particular theories and strategies as more workable than others relative to explaining and reducing gang-related offending.

Mitch Miller and Professor Emeritus Albert Cohen have opened this volume with an informative and insightful piece geared to provide readers with an overview of gang theories and their policy implications. Thus, how gangs are approached and dealt with by various community and law enforcement agencies can be best understood by examining the theories underlying the intervention strategies employed by agency personnel. Mark Hamm follows their introduction with an intriguing chapter that examines the methods whereby youth gangs are studied and explanatory and descriptive data are subsequently derived. Hamm's chapter abounds with direct eyewitness and participant observer accounts of those who are in direct contact with gang members in day-to-day activities. Such enriching information heightens our awareness of the many difficulties and obstacles encountered when attempting to acquire reliable data about gangs.

In their chapter, Thomas Winfree and Larry Mays discuss the significant role that family variables play in influencing gang involvement.

Beth McConnell's chapter highlights gang presence in school settings. More often than not, schools are ideal recruiting mediums for "wanna-be" prospective gang members. All too frequently, young gang members will admit to joining gangs only for self-protection. Once inducted into gangs, most youths must comply with gang rules, which are usually crime-related. McConnell describes recent programs and strategies designed to minimize and ultimately eliminate gang presence in schools. Several interventions are described.

George Knox, the editor of the *Gang Journal*, and his colleagues, Professors Jim Houston, Ed Tromanhauser, Tom McCurrie, and John Laskey, develop the theme of gang migration to account for the spread and persistence of gangs nationally. They describe numerous situational and geographical elements, including gang franchising and gang imperialism, to show the relative ease with which gangs in one part of the country are transplanted to other U.S. regions. They conclude their article with several thoughtful recommendations for law enforcement agencies and others interested in combatting gang proliferation. Jeff Rush's chapter follows Knox et al.'s contribution quite logically, as the matter of police response to gangs is addressed. Gang units in city police departments are described, as well as their functions and general interventionist activities.

In some respects, youth gang activity has been compared with organized crime. This is particularly true of youth gangs that traffic in illegal drugs. Greg Orvis describes the elaborate organizational structure of some of these corporate gangs and how they conduct their illegal business on an international scale. Orvis suggests that organized crime statutes, such as RICO, can be used to prosecute at least some of the more serious gangs associated with high-level drug trafficking.

One major development occurring over the last four decades or so is the formation and persistence of gangs in jails and prisons. Bob Fong, Ron Vogel, and Sal Buentello have contributed a colorful chapter depicting gangs behind prison bars. They describe prison gang slang or jargon and illustrate gang signs and graffiti. They provide readers with the latest figures relative to gang trends in prison settings and the spread of gangs throughout all U.S. prison and penitentiary facilities. They describe the current recruitment practices of prison gangs that are used to attract new members. Finally, they discuss several policy implications of prison gangs and what policies might be used to thwart their influence and persistence.

Finn Esbensen, a noted expert on delinquency and drug use, has written a particularly timely chapter about the adoption of a national gang strategy. This chapter is both novel and significant because it acknowledges the "gang problem" as a national one. Further, it outlines several practical actions that can be implemented by law enforcement and community agencies to counter problems generated and perpetuated by gangs. Esbensen interlaces his chapter with various pitfalls associated with previously suggested national panaceas for nefarious gang activities. Thus, learning about what *not to do* is as important as learning *what might be done* in future years as effective gang intervention and prevention strategies.

Ira Sharkansky follows Esbensen's chapter with a relevant policy analysis of gang violence. Sharkansky's piece revisits how gangs are conceptualized. His retrospective analysis is fitting here, because it reminds us of the array of gang-generated social problems we must face on a daily basis. The policy recommendations he includes are positive actions that can be implemented by more progressive and innovative agencies.

All in all, I believe that this volume is a valuable contribution to the Monograph Series. Particularly now, we need more than knee-jerk reactions of community officials who react only when a gang problem sporadically occurs. The gang-remedy agenda outlined by this volume is strong and consistent throughout the various chapters. An integrated effort with law enforcement and community intervention agencies is mandated to counter a seemingly local, yet national, gang problem. Once this fact is recognized by a significant number of people in the right political places, we will be able to pursue the most effective courses of action to bring under control a currently out-of-control gang problem in the United States. I am very pleased to have this volume in the Monograph Series under my general editorship.

Dean J. Champion
ACJS/Anderson Monograph Series Editor
Minot, ND

Preface

This monograph was developed in response to the observation that existing gang readers inadequately addressed the criminal justice system's treatment of the crime and other social problems presented by gangs. The social science literature on gangs deals with their composition, culture, and diversity, but seldom confronts, beyond general policy recommendation, formal social control efforts. The following collection of original theoretical and empirical works fill this space by speaking to actual enforcement, prosecution, and research issues and strategies. The contributions represent sociological, legal, political science, and criminal justice perspectives that, collectively, stress *response* to increasingly violent and utilitarian gang-related crime.

The volume's distinct criminal justice orientation was made possible by coeditor Jeff Rush. The individual chapter authors' enthusiasm, constructive comments, and professionalism made editing this volume an enjoyable and educational experience. Thanks are due to several people that helped in various ways: Jim Black and Kevin Bryant for reviewing chapters, Richard Wright for sagely advice, Jack Wilson for computer support, and Linda Robinson and Pam Morgan for secretarial support. Senior scholars Albert Cohen and Ira Sharkansky bolstered the overall quality of the volume and their participation is sincerely appreciated. Gail Eccleston from Anderson directed development and minimized much of the anxiety associated with my role of first-time editor. Last, I would especially like to thank Dean Champion, the ACJS/Anderson Series Editor, for providing an opportunity to, and demonstrating confidence in, a junior colleague.

J. Mitchell Miller
Knoxville, Tennessee

Contents

Section I

SOCIAL SCIENCE PERSPECTIVES ON GANGS

1

Gang Theories and their Policy Implications

J. Mitchell Miller
The University of Tennessee—Knoxville

Albert Cohen
University of Connecticut

Despite a well-noted lack of consensus on what constitutes a gang, researchers, the public, and certainly law enforcement personnel have come to perceive certain types of collectives as inherently deviant and socially parasitic (Klein, 1971; Pfohl, 1992). While these attributes almost invariably apply to gangs today, this has not always been the case. As Kornhouser (1978) observes, the term *gang* has not always been coterminous with *delinquent gang*.

Western culture has romanticized both actual and fictional gangs that were often, but not always, criminal or otherwise socially threatening. Fitting examples include Jean Laffite's famous crew of pirates, Robin Hood's group of merrymen, and numerous bands of Wild West outlaws, most notably the Jesse James Gang. Sociological characterizations of gangs are less denigrating and emphasize gang formation: consequences of maturation on childhood play groups (MacLeod, 1987), the solidification of neighborhood social clubs (Hagedorn, 1988; Jankowski, 1991), the escalation of breakdancing competitions to turf consciousness (Taylor, 1990; Moore, 1983) and most recently, the "prosocial gang" (Goldstein, 1995).

The fact that gangs did not always evoke a negative connotation suggests that attitudes toward them have changed over time and, almost without exception, for the worse. This change is not wholly a result of increases in the number or size of gangs nor the extent or seriousness of their delinquency. Rather, varying perceptions and levels of academic interest in gangs have been

3

explained as a result of four interrelated factors: dominant ideology, advances in methodology, the applicability of popular social theory to gang issues, and general sociopolitical conditions (Bookin-Weiner & Horowitz, 1983). While these factors suggest why gangs are likely to be of more or less interest at certain times, the actual gang knowledge base has resulted from the propagation of research from sociology to subdisciplines.

This chapter acknowledges the lead role of theoretical explanations in the scientific study of delinquent gangs and their import in the progression of criminology and the criminal justice sciences. Historical and current trends in gang theorizing and research are discussed through a near-chronologically ordered review of major theories. Beyond review, the implications for social and criminal justice policy are appraised.

THE IMPACT OF GANGS ON
THEORY, RESEARCH, AND POLICY

Theories about gangs and theories that use the gang to address broader social issues have had a tremendous influence beyond their focal topics. Much of theoretical criminology, for example, is actually explication and depiction of delinquent behavior by youth gangs. Subculture, strain, opportunity, and conflict theories of crime and delinquency are supported, to differing bounds, by gang derived data. Some of criminology's central theorem are gleaned from these theories: *delinquency is learned through interaction with others* and *most often occurs in a group context.*

The construction of gang theories has also been consequential to paradigmatic shifts in research methodology. Early attention to gangs helped make ethnography standard science, as researchers prior to the 1970s generally followed the example of fieldwork set by the "Chicago School" (e.g., Shaw, 1930, Shaw & McKay, 1942). Though fundamentally treated as delinquent, youth gangs were also considered primary groups (Cooley, 1909) and unique types of collectives (Asbury, 1927) to be explored firsthand via observational and interview techniques. Such techniques facilitated understanding of the processes of gang development, behavior, and member desistence. Contemporary theories reflect renewed interest in these topics and continuation of a similar field research orientation.

Gang study today is by no means limited to qualitative research designs. Typical limitations of fieldwork, such as gaining access to subject groups (initial entry), researcher bias, and the generalizability of findings, are considered especially acute in the study of gangs (Hamm, 1995; Hagedorn, 1990). These problems are supposedly offset by survey instruments fashioned to gang-related topics (e.g., Morash, 1983; Fagan, 1989; Spergel, 1989; Thornberry, et al., 1993; Esbensen & Huizinga, 1993). Such surveys reflect a renewed interest in previously assessed predictors of gangs and ganging (Topping, 1943; Dumpson, 1949; Glueck & Glueck, 1950; Klein, 1971) and have produced a wealth of new information on the prevalence, composition, and criminality of gangs.

Objections to the application of survey methodologies in gang research center on the value of the data. Erickson's "group hazard hypothesis" (1971), for example, contended official overrepresentation of gang delinquency due to the increased likelihood of arrest for acts committed in a group context. This position has recently been restated and expanded in the "courthouse criminology" debate which doubts the validity of gang knowledge derived from official data sources such as law enforcement and prison questionnaires (Hagedorn, 1990). Is a crime to be considered gang-related only when it occurs in a group context or also when gang members act alone? More fundamentally, how credible are responses by those with a vested interest in minimizing further conflict with authority? The answers to these and similar questions will necessarily affect, and possibly distort, the knowledge base from which theories are formed.

Gang theories have also had remarkable bearing upon criminal justice policy. This is not surprising given that some of the major theories were framed during the 1950s and 1960s in studies sponsored by federal grants specifying social control objectives (Miller, 1974). The theories of this era spoke to what was considered a timely problem of unprecedented proportion: juvenile delinquency. Rebellious youth associated with the emergence of the rock and roll era presented a new, visible threat to authority. In many ways, gangs were the epitome of this threat. Their banding and symbolism made them readily identifiable targets for criminal justice responses. Policing gangs was thus equated with addressing a larger social issue.

One noteworthy and lasting consequence of this application of theory is a tendency to define gangs as socially problematic by means of an enforcement rationale (Spergel & Curry, 1990). Social control is an important theoretical theme detectable throughout the history of gang research. As noted below, however, this perspective was not a forerunner to (nor necessarily of interest) to social scientists who first addressed youth gangs.

EARLY STATEMENTS: SOCIOLOGICAL ORIGINS

The pervasive social control problems presented by gangs have embedded them as primary research foci in criminology and criminal justice science. Gang research in both of these concentrations unquestionably arose out of a sociological tradition. Whereas sociology's impression was evident as early as the 1930s (Asbury, 1927; Thrasher, 1928; Bolitho, 1930; Whyte, 1943), the applied criminological literature overlooked gangs. The 1949 edition of *The Encyclopedia of Criminology* (a standard criminalistic/police science reference), for instance, contained no entry under the heading "gang."

Although sociologists had previously noted that delinquency habitually occurred in group contexts, Thrasher's *The Gang: A Study of 1303 Gangs in Chicago* (1928) is frequently considered to be the catalyst for several ground-breaking theories. He observed that gangs were:

1. interstitial,
2. concentrated in lower class neighborhoods,
3. responsive to a lack of conventional employment opportunities,
4. composed of young males lacking skills to compete for jobs and
5. a process by which delinquents were socialized into adult crime.

Thrasher's innovative conceptualization of *interstitial* merits brief comment. This descriptive term was used plurally in reference to the transitory and peripheral character of gangs who emerged in socially disorganized areas to replace order where there is little, although they seldom lasted more than a few years (Thrasher, 1928:22). The gang was more than a fleeting gathering of similarly circumstanced individuals but less than a permanent organization. Members, then usually immigrants, were only marginally incorporated into broader American culture and were typically between childhood and adulthood. Gang process was interstitial as well, wavering along a continuum from planning to spontaneity. Three decades later, instability was stressed again by the labeling of the youth gang as a "near-group" (Yablonsky, 1959), an idea that remains influential in contemporary explications (Taylor, 1990).

Perhaps what is particularly unique about Thrasher's study is its treatment of why and how gangs form. Whereas many later theories utilized the gang to describe, interpret, and explain delinquency, particularly its distribution in the social order, Thrasher was more directly concerned with identifying causal variables of gang formation. Weak social controls are often considered Thrasher's primary determinant of gang development, but his combined model also incorporated lower-class culture, status frustration, collective behavior, and social ecology.

Recent works cite Thrasher's study as a precursor to diverse theoretical traditions and present striking disagreement concerning his heritage. Hagedorn (1988:55) refers to "Thrasher and the Subculturists" but then curiously proceeds with an explanation of gang formation as a result of social disorganization, as does Kornhouser (1978:21). His legacy is also apparent in learning/subcultural and opportunity/strain-based theories (Merton, 1938; Cohen, 1955; Miller, 1958; Cloward & Ohlin, 1960).

Other early statements addressing gang formation and behavior have received less attention. Furfey (1928) hypothesized that gang cohesiveness was positively correlated with class and confirmed Thrasher's observation that gangs were concentrated in slum areas. Asbury (1927) focused on ethnicity and culture to describe the diversity of gangs in New York as early as the late 1920s. Quite differently, Bolitho (1930) submitted that ganging was a form of psychosis, an issue recently raised in an integrated model fusing "kind of person" and "kind of group" (Thornberry, et al., 1993). Ganging was similarly treated as a vehicle by which sociopaths vented hostility and anger (Yablonsky, 1962; Short & Stodtbeck, 1965). Psychological explanations of ganging are readily dismissed as passé in spite of repeated testimony by gang members that their acts of violence result from "just losing my head," that is, a temporary inability to reason (Currie, 1991).

Street Corner Society (Whyte, 1943) addressed lower-class Italian and Puerto Rican lifestyles and is frequently cited in discussions of gang theory. Its lasting relevance is due to the care afforded the relationship between social forces effecting minorities in depressed urban areas and conventionality rather than delinquent behavior by youth gangs per se. Although the racial and ethnic compositions of gangs have changed over time, they remain an overwhelmingly minority phenomenon (Moore, 1991). As one gang theorist notes: "To be white is to be an outsider to gang members" (Hagedorn, 1990:253).

Tally's Corner, a notable work by Elliot Liebow, appeared in 1967 and further placed gangs in a black and urban context. Gangs had become such a hot topic in academia that Dale Hardman published an article that same year titled "Historical Perspectives on Gang Research." Surprisingly, this sharp rise of interest in gangs was less affected by racial concerns as by an emerging theoretical order accenting the relationship between culture, class, and delinquency.

THE SUBCULTURAL ERA: 1950s AND 1960s

Subcultural theories dominated the study of gangs during the 1950s and 1960s. They stress that some environments are characterized by atypical, criminogenic value and normative systems, making deviant behavior more or less normal for those within the subculture. The subculture has been described in relation to the dominant culture with great clarity:

> A subculture implies that there are value judgements or a social value system which is apart from and a part of a larger or central value system. From the viewpoint of this larger dominant culture, the values of the sub-culture set the latter apart and prevent total integration, occasionally causing open or covert conflicts (Wolfgang & Ferracuti, 1967:99).

The subculture enables, via interaction with the subgroup, individual benefit that may be material, such as profits from drug sales, or psychological benefit through increased self-esteem and social status. These latter intangible advantages foster greater group cohesion and make the differences in value systems of the subculture and the larger society pronounced; the outcome is a we vs. them predicament. Repudiation of some societal standards and norms (particularly ones beneficial to and representative of the dominant order) becomes a defining characteristic of a subculture and necessarily results in cultural conflict (Vetter & Silverman, 1980).

Criminology and criminal justice text authors (e.g., Shoemaker, 1984; Reid, 1990; Lilly, et al., 1989; Martin, et al., 1990) often begin discussion of this theoretical school with *Delinquent Boys: The Culture of the Gang* (Cohen, 1955) wherein a general theory of subcultures is presented through extraction and characterization of the properties of gangs. Observation of the existing literature revealed that boys from the bottom end of the socioeconomic scale shared difficulty in conforming to the dominant society that largely rejected them. This difficulty is partially explained by differing degrees of drive and ambition that affect individual responsibility, but also by social structural constraints largely beyond their control.

Working-class youth experience a socialization process that devalues success in the classroom, deferred pleasure and satisfaction, long-range planning, and the cultivation of etiquette mandatory for survival in business and social arenas. Rather than participate in "wholesome" leisure activity, they opt for activities typified by physical aggression. Overall, the learning experience of lower-class males leaves them ill-prepared to compete in a world gauged by a *middle-class measuring rod* (Cohen, 1955:129). Deficiencies are most noticeable in the classroom, where working-class youth are frequently overshadowed and belittled by their middle-class counterparts. Turning to membership in a delinquent gang is but a normal adaptation to status frustration resulting from clashing cultures.

The emergence of subcultures, then, is an alternative by various persons to their mutual rejection, a collective response to a shared problem. The process by which subcultures form and evolve is one of trial and error, a redefining of accepted norms likened to crowd behavior. While "collective outbursts" as a way of solving problems are usually temporary and soon wane, they often succeed in establishing subcultures that, once created, assume a life of their own. This point has vast implications for social policy and criminal justice strategy and will be further discussed below.

While most reviews of Cohen's cultural deviance theory have been favorable, charges have been levied that inadequate support is presented for what is basically untestable theory (Kitsuse & Dietrick, 1959). In response to this criticism, others have rightly considered the matter to be one of perspective (Martin, et al., 1990). The criticism of verification has merit from a quantitative viewpoint, but Cohen's work is descriptive explanation of the cultural bases of gang delinquency's uneven distribution throughout society.

Whereas a strict chronological listing of subcultural theories would move from Cohen (1955) to Miller (1958), Cloward and Ohlin's (1960) theory of delinquency is naturally paired with Cohen. Their major work, *Delinquency and Opportunity: A Theory of Delinquent Gangs* (1960), also acknowledges the relationship between behavior and status frustration (Merton, 1938).

Cloward and Ohlin further Cohen's hypothesis through a detailed accounting of both subculture emergence and the traits of defiant outgroups via a typology of gangs. Often termed an "opportunity theory" (Bartol, 1980; Shoemaker, 1984; Lilly, et al., 1989), the basic premises are (1) limited and blocked economic aspirations lead to frustration and negative self-esteem, and (2) these frustrations move youth to form gangs that vary in type. In short, lower-class teenagers realize they have little chance for future success through the use of conventional standards and consequently resort to membership in one of three gang types. The ratio of conventional and criminal values to which a juvenile is consistently exposed accounts for the differences in the character of the gangs.

The Cloward-Ohlin gang typology is a hierarchy in terms of the amount of prestige associated with affiliation. At the top is the criminal gang whose activities revolve around stealing. Theft and other deviant acts serve to positively reinforce the mutual co-dependence between the juvenile and the group. Not all have the skills and composure to integrate into criminal gangs, which screen potential members for certain abilities and willingness to conform to a code of values necessary to the unit's success. Mandatory criteria include self-control, solidarity to the group, and desire to cultivate one's criminal ability. Those strained youth who are precluded from gangs that primarily steal congregate around violent behavior such as fighting, arson, and serious vandalism. Termed a "conflict subculture" (Cloward & Ohlin, 1960:171), this type of gang results from an absence of adult role models involved in gainful criminal behavior.

Some youth are neither violent nor successful in criminal endeavors. Having failed in both conventional and multiple deviant sectors of society, they retreat into a third type of gang that is characterized by drug use (Cloward & Ohlin, 1960:183). Members of this relatively unorganized gang resort to drugs as an escape from failure resulting from differential access to both legitimate and illegitimate opportunities, but also deficient familial and community support. A lack of interest by adults in the future success or failure of their sons and other young males in the neighborhood symbolizes rejection, the adaptation to which is "exploration of nonconformist alternatives" (Cloward & Ohlin, 1960:86).

Cloward and Ohlin's opportunity theory has been criticized for its unnatural rigidity (Empey, 1982:250; Lilly, et al., 1989). Delinquents do not choose exclusively between theft, vandalism, or drug use through a conscious affiliation with gang types. Instead, any one of the gang types may, and obviously do, engage in all or some combination of these behaviors (Cummings & Monti, 1993).

Unlike Cohen or Cloward and Ohlin, Walter B. Miller developed a theory that concentrated directly on culture. In an article titled, "Lower Class Culture as a Generating Milieu of Gang Delinquency" (1958), he argued the existence of a distinct and observable lower-class culture. Unlike the middle-class emphasis on conventional values, the lower class has defining *focal concerns* that include (1) trouble, (2) toughness, (3) smartness, (4) excitement, (5) fate, and (6) autonomy.

These concerns foster the formation of street corner gangs while undermining conventional values. "Smartness," for example, is a skill that warrants respect in the lower-class culture. This refers to the ability to con someone in real-life situations, rather than formal knowledge that is relatively inapplicable and even resented in poorer areas. A belief in "fate" discourages the work ethic, undermines prudence, and minimizes hope for self-improvement, all of which encourage risk-taking. "Excitement" rationalizes otherwise senseless acts of gang violence.

"Trouble," however, is perhaps the most defining of the focal concerns: you do not decide whether to do something on the basis of rightness or wrongness (i.e., morality), but rather on the basis of expediency, hassles, and practical consequences. Decisions not to commit certain acts center on whether the commission is likely to get you into trouble.

The theory rests on the supposition that deviance is normal and to be expected in segments of the lower class where culturally specified focal concerns make conformity to criminal behavior as natural as acceptance of conventional mores for the middle class. Juveniles accepting a preponderance of these "practices which comprise essential elements of the total life pattern of lower class culture automatically violate legal norms," typically in a gang setting (Miller, 1958:167).

Critiques have centered around three points. Foremost is the issue of whether the theory is tautological in that subculture is said to cause deviance, but deviance is an attribute of subculture. There is unclear separation of cause and effect (i.e., no real distinction between dependent and independent variables). Also, some of the focal concerns contended to be exclusive to the lower class are observable in the middle class (Shoemaker, 1984). Another issue concerns the use of race rather than class in assessments of the relationship between delinquency, matriarchal households and an exaggerated sense of masculinity exemplified by physical aggression (Berger & Simon, 1974). Focus on minorities and the inseparable issue of atypical family structure, however, moves discussion away from the presence of a lower-class value system to differences in racial groups.

In sum, subcultural explanations were pivotal for theoretical criminology, establishing an explanatory framework for subsequent gang analysis. Youth gangs were so linked with delinquency that in the future they would be considered inherently deviant. Moreover, subculture became a major concept in conservative and centrist ideologies, a convenient comparative device for highlighting normative standards.

AFTER SUBCULTURE

By the 1960s a number of closely related social movements (including the civil rights movement, anti-Vietnam protest, and the counterculture) were under way. In varying degrees they expressed the same themes: distrust and defiance of authority that was perceived to be used by elite factions to create and maintain hierarchy and exploitation of the weak. Criminology was profoundly affected by the spirit of the times. Its attention shifted from the construction of theory and the explanation of crime to opposing the oppressiveness of the criminal justice system.

As bandwagon shifts to the political left transpired, labeling theory replaced subculture as the leading theory (Bookin-Weiner & Horowitz, 1983). The main thrust of labeling theory was that crime and delinquency are definitions and labels that are assigned to persons and events by operatives of the criminal justice system. Explaining crime and delinquency, then, is explaining the way in which the labeling process works, and how it singles out certain people for labeling and not others. In its more extreme formulations, labeling theory was not concerned with the explanation of the behavior we call crime and delinquency because criminals and delinquents were not assumed to differ very much in their behavior from other people. Rather, the real difference is said to be the degree of vulnerability to the labeling activities of the criminal justice system.

During this period of interest in labeling, theoretically oriented research on gangs languished but did not disappear. More moderate versions of labeling theory propelled some research (e.g., research on gang behavior and emphasis on the role of official processing and labeling in the development of that behavior), but the leading cause of crime and delinquency was considered the criminal justice system itself (Werthman, 1967; Werthman & Piliavin, 1967; Armstrong & Wilson, 1973). Specifically, criminal and delinquent behavior was portrayed as responsive to social inequality and class oppression (Bookin, 1980).

Much of the fashionable literature of the period, not only on gangs but on social problems generally, was not only indifferent to subcultural theory but was actively opposed to it. This literature included works such as Chambliss' *The Saints and the Roughnecks* (1973) that emphasized a "conflict" perspective that viewed the subcultural theories as conservative. Social control was deemed reactionary because crime and delinquency were direct, reasonable, and even justifiable adaptations to injustice. Gangs in this view, then, were perceived as victims. Some went so far as to portray them as political revolutionaries (Frye, 1973).

The rise of social control/bonding theory (e.g., Hirschi, 1969) did not accelerate gang research either, though seemingly well-suited to do so (Bookin-Weiner & Horowitz, 1983; Vold & Bernard, 1986). The central elements of attachment to others, degrees of commitment to conventionality, daily routine, and belief in a moral order speak to why gangs exist and have implications for their actions. Ensuing research interests nonetheless moved toward macro-level determinants of crime and further away from culture and group behavior. Consequently, gangs were largely ignored until the mid-1980s when they were seriously connected with drug and violence problems of epidemic proportions (Curry & Spergel, 1988).

THE CURRENT STATE OF GANG THEORY

Just a decade ago, a theoretical commentary on gangs began with the statement: "We have extensive theory development—now dated—and some research" (Spergel, 1984:199). Five years later another theorist concurred: "Less is known about gangs and gang violence today than was known in the 1960s" (Jackson, 1989:313). Neither observation remains true today. In the last decade, social scientists have produced a plethora of theories and findings about youth gangs.

No doubt, much of the attention is a corollary of the war on drugs and associated violence. But academic interest in gangs transcends the U.S. drug problem and is driven, in good part, by the belief that gangs are deeply interwoven with numerous social problems of catastrophic proportions such as institutional racism, unemployment, familial disruption, education and, of course, crime. It is fair to say that gang research has reached an all-time high, evident in part by the 1992 creation of *The Gang Journal*. Indeed, the 1990s mark what is the "second era" of gang research in the social sciences.

Those currently crafting gang theories look to the earlier subcultural era for comparative purposes. Alleged shortcomings of cultural deviance theories, such as those discussed above, often serve as points of departure for establishing alternative theory. A debate has emerged that centers on whether the underlying causes of gang formation and behavior stem from cultural deficiencies or socioeconomic factors. Accordingly, contemporary gang theory is frequently categorized dichotomously: *subculture* vs. *urban underclass*.

URBAN UNDERCLASS

The urban underclass is contended to be an emerging, but already fixed, social class beneath the traditional lower class. This new class is predominately composed of minority urbanites negatively affected by economic and residential trends. Underclass theorists note that the shift from a manufacturing to a service industry, industrial exodus outside of the United States, and the effects of suburbanization ("white flight" and its impact on neighborhood tax bases) have concentrated and disadvantaged poorly educated minorities, especially Blacks, in areas increasingly deprived of employment opportunities. Unlike the traditional lower class that is occupationally marginalized (i.e., locked into unattractive wage labor), the underclass is outside of the conventional economic arena altogether (Kasarda, 1985; Wilson, 1987). For many in the inner cities, employment is neither available nor accessible.

Underclass theorists recognize that a distinct subculture has emerged that disrupts family and community controls and promotes a "getting paid" philosophy based upon quick income via the hustle (Sullivan, 1989). This attitude, however, is presented as an attribute of social inequality rather than a culturally specified correlate of various social problems, including gangs. The activities of gangs, as Hagan observes:

> are not intergenerationally transmitted expressions of cultural preferences, but rather cultural adaptations to restricted opportunities for the redistribution of wealth. Put another way, these youth have substituted investment in subcultures of youth crime and delinquency for involvement in a dominant culture that makes limited structural or cultural investment in their futures (1993:328).

Gangs and their involvement in utilitarian crime (theft and drugs) are viewed from the underclass position, then, as a natural response to the harsh influence of street life created by structural divestment. Divestment limits positive cultural and social opportunities and is interrelated with various social problems, particularly the quality of education and subsequent employment opportunities. Underemployment and unpreparedness for employment explain changes in gang composition from delinquent youth groups to quasi-criminal organizations. Unlike previous eras when most delinquents matured out of youth crime into legitimate employment, present-day "gangbangers" are comparatively much older (Horowitz, 1983; Spergel, 1984). Increasing adult participation contributes to portrayals of gangs as American enterprises and an institutionalized facet of urban minority life (Padilla, 1992).

The causal relation between the underclass and gangs is widely accepted today in sociological criminology (MacLeod, 1987; Moore, 1988; 1991; Hagedorn, 1988; 1990; Vigil, 1988; Sullivan, 1990; Hagan, 1993; Anderson, 1990; Padilla, 1992; Cummings & Monti, 1993). It is now accurate to view the underclass perspective as the dominant paradigm guiding gang research, but it has problems that become apparent in its policy agenda.

POLICY IMPLICATIONS OF GANG THEORY

There is a general reluctance on the part of social scientists to address the shortcomings of underclass and similar social philosophies. This reluctance stems from the proliferation of cultural diversity objectives throughout academia generally and the social sciences in particular. There is a tendency to avoid defining and analyzing gangs and similar social problems in a manner that may be labeled racial (and especially racist), even in light of well-documented racial or ethnic realities (Cummings & Monti, 1993). As Miller (1990:277) observes:

> The social context of gang life and the social characteristics of most gang members entail a set of extremely sensitive issues involving social class and ethnicity that are highly charged in U.S. society, and evoke strong passions.

Neglect of the influence of race consequently shifts attention to class, nowhere more apparent than in underclass models that rationalize crime within ethnic subcultures as an attribute or expression of inequality. The subcultural position, however, also focuses on class rather than race, as prominent underclass theorists have observed (Wilson, 1985; Hagedorn, 1988). Portrayals of subcultural theory as conservative or racist, while simply not true, augment the underclass approach that is more sympathetic to current liberal ideology. Because social inequality is believed to generate ganging, implications for policy are to alleviate blocked economic opportunities and conditions of institutional racism. Despite much rhetoric of addressing root causes and energizing economic opportunity via diversification, the prescription remains continuation of social welfare programs. If subcultural theory is correct and history any indicator, such a strategy will not work.

Social and fiscal resources were previously spent on lower-class problems during the 1960s in the "War on Poverty" but met with little success. Liberals presently bemoan the lack of government resources channeled toward the gang problem despite substantial social and economic investment in "Head Start," gang intervention and like youth service programs. Though problematic, numerous private sector agencies also service a gang clientele. An examination of 60 such programs well evidence that "the nation's failure to remedy its gang problems is not attributable to lack of effort" (Miller, 1990:267). Failed attempts to remedy or even allay social inequality as a means of addressing the U.S. gang problem, then, are not entirely a result of too few nor unequal distribution of resources.

Clearly, the totality of these efforts, public and private, are akin to shooting an elephant with a slingshot, but it is also logical to expect some return on gang problem investments. Instead of realizing even a modicum of improvement, the reverse appears to be the case. In inner-city areas where social programs for the disadvantaged or underprivileged are centralized, gang-related problems of drugs and violence have not tempered but continue to spiral.

The debate over the determinants of why we have gangs may be an ambiguous point in regard to whether gang policy will be social support or control oriented. Almost four decades ago, it was submitted that a subculture will become self-perpetuating once created (Cohen, 1955). Likewise, we were warned that eliminating poverty will not necessarily reduce lower-class delinquency (Miller, 1958).

Today, there is still a cultural reality that both passively undermines and actively overrides would-be answers. Moreover, the contemporary lower class is not so much a new social class as a pronounced and visible facet of the traditional lower class. The same focal concerns of excitement, toughness, and smartness identified by Miller in the 1950s have not disappeared. Rather, these subcultural components remain apparent today in much intensified forms, collectively constituting what is popularly labeled *gang culture*.

Due to the mass media (e.g., "YO! MTV RAPS!"), gang culture is promoted within and projected outside of the neighborhoods where gangs exist. This culture carries a message to American minority youth that gangs are *the* means for financial success, sex appeal, respect, and ethnic expression. A corresponding "Cop Killer" recording and beat-the-system mentality is too readily accepted and provides the conflict with authorities necessary for gang solidification. There can be little doubt that not only does lower-class culture persist, it has escalated in new ways that promote crime.

Other facts also make the underclass position suspect. The absence of gangs in many impoverished minority areas suggests that something other than deprivation is responsible for their existence. The fact that gangs constitute but a fraction of gang-age, lower-strata, inner-city residents also raises questions and exposes the variable force of inequality.

CONCLUSION

Theoretical explanations of gangs address the reasons they form and why they tend to be delinquent and criminal. Each of the major perspectives marks a different approach for gang policy. One thing is sure—gangs present a social policy conundrum and the consequences for criminal justice strategy are painfully unclear. A cultural approach lends credence to control initiatives now necessary in many urban areas, but policing gangs can be counterproductive. Proactive enforcement strategies too often provide the conflict necessary to unify and perpetuate gangs.

Subcultural theories are typically characterized by sociological criminologists as ideological reinforcement for selective law enforcement, in this case, the targeting of minority youth. Because the culture of gangs today clearly encourages crime, there is little doubt that police key on symbols, signals, and other visible indicators of gang activity. However, this is a matter of police responding to a problem where it is most apparent and not necessarily a reflection of a polarized ideological position wherein cultural awareness is a means to biased ends. After all, in the 1950s subcultural theory called attention to the very social issues which its critics now champion. Gangs and delinquency were then perceived as manifestations of broader social problems that might be remedied through various social, not enforcement, programs.

Theoretical work on gangs, and the policy recommendations that will follow, need not continue in this paradigmatic civil war. It is unwise to do so, for cultural and underclass theories are not as diametrically opposed as many would have us believe. Rather, they are partial truths, each incorporating the other's fundamental concepts (Horowitz, 1990:42; Lo, 1991). Cultural deviance theories, for example, near rest upon socioeconomic determinants of culture. Yet, injecting economic relief may only fortify rather than change aspects of the gang culture. The popular gang theory dichotomy should thus be discarded for it is a false taxonomy.

A more productive alternative remains elusive, and as many of the chapters in this volume indicate, bolstered enforcement efforts seem to be the preferred response. Given the present political agenda and power of the "new right," it seems inevitable that social programs will be drastically reduced, if not abolished, in the near future. It therefore becomes the role of theory to not only explain the presence and composition of gangs, but to also critically confront the effects sure to result from escalated enforcement.

2

Doing Gang Research in the 1990s: Pedagogical Implications of the Literature

Mark S. Hamm
Indiana State University

Social images of gangs abound in our world today. From the "white heat" of movies and television to the emotional volatility of militant rap music, urban gangs are portrayed as more violent now than ever before in the American experience. Ambitious politicians from all points on the political spectrum have decried the upsurge in gang violence; and in the wake of the Los Angeles riots of 1992, some politicians have predicted that gangs have the potential to become the major social problem facing urban America in the next century.

Not surprisingly, university courses exploring gang violence seem to attract more students of criminology and criminal justice than almost any other subject. This chapter explores—in desperate brevity—the pedagogical implications of American gang literature. The product is intended to serve as a primer that may be used by educators to introduce their students to the complexities of doing gang research in the 1990s.

GAINING ACCESS

The most important step in conducting gang research is the development of a pool of subjects. This demands that researchers overcome two major obstacles: paranoia and violence.

By its very nature, social science research creates conditions that can put gang members at risk for both arrest by police, and retaliation from other members of the gang. Thus, researchers—whose goal is to expose the individual and organizational features of gangs—are potentially seen as threats to the gang in general, and to its members in specific. Because the researcher is an intruder into the gang, members are likely to be paranoid about participating in any study. In turn, this paranoia can lead to violence against the researcher. Over the years, criminologists have relied on four primary strategies for entering the inner circle of American street gangs. Each has attempted, with varying degrees of success, to avoid the problems of paranoia and violence. I begin with the most traditional method.

PARTICIPANT OBSERVATION

Historically, scholars have entered gangs through the method of participant observation (also referred to as the field study approach or sociological ethnography). This technique has been preferred because of its ability to bring the researcher face to face with their subjects. Through this face-to-face interaction, researchers are afforded sensitizing and inductive methods for understanding the individual and organizational features of gangs.

In its most recent manifestation, participant observation is exemplified in the research of Martin Sanchez Jankowski (1991)—a work heralded by veteran gang researcher Ruth Horowitz in the liner notes to Jankowski's Islands in the Street, as "important and elegant . . . this will be the book on gangs for the next ten years, if not longer."

Jankowski offers a rare comparative study of 37 gangs from Los Angeles (n=13 gangs), New York City (n=20), and Boston (n=4), conducted over a 10-year period of intensive participant observation (1978-1988). The author successfully entered Irish gangs and African-American gangs; Puerto Rican gangs and gangs of Chicanos, Dominicans, Jamacians, and Central Americans. Jankowski conducted interviews with more than 1,000 gang members, and observed more than 5,000 acts of violence committed by them. He also provides extensive eyewitness accounts of gang beatings, stabbings, and drive-by shootings. To gain access to these gangs, Jankowski was required—first and foremost—to undergo a test of courage. He writes that:

> [In] all of the gangs . . . [t]his test had to do with determining how tough I was. While there were variations in exactly how the test was administered, it involved a number of members starting a fight with me. This was done to see how good a fighter I was and to see if I had "heart" (courage) . . . . The fact that I had training in karate did not eliminate the anxiety that such situations create, but it did help to reduce it. Although the tests often left bruises, I was

never seriously hurt. Quite remarkably, in the more than ten years during which I conducted this research, I was only seriously injured twice (1991:12).

In sum, Jankowski entered the inner circle of 37 violent gangs and recieved a physical beating each time he did. Once he endured this brutal rite of passage, Jankowski went on to commit gang violence himself—which resulted in two serious injuries.

> I participated in nearly all the things they did. I ate where they ate, I slept where they slept, I stayed with their families, I traveled where they went, and in certain situations where I could not remain neutral, I fought with them (Jankowski, 1991:13).

This study carries two overarching pedagogical implications for those of us who teach the criminology of gang research in the 1990s. First, in addition to teaching theory and research methods, we must begin to educate and train our students in the martial arts. The skill of self defense, it seems, is now a prerequisite for entering violent youth collectives. Second, because researchers themselves are often required to commit gang violence, students must be educated in the morality of vengeanace—which makes interpersonal aggression justifiable in those situations where researchers cannot remain neutral. Learning this morality of violence is now just as important to doing gang research as the lessons of Sutherland and Cressey, Hirschi, Quinney, and Campbell and Stanley. Alas, the pedagogical implications of "the book" on American gangs are quite grim.

The Purists

Jankowski's experiences are highly unique to the tradition of participant observation research. In fact, never before in the entire corpus of American gang literature has a researcher documented so many personal experiences with violence. This can be explained by the researcher's introduction to the various gangs. In each of the 37 gangs studied, Jankowski relied on the assistance of community leaders, social workers, and/or clergy to make his initial contact with gang members—any gang member.

First impressions, according to a vast body of social psychology, are profoundly important. The first impressions made by Jankowski—especially among the hundreds of gang underlings he met—marked him as being associated with a system of gang control (see Klein, 1971 for a concise discussion of this problem). This wavering from the purity of participant observation research led to Jankowski's tests of courage—which resulted in his 37 beatings and two serious injuries. Jankowski's rationale for using social control agents was that they were instrumental in gaining access. "[H]aving decided what gangs to study," he argues, "one does not simply show up on their streetcorners and say, 'I am a professor and I want to study you.' This would be naive and quite dangerous." (1991:9)

Yet, this was precisely the method used for gaining access to gangs in such participant observation classics as William J. Chambliss' (1973) *The Saints and the Roughnecks,* R. Lincoln Keiser's (1969) *The Vice Lords,* Walter Miller's (1958) *Lower Class Culture as a Generating Milieu of Gang Delinquency,* Irving Spergel's (1964) *Racketville, Slumtown, Haulburg,* and William Foote Whyte's (1943) *Street Corner Society.* Participant observation was probably used by Fredric M. Thrasher (1927/1963) in his historic work, *The Gang* (see Short, 1963:viii). It was also the method used in more recent criminological studies of collective violence such as Adler's (1985) analysis of cocaine smugglers in Northern California, Campbell's (1987) study of Puerto Rican gangs in New York City's South Bronx, Hamm's (1993) analysis of violence among American neo-Nazi skinhead youth, Horowitz's (1983) exposé on a Chicano gang in Chicago, Mieczkowski's (1986, 1988) studies of African-American heroin and crack cocaine dealers (drug crews) in Detroit, and Vigil's (1988) research on the barrio gangs of East Los Angeles.

In these studies, researchers have entered the field as criminology natives unaffiliated with agents of social control. They presented themselves alone; as impartial social scientists with a purely academic interest in the lives and behaviors of individual gang members. Often, these researchers have focused on gang leaders, assuming that leaders will display the highest rates and severity of violence. Based on face-to-face interaction and interpersonal trust, researchers have convinced gang leaders that they had nothing to fear. In this way, the purists removed the dual threats of paranoia and violence. And through their honesty, they displayed courage.

For example, Chambliss (1973) simply approached the leaders of the Saints and the Roughnecks outside a Seattle pizza parlor. Working independent of community agencies, social workers, or the clergy, Chambliss established trust with his subjects and went on to observe numerous acts of violence perpetrated by the Saints over a two-year period. Because of the trust established with his subjects (by working alone and first introducing himself to gang leaders), Chambliss never once had to defend himself. And, to be sure, Chambliss never engaged in gang violence.

Perhaps more instructive is Horowitz's (1983) research on a Chicano gang called the Lions. "Readers may wonder," she asks in the Introduction to *Honor and the American Dream,* "how a woman could possibly have joined gang members as they loitered on street corners and around park benches and developed relationships that allowed her to gather sufficient and reliable data" (1983:6). After all, she laments, "I am Jewish, educated, small, fairly dark, a woman, dressed slightly sloppily but not too sloppily, and only a few years older than most of those I observed" (1983:6). Horowitz solved this research dilemma by entering the gang "without local sponsorhip" (1983:7). She simply walked into a poverty-stricken area of South Chicago, by herself, and took a seat on a bench in a park where Chicano gangs were known to congregate. Horowitz sat on this park bench—alone, from noon until midnight, for three days straight. Then,

> On the third afternoon of sitting on the bench, as I dropped a softball that had rolled toward me, a young man came over and said, "You can't catch" (which I acknowl-edged) and "You're not from the hood (neighborhood), are you?" This was a statement, not a question. He was Gilberto, the Lions' president. When I told him I wanted to write a book on Chicano youth, he said I should meet the other young men and took me over to shake hands with eight members of the Lions (1983:7).

So began Horowitz's three-year study of the Lions, during which time she observed numerous fights involving clubs, baseball bats, chains, bricks, and guns. Horowitz describes the precipitating phases of a gang war and the build up of a veritable arsenal of shotguns and pistols. She observed it all from her park bench. Horowitz was never injured by the Lions or any rival gang member. Indeed, she was often protected by the Lions who, over the course of the study, came to see her as a friend. Her favorable first impression had allowed Horowitz to enter the Lions peacefully. This allowed her to follow the gang and make observations. And this experience allowed Horowitz to formulate her provacative sociological treatise on gang violence.

The pedagogical implications of the purist approach are these: Students—especially women—must be taught how to walk into depressed and dilapidated urban areas alone, demonstrating no fear whatsoever, where they must hunt down and introduce themselves to gang leaders and negotiate interviews with leaders and their gang underlings. This implication is important and must be stated as clearly as possible: Always go to gang leaders first, and never go to a gang underling first. In short, students must be taught courage. Not courage through karate as suggested by Jankowski, but courage through honesty which has proven to be effective in controlling paranoia and violence by Chambliss, Horowitz and a legion of gang scholars dating back to the Chicago School of the 1920s. Courage overcomes fear, and fear is the wellspring of all violence. The following quote, given to Jankowski by a gang member after he had sav-agely beaten an innocent bystander, describes eloquently the importance of overcoming fear when doing gang research in the 1990s.

Shit, I don't know, the guy just pissed me off. Did you see how he was walking down the street scared as a motherfucker? He was just tiptoeing along worried somebody was going to mess with him. He showed no guts. Shit all sorts of people, including me, go to neighborhoods they don't know and where something might happen to them, but they walk with balls, not like this guy. This guy disgusted me, so I blasted him (1991:156).

COMMUNITY AGENCY FIELD STUDIES

Other researchers have collaborated with gang members, former gang members, and/or university graduate students to enter gangs under the auspices of community agencies. Through this collaborative effort, researchers have protected themselves from paranoia and violence by handing these pressures over to those gang members, former members, and/or students who were in their employ. However, these arrangements have always had a significant affect on the research process itself. As a result, studies conducted in the community agency field study tradition have never documented the extreme levels of gang violence found in participant observation research (e.g., Hamm, 1993; Jankowski, 1991; Vigil, 1988).

The community agency field study approach began with the work of Lewis Yablonsky (1962/1983) who—according to one textbook—"made an important contribution to the understanding of gang behavior" (Siegel and Senna, 1981:255). During the late 1950s, Yablonsky was appointed by a government-funded community agency to develop and direct a New York City gang prevention program on the upper West Side of Manhattan called "Morningside Heights, Inc." Yablonsky lived and worked in the area and gang members would "often hang out" at his office and occassionally visit his home (1983:xi).

Yablonsky's contribution to gang research was built on 51 gang members' responses to 16 open-ended questions related to the structure and behavior of one Morningside Heights, Inc. gang called the Balkans. The Balkans were a group of Puerto Rican youths responsible for an unspecified number of homicides, assaults, robberies, burglaries, and drug addictions. Yablonsky called them The Violent Gang.

Yet unlike those gang researchers working in the participant-observation tradition, Yablonsky did not conduct his interviews in a face-to-face fashion. Instead, he used his influence as the director of Morningside Heights, Inc. and offered two Balkan leaders—named Duke and Pedro—$10 apiece for each completed questionnaire they administered to their gang underlings. This was an unprecedented strategy for entering a gang. Gang leaders were now themselves employees of the research project, and their behaviors were viewed as legitimate (see Bookin-Weiner & Horowitz, 1983 for a splendid account of this important shift in American gang research).

Duke and Pedro's method of administering the questionnaire was also unprecedented. Unlike the purists who invoked honesty and interpersonal trust in their collection of interview data, Yablonsky trained Duke and Pedro to use coercion and intimidation to administer his survey. "Their approach," recalled Yablonsky, "seemed to vary between a polite request for information at one extreme and a threatening 'You fill it out 'cause I say so' interview at the other" (1983:103). In essence, Yablonsky recognized Duke and Pedro's coercive authority within the Balkans, and he began to train them in methods of data collection through the threat of violence. The following role-playing account is taken from Yablonsky's training sessions with Duke wherein Yablonsky plays the role of the recalcitrant subject.

> YABLONSKY: (referring to the questionnaire): Well, what's that for?
>
> DUKE: A guy I know is writing a book on gangs and I'm doing it for him.
>
> YABLONSKY: No, man. I don't know whether I want to do that, 'cause it's liable to get in the papers or liable to get to the cops or something like that.
>
> DUKE: I'm not giving it to the cops or anybody else; this is just for this guy.
>
> YABLONSKY: How do you know he isn't a cop?
>
> DUKE: Well, you know me—I wouldn't give it to the cops.
>
> YABLONSKY: Yeah, but I can't be sure.
>
> DUKE: Just don't bullshit me; just fill it out (getting angry) (Yablonsky, 1983:103-104).

Yablonsky found that "Duke's interview technique was 'forceful,' he had a talent for getting information" (1983:104). Indeed he did. Within three weeks, Duke and Pedro conducted a total of 51 interviews for Yablonsky, and they were rewarded $510 for their efforts. (In 1993 prices, this reward would equal about $1,500.) Thus, Yablonsky remained safe from the threats of paranoia and violence by handing these pressures over to Duke and Pedro for a handsome price. Yet Duke and Pedro would ultimately pay for their participation in gang research.

> The gang-boy respondents had mixed reactions to Duke and Pedro as researchers. Some . . . felt they were stoolies working for the cops, and some non-Balkans reacted with overt hostility. On one occassion, Duke arrived at my office,

displaying some . . . fresh lacerations on his face, and claimed he had been beaten and robbed of 10 filled-out questionnaires by six unidentified Negroes in central Harlem (Yablonsky, 1983:103).

The Managers

Despite the ethical ramifications of bringing harm to the subjects of social science research (Babbie, 1992), Yablonsky's techniques have been duplicated by others. Most notable is the often-cited work of Joan Moore (1978) who founded a community-based research project that utilized a combination of former East Los Angeles gang members (known as pintos, or ex-convicts) and graduate students. Like the research of Yablonsky, Moore's collaboration was funded by outside sources (the National Science Foundation and the National Institute of Drug Abuse). And also like Yablonsky, her collaboration produced a litany of problems. In the Introduction to *Homeboys*, Moore regrets that her research staff "shared collective traumas and most of us went through individual crises in connection with the work" (1978:x).

These problems all arose from paranoia. But not paranoia between the researcher and the gang member (indeed, there is no evidence that Moore actually met an active gang member herself)—but between the pintos and the academic students who comprised the research team. According to Moore, the pintos feared negative stereotyping from students, and students feared that pintos could not "identify with contributing to knowledge as a goal" (1978:184). The pintos feared manipulation on the part of students, and vice-versa. Pintos mistrusted students and students were fearful and contemptuous of the pintos' capacity to engage in illegal behavior (e.g., shooting heroin). Both groups distrusted the long-range goals of the research. And, most important, Moore's research organization was brought to its knees by the problem of gossip.

> Rumors about criminal activity are a great and obvious hazard to a pinto project . . . . In an atmosphere of mixed conceptions of normality, gossip is dangerous. The academic people suffered from rumors among fellow academics about neurotic motivations. . . . The pinto staff was accused of selling out to the establishment for personal profit. The charges were always accompanied by negative implications. [The] gossip implied that both the pinto and the academic staff were using each other for unspeakable reasons (Moore, 1978:185-186).

The cumulative effect of this was a total transformation of the research project. "The experiment was stressful," Moore concluded, "—so much so that one major element, most of the graduate student assistants, became alienated and withdrew" (1978:187). This resulted in a major modification of the research goals. Originally designed as a survey-driven study of the individual and organizational charcateristics of modern barrio gangs, Moore's research now turned toward an oral history and conceptualizing approach emphasizing the socialization of Chicano males. Accordingly, no new data were generated on the proclivity of urban gangs to engage in violence. The scholastic energy to understand such complex phenomena had been consumed by an inept bureaucracy.

During the mid-1980s, Moore and John M. Hagedorn—a Milwaukee gang prevention specialist and community activist—became co-principal investigators of the "Milwaukee Gang Research Project" funded by a small grant from a private organization called the Milwaukee Foundation. This collaboration led to the publication of Hagedorn's (1988) *People and Folks*—"the most insightful book ever written on inner-city gangs," according to William Julius Wilson's liner notes to the work. Although Hagedorn (1988:25) recognized that "Moore's collaborative research became the methodological starting point" for his study, Hagedorn made four important modifications to the community agency field study approach.

Hagedorn's Contribution. First, Hagedorn adopted a stripped-down version of the "collaborative model" that proved to be so troublesome in East Los Angeles. Gone were the numerous graduate students and ex-convicts. Instead, Hagedorn chose to work with only one former gang leader and ex-prisoner, named Perry Macon. Second, Hagedorn focused specifically on 47 founding street gang members. "Those interviewed were the 'top dogs' of Milwaukee's gangs," he wrote, ". . . [and] We paid twenty dollars for each interview" (1988:32). Third, Hagedorn conducted most of the 47 interviews himself. He conducted these interviews in his home or at his office at the University of Milwaukee research center which housed his project. Macon's job was to recruit former top dogs off the streets and deliver them to Hagedorn for interviewing. Finally, rather than asking gang members to fill out questionnaires on their attitudes and behaviors, Hagedorn's subjects spoke into a tape recorder.

Hagedorn's methods contributed significantly to the commmunity agency field study tradition because they brought the researcher back to his historical roots where he was provided inductive and sensitizing methods for understanding gangs. By eliminating bureaucracy, Hagedorn came face to face with his subjects and developed rich insights into the social dynamics that lead young people to join urban gangs in the first place. But unlike the participant-observation researchers, Hagedorn discovered that violence played only small role in Milwaukee gangs. He concluded that:

> All gangs we studied in Milwaukee were "fighting gangs,"
> but the fighting period was generally when the gang mem-
> bers were "juniors" or in their early teens. As the gang
> matured, their interests turned to fundamental problems of
> survival (Hagedorn, 1988:100).

Now, there may be four interrelated reasons why Hagedorn discovered low
levels of violence among Milwaukee gangs.

1. The majority of Hagedorn's subjects were gang founders who had
   subsequently left their gangs. Hence, Hagedorn's subjects may
   have held negative attitudes about gangs. If so, they may have
   underreported what they could remember about violence back in
   the days when they were the top dogs.

2. The role of the intermediary (Macon) may have influenced the
   selection of subjects brought before Hagedorn for interviewing.

3. Hagedorn's use of an electronic recording device may have
   affected subjects' responses.

4. Hagedorn may not have asked the right questions. Of the 124
   questions used in the interviews, only three related to violence.
   Hagedorn made no attempt to study the effects of social processes
   (e.g., gun ownership, alcohol and drug use, ideology, religion, and
   contemporary music) on the incidence of gang violence.

Thus, the pedagogical implications of the community agency field study
approach are complicated. Yablonsky's (1983) research suggests that we begin
to train our students in the art of persuasion, so that students may one day
train gang leaders to coerce and intimidate gang underlyings into filling out
questionnaires. Moore's (1978) research suggests that the managerial complications of community agency field study approach are so overwhelming that
they deform the very process of social science itself. Therefore, students
should be taught a healthy skepticism of the community agency field study tradition. Yet Hagedorn (1988) shows that a community researcher can effectively
overcome the obstacles of paranoia and violence by working with a single former gang member, and by studying only former gang leaders in a face-to-face
exchange. And if students follow his procedures, Hagedorn's work indicates
that students will almost never witness an act of gang violence.

DETACHED CASEWORKER STUDIES

Levine (1972:132) argues that "deductive reasoning can prove nothing."
By this, Levine implies that at least something may be learned from inductive

reasoning. The most reliable source of information on gang violence is the observed behavior of, and testimony of, gang members themselves. This observed behavior and testimony served as the intellectual grist for gang scholars working in the participant-observation tradition. From specific instances of violence, the participant-observation researchers looked "outward" in search of general theoretical principles to explain their observational and interview data. This is the essence of inductive reasoning. Other researchers have worked from a deductive model: They began with a general theory of gang violence, and then went in search of specific gangs to confirm their theoretical expectations. However, consistent with the community agency field study approach (e.g., Hagedorn, 1988; Moore, 1978), these researchers have provided little meaningful knowledge on gang violence.

The Corporate Executives

Another community-oriented technique for entering gangs has been survey research conducted in conjunction with social workers. This technique began with the research of James F. Short and Fred L. Strodtbeck (1965)—a work which many consider the high-water mark of empirical analysis on American street gangs (e.g., Gottfredson & Hirschi, 1990; Spergel, 1990; Wilson & Herrnstein, 1985).

In their pathbreaking study, Group Process and Gang Delinquency, Short and Strodtbeck examined 38 Chicago street gangs through what they called "detached caseworkers" affiliated with the City's YMCA. The detached caseworkers spent most of their time with gang members; gaining their trust, steering them away from delinquency, and encouraging participation in more conventional activities—such as playing basketball. Relying on a five-year grant from the National Institute of Mental Health (1959-1962), Short and Strodtbeck were the employers of these detached caseworkers. The researchers directed their employees to fill out an extensive questionnaire on each gang members' norms, values, and self-reported acts of delinquency and violence.

Essentially, they found nothing. But this is not the message transmitted in textbooks. Orcott, for instance, describes Short and Strodtbeck's gang theory as being capable of "explaining consistent and revealing patterns of social interaction leading to violence" (1983:171). Yet after two years of interviewing (1959-1961), Short and Strodtbeck's detached caseworkers produced a total of 598 completed questionnaires that failed to identify a single delinquent gang member in the entire City of Chicago. This happened despite the fact that the Chicago street gangs accounted for 25 percent of all teenage homicides during the late 1950s (see Spergel, 1990). The authors fully acknowledge this severe limitation of their research with the following caveat.

> The failure to locate a full-blown criminal group, or more
> than one drug-using group, despite our highly motivated

> effort to do so, is a "finding" of some importance, for it
> casts doubt on the generality of these phenomena, if not on
> their existence (Short & Strodtbeck, 1965:13).

In other words, the subjects in Short and Strodtbeck's historic research were not violent at all. Hence, there can be no "consistent and revealing patterns of social interaction that leads to violence" among youths who have never engaged in violence to begin with. At bottom, Short and Strodtbeck were left with exhaustive survey data on nearly 600 youngsters who were guilty of nothing more than horseplay. "We were led in the end," they write, "to seek groups not primarily oriented around fighting, but with extensive involvement in the pursuit of 'kicks'" (1965:13).

The pedagogical implications of Short and Strodtbeck's research are these. First, students must be taught skills in grant writing and management. They must aspire to become corporate executives of large-scale research projects dedicated to understanding the pursuit of kicks. Because the detached caseworker approach consistently fails to discover delinquency and violence—and because the researcher never actually comes into contact with gang members—lessons in courage are irrelevant. Second, skills in corporate executive management are of utmost importance in today's marketplace of ideas on doing gang research. Currently, nearly every federal agency concerned with research on gangs assumes the efficacy of the detached caseworker approach and consequently limits research outside this tradition on the grounds that alternative methods are less likely to produce results of policy significance (see U.S. Department of Justice, 1992).

The Mathematical Olympian. This trend is exemplified by the federally funded research of Jeffrey Fagan (1989, 1990; see also Wilson, 1990). Like the YMCA research of Short and Strodtbeck, Fagan recruited his subjects through gang prevention programs sponsored by social service agencies, neighborhood advocacy groups, and community centers in Los Angeles, San Diego, and Chicago. Fagan called this group of gang prevention specialists "intermediaries." The intermediaries, who lived and worked in the field, persuaded active gang members to come to neighborhood community centers, where gang members were asked to fill out questionnaires by yet another group of "proctors" (community center employees) who were also part of the research team. On completion of their questionnaires, gang members were rewarded T-shirts, baseball caps, and music cassettes. Across three cities, this entire operation (i.e., prices paid to intermediaries, proctors, and gang members) was funded by Fagan's grant from the National Institute of Justice.

This research enterprise led to 151 usable questionnaires on gang organization and behavior. Fagan's sample, therefore, provided enough statistical power to establish grounds for quantitative criminology. Through an unprecedented display of complex statistical proofs, Fagan made two discoveries about the nature of violent gangs in America today: (1) the organizational structures of gangs facilitates violence, and (2) gang violence is usually presaged by drug use and/or drug dealing.

Fagan's study was successful because it was safe. While gang members were encouraged and rewarded for participating in the study, Fagan did not come in contact with his subjects. Thus he was spared the threats of paranoia and violence. Ultimately, however, Fagan's research was also affected by the detached caseworker approach. While Fagan discovered a uniform prevalence of violence among his subjects, he also found variance in the incidence of violence. Fagan notes that:

> Differences were evident . . . Los Angeles gang members in this study underreported gang involvement in violence. Their responses may reflect the complex role of the intermediary group with gangs (1989:652).

The pedagogical implications of Fagan's research are as follows. To do gang research in the 1990s, it is first of all necessary to be the proprietor of a large government grant. This grant will provide resources to overcome paranoia and violence by removing the researcher from his or her subjects, and by rewarding research staffs and gang members for participating in the study. Second, students must be taught to manage large and complex statistical files on high-speed mainframe computers. And third, students must be taught this: The detached caseworker approach will automatically introduce error variance into statistical predictions of gang violence whenever it is computed.

PRISON FIELD STUDIES

Perhaps the most untapped sources of information about gangs are the *post hoc* recollections of former gang members who are now incarcerated in prison. In the prison field study approach, the researcher conducts interviews with incarcerated former gang members who have been identified by correctional officials. Therefore, the researcher has a steady pool of subjects and the safety of a nearby prison guard who is trained to eliminate paranoia and violence. This arrangement places the researcher face-to-face with subjects, and it places subjects in less danger than if they were being interviewed in the community while at large for a violent crime (see Polsky, 1967).

This emerging strain of gang research is represented in the work of Skolnick (1988) who drew a purposive sample of 39 incarcerated former gang members who were heavily involved in the California crack trade. And by the research of Winfree, Vigil, and Mays (1991) who posit a stochastic model of gang violence based on the results of questionnaire data drawn from a purposive sample of former gang members incarcerated in New Mexico prisons.

The pedagogical implications of the prison field study method are that students must be taught how to construct reliable and valid survey questionnaires based on extant gang research and theory. Then, they must convince correctional administrators that their research is worthwhile. Students can do this without a grant. All they need to do is contact the warden of a nearby prison, and explain—with impeccable clarity—the goals of their research; and then, follow the warden's advice for implementing a research project to meet these goals. In strictly criminological terms, the overarching goal of all gang research is to explain the propensity for violence (Thrasher, 1927, Chapter IX).

CONCLUSIONS

Klein (1992) offers a helpful comment on conducting gang research in the 1990s. In his critical review of Islands in the Street, Klein argues that "It is difficult to sep[a]rate the [researcher's] attempts to take new ground from his procedures—both research and presentation" (1992:81). Consistent with this, I have attempted to show that as researchers move farther and farther away from inductive reasoning—and therefore, farther away from explanations concerning the way gang members view their own world—researchers tend to rely more and more on their own value-laden assumptions (derived from deductive reasoning) about human nature and the way society should and does operate. Along the way, these researchers tell us almost nothing about the problem of gang violence. If the goal of gang research is to understand violence, then the end result of the community agency and detached caseworker methods is scientific ossification.

Reified scientific beliefs confirm prevailing opinions among law enforcement officers, community activists, legislators, correctional administrators, citizens, rap artists, and students of criminology and criminal justice. These mainstream opinions—shaped by the social and political contentions of the times—support and sustain the views of social control agents, rather than the empirical realities of the criminal phenomena researchers are interested in to begin with.

I have suggested that this academic and public policy stagnation can be corrected through university courses that encourage students to return to a more traditional approach to doing gang research. Following Mills (1959), I have attempted to show that government grants and advanced technology have been responsible for transforming gang researchers into bureaucrats and technicians. Mills explained that a "quality of mind" was necessary to "achieve lucid summations of what is going on in the world." In distinguishing the social scientist from the bureaucrat/technician, Mills described the former as having a capacity to shift from one intellectual perspective to another, a playfulness of mind that integrates ideas in novel ways, and a "fierce drive to make sense of the world" (1959:211).

With respect to gang violence, such "playfulness of mind" can be achieved only by seeing gang violence first-hand, and/or by directly interviewing gang members who have committed violence. This criminological lesson is not learned in the cloistered hallways of a university; nor is it learned at a computer keyboard. It is never learned in an office of grants and contracts. It is learned only on the streets—through courage.

Section II

THE SOCIAL EMBEDDEDNESS AND SPREAD OF GANGS

3

Family and Peer Influences on Gang Involvement: A Comparison of Institutionalized and Free-World Youth in a Southwestern State[1]

L. Thomas Winfree, Jr.
New Mexico State University

G. Larry Mays
New Mexico State University

In the mid-1980s, a new wave of academic gang research began to focus on a wide range of descriptive and causative factors, including gang ethnicity (Chin, 1990, 1993; Curry & Spergel, 1992; Sanders, 1994; Vigil, 1990; Vigil & Long, 1990; Vigil & Yun, 1990), gender (Bjerregaard & Smith, 1993; Campbell, 1990), members' ages (Lasley, 1992), involvement in drugs (Esbensen & Huizinga, 1993; Fagan, 1989, 1990), organizational patterns (Taylor, 1990), sociodemographics (Vigil, 1988), offense patterns (Winfree, Mays, & Vigil-Backstrom, 1994), and intervention programs (Conly, Kelly, Mahanna & Warner, 1993; Goldstein & Huff, 1993; Thompson & Jason, 1988). Conspicuously absent from most of the research on gangs is the role played by family variables in the likelihood that youngsters will join, not join, and/or remain in youth gangs.

This is not to say that no one addresses the significance of families on gang delinquency (see, e.g., Goldstein, 1991; Goldstein & Huff, 1993). For instance, Conly et al. (1993:39) note that "Although families are often viewed as central to solving the problems of youths who live in neighborhoods with gangs, none of the gang programs surveyed [by the National Institute of Justice] focuses exclusively on families, although many include family outreach among their program components." Conly and her colleagues (1993:39) maintain further that prior research "suggests that parents are a negligible influence in the lives of gang members." Indeed, Lyon, Henggeler and Hall (1992) failed to find differences in gang behavior between groups of incarcerated Hispanic and Anglo children. They, unlike Conly et al., did not infer from these findings that family relations do not matter: "The lack of between-group differences does not discount the important role of family relations in serious antisocial behavior, but such findings suggest that family problems are no more associated with gang membership than with serious antisocial behavior in general" (Lyon et al., 1992:447).

Given the relatively sparse treatment of gang members' family variables, the previous research on this subject cannot be viewed as definitive. Therefore, the present piece is designed to provide one more part of the puzzle to aid in our understanding of gangs and the significance of families.

WHY FAMILIES?

The family is assumed to play a major role in a child's formative years. Goldstein (1991:218) says, for example, "The family and community are both essential to a child's moral, social, spiritual, emotional, physical, and intellectual development. The extent to which youngsters learn social rules, employ prosocial behaviors, internalize moral development and structure values is directly related to their interactions with family and community members." As a result of the general importance of families in shaping behavior, control theory (among other theories) indicates that family factors exert a "broad and deep influence . . . upon the likelihood of delinquent behavior" (Goldstein, 1991:14).

Studies of other forms of youthful misconduct, including drugs, alcohol, and delinquency, have provided insights into parental influences. For example, Winfree (1985), in a two-wave panel study of adolescent drug use, observed that youths who reported increased levels of conflict with one or more of their parents at Time 2 were more likely to report problem drug use.

Perhaps a partial understanding of this . . . finding lies in our contention that, whereas changes in peer-related orientations are part of the process of growing up, significant alterations in the more primary relationships with one's parents can be far more traumatic, and these relationships can thereby create a set of social-psychological conditions conducive to drug use (Winfree, 1985:510).

Parental conflict is clearly an important contributor to our understanding of youthful misbehavior, including not only drugs (Jensen, 1972; Kandel, Treiman, Faust & Single, 1976; Winfree & Griffiths, 1985), but also more traditional forms of delinquency (Aultman & Wellford, 1978; Burkett &

Jensen, 1975; Dull, 1984; Hirschi, 1969; Matsueda & Heimer, 1987; Williams, Clinton, Winfree & Clark, 1992). Other studies of adolescent alcohol use have found that parents and immediate family members can have a strong influence on rates of self-reported use, particularly if the family is a source of permissive norm qualities (Krohn, Akers, Radosevich & Lanza-Kaduce, 1982; Larsen & Abu-Laban, 1968; see too Sellers, Winfree & Griffiths, 1993).

Not only are families important generally in a child's development, but also within certain ethnic cultures the family seems to occupy a particularly significant place. Vigil (1988), in his study of Hispanic gangs in Southern California, repeatedly notes the importance of families or particular family members in inhibiting or encouraging gang activity. For example, he asserts that some gang-involved youngsters have male family members who serve as role models that encourage them to join a gang (Vigil, 1988:88). Vigil (1988:87-88) also says that the gang members in his study shared "a background of family stress;" the outcome of a lack of firm grounding in the family often was a "lack of success in and subsequent alienation from school, and a disinclination toward many conventional pursuits of childhood and adolescence."

If the family occupies a significant place in child development, and there is general agreement that it does, then the impact of various family factors on delinquency need to be examined. Potential family factors related to gang-based delinquency include: economic status (particularly low income, prolonged unemployment, and/or welfare support), family stress (including death of a parent, divorce, or general family chaos), and little family interaction such as lack of shared leisure time (Goldstein, 1991; Vigil, 1988).

Horne (1993:190) characterizes these key factors as "contextual variables that contribute to disrupted family management practices." Among these variables he identifies the following: "intergenerational antisocial behavior; demographic variables such as ethnicity, socioeconomic status, and parental education; and family stressors such as marital conflict, divorce, and unemployment" (Horne, 1993:190). While this chapter will not look at all of these family elements, we will focus on a number of variables that could potentially influence a youngster's decision to join, or not join, a gang.

There is clearly a dearth of information about family influences on gang involvement, especially relative to those of youthful peers. In this chapter we offer an analysis of two samples of similar-aged individuals, one free-world and one institutionalized. These two groups can be further divided into gang and nongang, creating four subgroups (i.e., free-world non-gang, free-world gang, institutionalized non-gang, and institutionalized gang). We suspect that in terms of parental and peer influences these groups will differ from one another in significant ways. In particular, free-world non-gang youths should least resemble the other three groups. The extent to which the other three differ from and resemble each other is an empirical question. In some ways, gang youths should be the same, irrespective of where they live. Then, too, institutionalized youngsters share experiences, outlooks, and attitudes largely unknown to most free-world youths. These possible variations constitute the primary research question addressed in this chapter: In terms of peer and parental influences, how do groups of gang and non-gang, institutionalized and free-world youths differ from one another?

METHODS AND MEASURES

The present research stems from a year-long effort to understand gangs in one southwestern state, New Mexico. Survey instruments were developed to measure the background characteristics and attitudes of two groups. The first group consisted of a free-world population of 9th and 11th grade students in two public school districts located near the U.S.-Mexico border. The sampling procedures used are described elsewhere in detail (Winfree, Vigil-Backstrom & Mays, 1994). The administrators of two high schools and one junior high school provided the names of 1,755 students; subsequently, we selected 630 names from this list, making certain that each school provided the proportionate number of youths to the final sample. Given the fact that the literature clearly defines youth-gang behavior as a male-dominated problem, we oversampled males 3 to 1; however, the sample size and expected return rate guaranteed the inclusion of at least 100 females in the final sample.

The questionnaires were administered in group settings by calling the sampled individuals to school cafeterias. The general purpose of the study was explained to them at that time ("We want to learn about gangs in New Mexico . . .") and the confidentiality of their responses was assured. All of the participants received the opportunity to withdraw without prejudice at that time. (We explained that they could simply stay in the room until all the others were finished so that no one would know who did and did not participate.) At the end of one hour, all questionnaires were placed in a locked box by the students. A total of 408 questionnaires were returned; only about one dozen students at all three sites refused to complete the questionnaire. Thirteen questionnaires were subsequently eliminated owing to failure to follow instructions or nonresponsiveness, leaving 395 completed and usable instruments. Of the 630 projected members of the sample, fully 10 percent were absent on the administration day, leaving 560 possible members of the sample. The final sample of 395 youths represented 69.6 percent of the students in attendance on the administration day, or 62.7 percent of the 9th and 11th grade students in all three schools originally selected for the study.

The second group consisted of officially adjudicated juvenile delinquents (see Winfree, Mays & Vigil-Backstrom, 1994). Given the relative small size of the population incarcerated at the state's juvenile correctional facilities, we decided to conduct a census. Three separate institutions were approached about the study; all three agreed to participate. The boys' school consists of nine one-room cottages located in a rural part of the state; it houses approximately 200 boys. The instruments were administered in groups of 20 to 25 boys. We followed the identical administration protocol as described for free-world youths. One additional element was that if the youths could not read the instrument, which had been pretested at the fifth-grade reading level, it was read to them and each youth recorded his own responses. Five youths refused to participate; the responses of another 13 were dropped from the analysis because of missing or inconsistent answers, most of which (we suspect) were due to problems with reading English, or generally low reading levels. The remaining 152 completed responses represented nearly 90 percent of the institutional population during the three-day administration period.

The administration procedure used at the boys' school was followed at the Youth Development and Diagnostic Center, located in the state's largest city. This facility, consisting of five cottages, is the reception and diagnostic center for all male and female admissions to state custody; most of the 100 or so residents are sentenced to a 90-day diagnostic screening (see Lozano, Mays & Winfree, 1990). Attached to the YDDC is a single 20-inmate cottage designed to house youthful female offenders.

Approximately 30 youths, almost all residents of YDDC, refused to participate in the survey. We obtained completed questionnaires from 101 male and female inmates; however, two were dropped from the analysis owing to extensive missing data. The remaining 98 questionnaires obtained from the YDDC/Girls' School facility represented nearly 80 percent of the youths in residence on the administration day.

The Variables

Self-Reported Delinquency. We employed a self-report delinquency (SRD) inventory. Respondents were asked to indicate the level of their involvement in any of 22 different norm- and rule-violating behaviors. The specific content for these items was derived from a rather large body of work on SRDs (cf., Gold, 1970; Hindelang, Hirschi & Weis, 1981; & Osgood, O'Malley, Bachman & Johnston, 1989). The current study focuses on serious youth misconduct, particularly that which is often associated with gangs and gang behavior. As a consequence, seven forms of minor self-reported misconduct (e.g., status offenses and rumor-spreading behavior) were dropped from the analysis, as were several of the even more serious forms of misbehavior, including property crimes. These deletions left the following forms of SRD as the focus of this analysis: (1) *Group-Context Personal Crimes* (i.e., taken part in fighting involving more than two people where only fists were used; taken part in a fight involving more than two people where weapons other than fists were used; shot at someone because you were told to by someone else); (2) *Drug-Related Crimes* (i.e., bought or drank beer, wine, or liquor; used illegal drugs such as marijuana or cocaine; sold illegal drugs such as marijuana or cocaine); and (3) *General Personal Crimes* (i.e., had a fistfight with one other person, "beat up" on kids who hadn't done anything to anyone; hurt or inflicted pain on someone else to see him or her squirm).

Respondents were asked to indicate how often they had "broken these rules since leaving the eighth grade." This self-report anchoring point proved to be problematic. The time frame was slightly less than one year for some of the youths (i.e., mostly freshmen) and up to three years or longer for others. To minimize the effects of this shortcoming, we elected to focus on the level of involvement as opposed to the specific rates of offending. Hence, we assigned a value of "1" to each offense for which the specific rate of offending exceeded "once or twice." Individuals who, for a specific offense, did not report any offending, or reported engaging in the act only once or twice, were assigned a value of "0" for that particular offense.

The nine offenses were grouped into the three composite indexes (i.e., group-context crime, drug crime, and general personal crime) and summed across each index. The composite scores reflect how many of the offense-specific crimes the youths reported committing three or more times. For each of the three separate indexes, the summated scores ranged from 0-3. Chronbach's alpha provided an indication of scale reliability: group-context crime (alpha = .76); drug-related crime (alpha = .72); and general personal crime (alpha = .57). The mean scores for each crime index, as reported in Table 3.1, suggest that the highest level of involvement was for drug-related crime (X = 1.69), with slightly lower levels of involvement reported for general personal crime (X = 1.56) and group-context crime (X = 1.34).

Gang Membership. We also employed a combination of self-definitional and criterion methods to determine whether any given respondent was a *youth-gang member* (cf., Curry & Spergel, 1992; Klein, 1971; Miller, 1990; Short, 1989). The survey instrument contained a series of wide-spaced questions related to the respondent's gang involvement. At one point, we asked the following question: "Have you ever been in a gang?" The group to which the youth claimed membership had to (1) have a name, (2) incorporate at least one cultural element (e.g., an initiation ritual, a specific leader or leaders, and gang "nicknames" for members); (3) exhibit at least one symbolic element (e.g., "colors," use of body tattoos, hand signals or signs, and jewelry); and engage in at least one illicit activity (e.g., sex, drugs, and drinking) or one illegal activity (e.g., fighting, committing crime, or vandalism). By this restrictive definition, we identified 214 gang members, or 33.2 percent of the free-world and institutionalized youths we surveyed.

Family and Peer Influences. We had access to seven separate measures of family and peer influences. With respect to the respondents' families, we inquired about *mother's education* (or that of the youth's female guardian) and *father's education* (or that of the youth's male guardian). In both cases most of the mothers and fathers had graduated high school or had received a General

Table 3.1.
Key Variables

Variable Names	Values	% (N)/ Mean (S.D.)
Sex	0. Female	24.2% (156)
	1. Male	75.8% (489)
Age	In years	$\overline{X}$ = 16.63
		(S.D. = 1.22)
Ethnicity	0. Other	32.9% (212)
	1. Hispanic	67.1% (433)
Grades	1. Mostly D's & F's	13.5% (87)
	2. Mostly C's	42.9% (277)
	3. Mostly B's	33.2% (214)
	4. Mostly A's	10.4% (67)
Work hours	Hours per week	X = 8.46
		(S.D. = 14.01)
Home alone: At night	1. Never	33.6% (217)
	2. Sometimes	42.8% (276)
	3. Frequently	23.6% (152)
Family Status	0. Other arrangement	38.9% (251)
	1. Intact family	61.1% (394)
Current Personal Status	0. Non-incarcerated	61.2% (395)
	1. Incarcerated	38.8% (250)
Gang Member	0. No	66.8% (431)
	1. Yes	33.2% (214)
Father's support	Higher the scale score, the greater the support provided by the father (range: 1-4)	$\overline{X}$ = 3.13 (S.D. = 0.65)
Father's education	1. Less than H.S.	26.4% (170)
	2. H.S./G.E.D.	44.5% (287)
	3. More than H.S.	29.1% (188)
Mother's support:	Higher the scale score, the greater the support provided by the mother (range: 1-4)	X = 2.96 (S.D. = 0.72)
Mother's education	1. Less than H.S.	27.0% (174)
	2. H.S./G.E.D.	45.7% (295)
	3. More than H.S.	27.3% (176)

Table 3.1 *(continued)*

Variable Names	Values	% (N)/ Mean (S.D.)
Friend's support	Higher the scale score, the greater the support provided by friends (range: 1-4)	$\bar{X} = 2.07$ (S.D. = 0.64)
Reaction of parents: Knowledge that youth is a gang member	−1. Respond negatively 0. Respond neutrally +1. Respond positively	58.0% (374) 5.3% (34) 36.7% (237)
Reaction of friends: Knowledge that youth is a gang member	−1. Respond negatively 0. Respond neutrally +1. Respond positively	34.9% (225) 18.8% (121) 46.4% (299)
Best friends in gang	1. None 2. Less than 1/2 3. More than 1/2 4. All	42.0% (271) 19.2% (124) 11.8% (76) 27.0% (174)
Pro-gang definitions	Higher the scale score, the more pro-gang the personal definitions (range: 1-3)	$\bar{X} = 7.14$ (S.D. = 2.52)
Group-context crime	Index score: 0-3 offenses	$\bar{X} = 1.34$ (S.D. = 1.17)
Drug crime	Index score: 0-3 offenses	$\bar{X} = 1.69$ (S.D. = 1.13)
General personal crime	Index score: 0-3 offenses	$\bar{X} = 1.56$ (S.D. = 1)

Equivalency Degree. We also created a scale to measure the level of parent support by asking the respondents, in the case of their mothers, a single question ("In your opinion, does you *mother* or *female guardian* . . .") followed by a series of statements: (1) praise, compliment or encourage you, (2) find fault or discourage you, (3) make you feel close to her, (4) do things for you that make you happy, and (5) give good advice. The same questions were asked of the respondents' fathers/male guardians. In both cases, the respondents were asked to indicate which statement best described how they felt about the question: (1) never, (2) seldom, (3) sometimes, and (4) usually.[2] The individual responses were summated and divided by the number of items to give an average scale score: The higher the scale score, the greater the support provided by the respective parent. Chronbach's alpha scores suggest that both *father's support* scale (alpha = .77) and *mother's support* scale (alpha = .79) are reasonably reliable. Finally, we asked each youth how his or her parents would respond if they thought the youth was a gang member. The possible responses included the following: (1) encourage you, (2) disapprove but do nothing, (3) scold or punish you, (4) kick you out of the house, and (5) turn you over to the police. In addition to these forced-choice responses, the respondents could give other possible responses. This latter group, along with the other five responses, was collapsed into a *parents' reaction* continuum that included negative responses (−1), neutral responses (0), and positive responses (+1).

Two measures of peer influence were similarly created. The first scale was *peers' support*, created with items identical to those used for both mother's and father's support, except the referent was one's peers. This scale, with an alpha score of .64, was viewed as marginally reliable. Second, we asked the youngsters to indicate how their friends would respond to the news of their gang membership. *Friends' reactions* was identical to parents' reaction except, once again, the emphasis was on one's friends.

Differential Associations. Perhaps the most common indicator of Sutherland's (1947) differential associations is the proportion of one's peers who belong to the target population, in this instance youth gangs (Winfree, Mays & Vigil-Backstrom, 1994; see also Akers, Krohn, Lanza-Kaduce & Radosevich, 1979). Specifically, we asked: "About how many of your *best friends* are gang members?" Thus, the question included Sutherland's "intensity" element from differential association theory. We provided the following response categories: (1) none or almost none, (2) less than half, (3) more than half, and (4) all or almost all. Over 4 in 10 youths indicated that none of their best friends were gang members. At the other extreme over one-quarter of the respondents reported that all or nearly all of their best friends were gang members.

Personal Pro-Gang Definitions. The idea that gang members might express more pro-gang definitions is borrowed directly from Sutherland's differential association theory (1947) and Akers' (1985) social learning theory (see also, Sellers & Winfree, 1990; Winfree, Vigil-Backstrom & Mays, 1994; Winfree, Sellers & Clason, 1993). It is conceived to be a by-product of the process whereby the individual, through interaction with others, learns evaluations of behavior as good or bad. As Akers et al. (1979:638) observe, the definitions are "themselves verbal and cognitive behavior which can be directly reinforced and also act as cue (discriminative) stimuli for other behavior." The pro-gang definitions used in this study were grounded in "gang experiences." The subjects were asked whether they (1) disapproved, (2) neither approved nor disapproved, or (3) approved of the following: (1) having friends in gangs, (2) being in a gang yourself, (3) taking part in illegal gang activities like fights, and (4) doing whatever the gang leaders tell you to do. These items formed a reliable measure of personal pro-gang attitudes (alpha = .86). The scores were summed and divided by four. The scale scores ranged from 1 (disapproval) to 3 (approval): the mean score for the sample of free-world and institutionalized youths was 2.5.

Personal-Biographical Characteristics. Seven personal-biographical characteristics are of substantive interest to this study. First, gang behavior, especially gang-related crime, is primarily but not exclusively, a male phenomenon (see Bowker, Gross & Klein, 1980; Campbell, 1987; Spergel, 1986, 1990). We acknowledge the importance of gender in this differential status and involvement by including both free-world and institutionalized female subjects. Nearly one-quarter of the sample is female. For this study we coded gender as *male* (1) or *female* (0).

Second, age is important, if only as a control variable. Older youths typically report far more extensive crime histories and a broader range of self-reported delinquencies (Spergel, 1986, 1990). We treated age as an interval variable. The average age was 16.6, with a standard deviation of 1.2 years.

Third, the gang phenomenon has long been associated with minority-group membership, or, in the southwest, the Hispanic-American culture (Spergel, 1990:212; Vigil, 1988). Critics of this viewpoint, however, point out that nothing endemic to the Chicano barrio supports the view that it is more gang- or violence-prone than other subcultural communities (Erlanger, 1979). Vigil (1988:7), in particular, maintains that while Chicano gangs are notable for their prevalence and persistence; only about 4 percent to 10 percent of barrio youths—the population at greatest risk—are associated with gangs. Most studies of youth gangs, however, focus on the minority status of gang members (see Curry & Spergel, 1992; Fagan, 1989; Fagan, Piper & Moore, 1986; Miller, 1975, 1982; Spergel, 1990). Given the relatively small number of non-Hispanic minority group youths either incarcerated or in the free-world sample, we coded ethnicity as *Hispanic* (1) and non-Hispanic (0). Two-thirds of the youths sampled were Hispanics.

The fourth characteristic, work outside the home, has been linked to youthful misconduct in previous studies (Huizinga, Loeber & Thornberry, 1992). We first asked the youths if they had a "paying job." We then asked them about how many hours per week they worked. On average, the youths in our survey worked 8.46 hours per week; however, the responses were clearly not normally distributed as the mean was 14 hours. A relatively large number of youths (11.6%) answered this question by indicating 40 hours per week; fully one youth in four worked more than 10 hours per week. At the other extreme, two-thirds reported no outside employment.[3]

We asked the youngsters to characterize their grades using the following categories: (1) Mostly D's and F's, (2) Mostly C's, (3) Mostly B's, and (4) Mostly A's. Most of the students (42.8%) reported being "C" students; however, one in three indicated that they received mostly B grades. Finally, mostly D's and F's and mostly A's were claimed by roughly equal parts of the students surveyed (13.5% and 10.4%, respectively).

Two family-related items were included as personal-biographical information. First, we asked the youths how often they were left home alone at night.[4]

The possible responses, with frequencies, are as follows: (1) never (33.6%), (2) sometimes (42.8%), and (3) frequently (23.6%). Second, we asked the youths to indicate the adults with whom they lived.[5] Their responses were collapsed into (1) intact/traditional families (i.e., both parents were present in the home), or (0) other arrangements. By far the most common residence pattern was intact family (61.1%).

FINDINGS

Four-Group Comparisons: Personal-Biographical Information

For the purposes of this analysis, the two samples of youths, free-world and institutional, were further divided into four groups: (1) free-world/non-gang youths, or Group 1; (2) free-world/gang youths, or Group 2; (3) institutional/non-gang youths, or Group 3; and (4) institutional/gang members, or Group 4. Table 3.2 contains a comparison of these four groups on the five key personal-biographical characteristics. All four groups differ in significant ways from each other. Group 1, as expected, has significantly more females than any of the other comparison groups. Members of this group are significantly younger than members of the institutionalized youths. Ethnicity exhibits no clear pattern: Group 1 has about the same number of Hispanic members as the institutionalized gang subsample, but significantly more Hispanics than Group 3, the institutionalized non-gang subsample. There are significantly fewer Hispanics in Group 1 than the free-world gang subsample (Group 3). The reported grades for Group 1 are also significantly higher than any other group. Finally, both institutionalized groups reported significantly higher work hours than Group 1; however, the hours reported for Group 2 were not significantly higher than Group 1.

Group 2 differs in significant ways from Groups 3 and 4 as well. For example, Group 2 has significantly more Hispanic members than either Group 3 or Group 4. Group 2 is also significantly younger than Group 4. Finally, members of Group 2 work far fewer hours than members of either Group 3 or Group 4.

Finally, comparisons of Groups 3 and 4 yield three significant differences. First, Group 4 has more males than Group 3. Second, Group 4 is older than Group 3. Finally, Group 4 consists of significantly more Hispanics than Group 3. It would appear that in the state's correctional facilities, gang members are significantly more likely to be male than female, older than younger, and Hispanic as opposed to non-Hispanic.

Given the high number of significant differences on these variables, multivariate analysis must control for all five. Next, however, we turn to a straightforward comparison of the four groups in terms of (1) family and peer influences and (2) criminal activities and personal pro-gang definitions.

Table 3.2
Personal-Biographical Information: Four-group comparison,
Means and T-test scores

	Groups (Mean Scores)				Comparisons (T-test scores & Alpha levels)					
	Free/ Non-gang (Group 1)	Free/ Gang (Group 2)	Inst/ Non-gang (Group 3)	Inst/ Gang (Group 4)	1/2	1/3	1/4	2/3	2/4	3/4
Sex	0.66	0.85	0.80	0.90	-3.41^c	-2.92^b	-5.27^c	0.88	-0.93	-2.04^a
Age	16.43	16.46	16.77	17.08	-0.21	-2.71^b	-5.39^c	-1.74	-3.55^c	-2.00^a
Hispanic	0.71	0.83	0.49	0.65	-2.13^a	4.40^c	1.33	5.15^c	2.88^b	-2.57^a
Grades	2.66	2.20	2.22	2.09	4.70^c	4.99^c	6.99^c	-0.21	1.01	1.31
Work activities	3.65	5.19	13.71	17.19	-1.38	-8.35^c	-10.84^c	-4.12^c	-5.45^c	-1.59

^{a}p < .05
^{b}p < .01
^{c}p < .001

Four-Group Comparisons: Family and Peer Influences

The family and peer measures for members of Group 1 (free-world non-gang), as summarized in Table 3.3, are significantly different from those observed for members of Group 2 (free-world gang) in only three ways: Not surprisingly, the parents of youth in Group 1 would respond more negatively than those in Group 2; similarly, Group 2 reports more positive peer reactions about possible gang membership and more best friends in gangs. These three differences hold true for comparisons of Group 1 with both Group 3 (institutional non-gang) and Group 4 (institutional gang). In addition, members of Groups 3 report significantly higher support from peers, and significantly more members report living in non-intact families. As predicted, the members of Group 1 differ most from those in Group 4; significant differences were observed for higher rates of being left alone at night and more support from fathers, plus the five other significant differences observed between members of Groups 1 and 3.

Group 2 (free-world gang) youth were, in most ways, similar to the institutionalized youth; however, we observed several interesting differences. For example, in comparison to both Groups 3 and 4, Group 2 members reside in more intact families. Group 2 members receive less support from mothers than those in Group 3 and less support from fathers than members of Group 4. Consistent with prior gang research, members of Group 2 have more best friends in gangs than members of Group 3 and less than those in Group 4.

Table 3.3
Family and Peer Influences: Four-group comparisons,
Means and T-test scores

	Groups (Mean Scores)				Comparisons (T-test scores & Alpha levels)					
	Free/ Non-gang (Group 1)	Free/ Gang (Group 2)	Inst/ Non-gang (Group 3)	Inst/ Gang (Group 4)	1/2	1/3	1/4	2/3	2/4	3/4
Family status	0.71	0.69	0.45	0.46	0.39	5.16[c]	−5.27[c]	3.39[c]	3.39[c]	−0.09
Alone at night	0.83	0.93	0.94	1.01	−1.08	1.39	−2.29[b]	−0.13	−0.73	−0.65
Father's support	3.07	3.03	3.20	3.32	0.48	−1.77	−3.69[c]	−1.86	−3.31[c]	−1.62
Father's education	2.02	1.98	2.09	2.02	0.49	−0.87	0.09	−1.16	−0.57	0.87
Mother's support	2.94	2.81	3.01	3.06	1.41	−1.00	−1.65	−2.02[a]	−2.37[a]	−0.56
Mother's education	1.93	2.02	2.09	2.08	−0.97	−1.89	−1.94	−0.59	−0.57	0.03
Reaction of parents	−0.45	−0.04	−0.08	0.12	−3.72[c]	−3.81[c]	−6.10[c]	0.29	−1.16	−1.60
Friend's support	2.00	2.06	2.13	2.14	−0.77	−2.01[a]	−2.19[b]	−0.78	−0.86	−0.07
Reaction of friends	−0.12	0.31	0.18	0.47	−3.67[c]	−2.90[b]	−6.47[c]	1.06	−1.62	−3.02[c]
Best friends in gang	1.60	3.00	2.09	3.43	−11.73[c]	−4.66[c]	−19.54[c]	5.36[c]	−3.08[b]	−10.08[c]

[a]p < .05
[b]p < .01
[c]p < .001

Groups 3 and 4, the two institutionalized subsamples, differed from each other in only two respects: reaction of friends and the number of best friends in gangs. Gang members reported more positive responses from peers and more best friends in gangs than nongang members. Otherwise, among the institutionalized youth, there were no significant differences between gang and nongang youth on family and peer factors.

The four groups differed most in terms of family status, reactions of parents and friends, and best friends in the gang. Comparisons based on education, whether mothers' or fathers', failed to provide any significant differences; the groups failed to differ in terms of being alone at night and, to a lesser extent, mothers' and fathers' support. In short, the findings for family and peer differences were mixed.

Four-Group Comparisons: Criminal Activities and Personal Pro-Gang Definitions

It is difficult to find a comparison in Table 3.4 in which the differences are not significant. Group 1 is significantly less pro-gang than any of the other three groups; its members also reported significantly lower rates of offending than the remaining three groups. The only two insignificant comparisons both involve Groups 2 and 3: the levels of group-context offending and drug-related crime reported by members of both groups are not significantly different. Also, consistent with previous findings reported in this chapter, the greatest differences are between members of Groups 1 and 4. Finally, free-world gang members (Group 2) report more pro-gang definitions than the institutionalized nongang members (Group 3).

Table 3.4
Crime and Personal Attitudes: Four-group comparisons, Means and T-test scores

	Groups (Mean Scores)				Comparisons (T-test scores & Alpha levels)					
	Free/ Non-gang (Group 1)	Free/ Gang (Group 2)	Inst/ Non-gang (Group 3)	Inst/ Gang (Group 4)	1/2	1/3	1/4	2/3	2/4	3/4
Pro-gang definitions	5.93	8.72	6.75	9.39	−11.03^c	−3.73^c	−17.18^c	5.90^c	−2.27^b	−9.81^c
Group-context crime	0.61	1.78	1.68	2.51	−10.35^c	−10.78^c	−22.86^c	0.68	−6.38^c	−7.81^c
Drug-related crime	1.06	1.88	2.10	2.70	−6.91^c	−9.98^c	−18.92^c	−1.46	−7.27^c	−5.48^c
Personal crime	1.13	1.54	1.92	2.24	−3.71^c	−9.15^c	−12.49^c	−2.69^b	−5.52^c	−2.76^b

^{a}p < .05
^{b}p < .01
^{c}p < .001

The comparisons of self-reported delinquency and pro-gang attitudes summarized in Table 3.4 support the view that, with few exceptions, those youths who have experienced both gang involvement and institutionalization are far more likely to embrace pro-gang attitudes and report more criminal activities than the other subgroups we studied. Institutionalized gang youths may not be uniquely different in terms of peer and parental influences, but they are in terms of SRD and pro-gang attitudes.

We turn next to the final remaining research question: To what extent do peer and parental influences and personal orientations provide insights into self-reported delinquency? We have already observed that the various subsamples differed significantly in terms of certain personal-biographical characteristics (Table 3.2). Moreover, inter-subsample differences emerged for examinations of both peer/family influences and SRD/pro-gang attitudes (Tables 3.3 and 3.4, respectively). Consequently, in order to provide as complete an answer to this question as possible, we include both personal-biographical characteristics and subsample membership (i.e., Groups 1, 2, 3, and 4) as controls.

Understanding Youthful Misconduct: Personal, Family, and Peer Influences

Table 3.5 contains the summary results of three separate ordinary least squares regression analyses. Group-context crime is the one most closely related to gang membership. The regression equation summarized in the first column in Table 3.5 suggests that several personal-biographical factors are important to understanding this particular SRD. That is, group context offending is highest for males and those who reported lower grades. Among the family-related variables, the most productive ones were living in non-intact families, left home alone at night, and low support from one's father. None of the other family-related variables made significant contributions to the regression equation for group-context offending.

The greatest insights into group-context offending, as measured by the standardized regression coefficients, were provided by peer influences, personal definitions, and subsample membership. The number of best friends in gangs made a significant contribution: The higher the number of best-friends-as-gang-members, the higher the level of reported group-context offending. Personal pro-gang attitudes make a very similar contribution in the first equation: The more pro-gang the personal attitudes, the higher the level of group-context offending. Finally, the members of the institutionalized gang subsample (Group 4) reported high levels of offending compared to free-world non-gang members (Group 1), followed in decreasing order by institutionalized non-gang (Group 3) and free-world gang members (Group 2). Overall, this equation explained 60 percent of the variance in group-context offending.

The only personal-biographical or parental variable to make a significant contribution to our understanding of drug-related crime is age: Drug-related offenders are likely to be older members of all four subsamples. Otherwise, this form of offending is highest among members of Groups 4 and 3 and, to a lesser extent, members of Group 2. The single best predictor is membership in Group 4. Personal pro-gang definitions, however, make a contribution to the equation on a par with that provided by membership in Group 3. Drug-related offending, more so than group-context crime, appears to be related primarily to legal status (i.e., adjudicated delinquent versus either free-world gang member or non-gang youth). The overall explained variance for this equation, while substantial (R-squared = .46), is less than that reported for group-context offending.

Table 3.5
Self-Reported Delinquency: Family, Peer and Personal Influences
(Standardized coefficients and, in parentheses,
unstandardized coefficients)

Independent Variables	Group-context crimes	Drug-related crimes	Personal crimes
Sex	0.18[c]	0.02	0.14[c]
	(0.48)	(0.06)	(0.32)
Age	0.04	0.13[c]	−0.05
	(0.04)	(0.12)	(−0.04)
Hispanic	−0.01	0.02	−0.03
	(−0.03)	(0.06)	(−0.07)
Grades	−0.11[c]	−0.10	−0.13
	(−0.16)	(−0.13)	(−0.15)
Work activities	0.06[a]	−0.02	−0.00
	(0.01)	(−0.00)	(−0.00)
Family status	−0.06[a]	−0.13	−0.06
	(−0.14)	(−0.31)	(−0.11)
Alone at night	0.05[a]	0.11	0.09
	(0.08)	(0.16)	(0.12)
Father's support	−0.06[a]	−0.01	−0.01
	(−0.11)	(−0.00)	(−0.14)
Father's education	0.01	0.04	−0.00
	(0.02)	(0.06)	(−0.00)
Mother's support	0.04	−0.05	0.01
	(0.03)	(−0.07)	(0.02)
Mother's education	−0.02	0.04	0.03
	(−0.03)	(0.05)	(0.04)
Parents reaction	−0.01	0.03	−0.03
	(−0.01)	(0.03)	(−0.03)
Friends' support	−0.02	−0.03	−0.01
	(−0.04)	(−0.05)	(−0.01)
Friends' reaction	0.05	0.05	−0.01
	(0.07)	(0.07)	(−0.02)
Best friends in gangs	0.25[c]	0.14	0.11[b]
	(0.23)	(0.13)	(0.09)
Personal definitions	0.21[c]	0.17[c]	0.24[c]
	(0.40)	(0.31)	(0.37)
Group 4 (Inst/Gang)	0.27[c]	0.30[c]	0.19[c]
	(0.78)	(0.84)	(0.48)
Group 3 (Inst/Nongang)	0.20[c]	0.24[c]	0.21[c]
	(0.62)	(0.71)	(0.54)
Group 2 (Non-inst/gang)	0.11[c]	0.08[a]	−0.03
	(.37)	(0.16)	(−0.11)
R[2]	0.61	0.48	0.34
Adjusted R[2]	0.60	0.46	0.32

[a]p < .05
[b]p < .01
[c]p <.001

The pattern of variable contributions for this equation is substantively the same as that reported for drug-related crime: Offending is highest for those youths who indicated that they were males, had high numbers of best friends in gangs, and possessed pro-gang personal attitudes. Offending was significantly higher for members of Groups 3 and 4, as compared to Group 1; however, Group 2 members did not report significantly higher levels of personal crime offending. This equation explained 34 percent of the variance in personal offending.

Overall, only a few variables contributed to more than one equation; a relatively large number made no contributions at all. In the first group, being male was important to both group-context and personal offending, as was having one's best friends in the gang; personal definitions and membership in Groups 3 and 4 were important to our understanding of all three forms of offending; being a member of Group 2 helped us understand the more gang-oriented forms of offending, but not personal offending. Interestingly, the family context variables made significant contributions only to group-context crime. Finally, family variables such as parents' education, parents' reaction to putative gang membership, and mothers' support were silent on all forms of offending examined in this chapter. Even peer support and peer reactions failed to contribute to our understanding of any other offense indexes.

SUMMARY AND CONCLUSIONS

In this section of the chapter, we will summarize both the results of this research and draw conclusions based on those results, as well as speculate on future implications for students of youth gangs. First, the use of four comparison groups proved useful. The between-groups comparisons found, for example, that there are significant differences between free-world and institutional populations and between gang-involved and non-gang-involved youngsters. As we would expect, free-world nongang youths are conspicuously and statistically different from the other groups on most variables. For instance, these youngsters have parents or guardians who are perceived by the students to hold more negative attitudes toward gangs.

Second, the use of four comparison groups in the present research also proved frustrating. The four-group comparisons revealed that there were significant differences among the four groups in terms of family variables; the most consistent differences included family status, perceived reactions of parents, perceived reactions of friends, and the number of best friends in gangs. especially parents' reaction to the gang status of their child. In terms of offense-specific behavior, however, the findings for family (and peer) differences were mixed. The family variables are significant only for group-context crimes (from a results standpoint the good news is that these are the most gang-related crimes). These relationships were not observed for the other types of offenses. In simplest terms, offending patterns are not the same for gang and nongang youngsters, and for institutionalized and free-world groups. The institutional groups are very similar on all except a couple of variables. The unresolved question at this point is whether the attitudes shared by these subgroups are formed before or after incarceration. (Even comparisons of institutional gang youths with their free-world cohort cannot answer this question, as we do not know how many of the latter group have been institutionalized at some point in the past.)

Ethnicity posed a similar interpretive problem to the family and peer variables. Whether in the free society or in the correctional facilities, Hispanic youth were significantly over-represented as members of gangs. Only the comparison between the free-world non-gang and institutional gang groups failed to produce a statistically significant difference. Yet in the multivariate analysis of the SRD, ethnicity failed to make a significant contribution to any of the three equations. All things being equal, none of the offending examined in this study is more the domain of Hispanic-American than the other youths in our study. This finding suggests that those who contend that there is nothing unique about ethnic minorities, including Hispanics, to suggest that they are more prone to violence, gang-related or otherwise, are correct (Erlanger, 1979; Vigil, 1988).

There are several implications of this research for future study on the links between parents, peers, and youth gangs. First, family variables contributed to our understanding of gang behavior, although not to the degree we anticipated. This does not mean, however, that family factors are not major influences. In fact, these findings warrant revisiting the conclusion drawn by Lyon et al. (1992:447) "Family problems are no more associated with gang membership than with serious antisocial behavior in general."

Second, the free-world gang population seems as delinquent—in attitudes and actions—as the institutionalized groups; however, the free-world non-gang group reported significantly lower offending rates for the three crime indexes we examined than either institutionalized subgroups or the free-world gang subgroup. These observations run counter to the conventional wisdom that the self-reported offending rates of adjudicated delinquents and other youth are very similar (Short & Nye, 1958). This set of observations may mean that the gang populations we studied, free-world and institutional, are committed to behaviors that eventually will lead many members into the institutional group. At this point, they are engaging in what can be considered threshold behaviors. Free-world gang members are in transition: Not all will "earn" adjudicated delinquent/institutionalized status, but they possess the necessary behavioral predispositions to warrant that status.

Perhaps the best way to examine family influences is to look at the free-world non-gang group. The youths that populate this group are the most law abiding and the most likely to have supportive and intact families. Rather than asking the question of why youngsters get involved in gangs, the free-world non-gang group may lead us to ask the question posed by Rogers (1977): "Why are you not a criminal?"

NOTES

[1]   The authors would like to acknowledge the work of Kathy Fuller and Teresa Vigil-Backstrom, particularly their collective efforts during the data collection and data entry phases. We would also like to acknowledge the assistance of the school administrators and the students who participated in the survey: Thank you.

[2]   In cases where the youth failed to respond or indicated "don't know," we assigned the mean value for all other respondents. In no case did more than 10% of the respondents fit into both of these categories.

[3]   In the case of the institutionalized population, the youngsters were asked about jobs prior to their present incarceration.

[4]   It should be noted that a similar question was asked about being left alone in the daytime. The percentage responding in the affirmative was so high as to make this item a monotonic variable. Analyses were performed with and without this variable. Its inclusion did little to alter the results, and the analyses were far simpler without it.

[5]   Once again, the institutionalized youths were asked to indicate the parent(s) with whom they lived prior to incarceration.

4

The Impact of Gangs on Schools

Elizabeth McConnell
Valdosta State University

The message from the popular press these days is that public schools, once considered a safe environment for children to learn, laugh, and play, is now a battleground. The academic community, through their research, have demonstrated that violent crime and gangs are problems associated with schools. For example, from a 1986 national survey it was determined that 3 million incidents of street crime took place inside schools or on school property (Wetzel, 1988). Research by Chance (1990) indicated that 24 percent of all violent crime involving teens occurred in the schools. Moriarty and Fleming (1990) suggested that many of the street crimes committed at school resulted from youth gangs, a phenomenon which was growing, spreading from urban to rural areas. In a national survey of public and private schools, 15 percent of the student respondents reported the presence of gangs in the respective schools, while 5 percent reported that they were unsure about the presence of gangs in schools (Bastain & Taylor, 1991). These findings reflect a daunting image of primary and secondary education.

Crime in schools causes significant problems for both victims and offenders. Violence and gang-related activity disrupts the learning environment and negatively affects the entire school. Many schools have responded to the growing problem by instigating a variety of in-school policies and procedures. Some school administrators are fighting the gang problem by simply trying to eliminate gang-related behavior at the school. It appears that this approach merely displaces the problem from the school to the community. Other schools and communities have developed joint programs to fight crime and gangs in schools, as well as in the community. Comprehensive programs are necessary to combat gangs in schools.

FEAR OF CRIME IN SCHOOLS

Fear of crime in schools is an increasing problem that must be confronted. For example, in a 1983 study researchers found that 55 percent of students were not fearful of being a victim of crime at school, 28 percent were slightly fearful, 15 percent were moderately fearful and only three percent were very fearful (McDermott, 1983). However, in a subsequent study, researchers found that students' fear of crime at school had increased from 19 percent to 53 percent between 1983 and 1991 (Bastian & Taylor, 1991). Overall, students had become more fearful of crime in school, as well as when traveling to and from school. Bastian and Taylor reported that students' fear of crime was directly related to the presence of gangs in schools as well as the mode of transportation used to travel to and from school. Other researchers found that middle school students, who used public transportation or walked to school, reported significant amounts of fear (see Pearson & Toby, 1991; Moles, 1987).

As the presence of gangs in schools increases, researchers have attempted to measure the impact of gangs on students' fear of in-school crime. This has been problematic for those schools that are characterized by gang presence as many of the victims of in-school crime are also gang members. It is not uncommon for perpetrators of in-school crime to have histories of criminal victimization. This is especially true when gang activity is involved since gangs tend to victimize one another. It was found that fights between rival gangs is one of the more common forms of violent victimizations in schools characterized by the presence of gangs (McConnell, 1993). Based on data collected from a survey of high school students and from interviews with gang members, the researcher found that gang members threaten rival gang members with violence at school more than three times as often as they threatened non-gang members.

Other researchers have examined in-school crime and gangs by studying the influence of environmental factors on. For example, in a recent survey of 6th and 8th grade teachers and students in two Chicago schools, researchers studied the influence of the community on in-school crime (Menacker, Weldon & Hurwitz, 1990). The following were concluded by the researchers (1990:71):

> Almost half of the students (44%) surveyed did not feel safe in school.

> Almost half of the teachers in the sample (42%) hesitated to confront misbehaving students for fear of their personal safety.

> Only 38 percent of the teachers reported feeling very safe in their classrooms.

Nineteen to 20 percent of the students avoided the shortest routes home and the school parking lot because of fear for their personal safety.

From a survey in which violent in-school crime was measured nationally and more than 10,000 students were interviewed, it was reported by 15 percent of the students that gangs were present in their schools (Bastain & Taylor, 1991:1). Sixteen percent of the sample reported that a student had attacked or threatened a teacher at their school in the six months before the interview (1991:8). The researchers compared reported fear levels between students who attended schools where drugs were available with fear levels of students in schools who reported unavailability of drugs at school. The researchers determined that students who attended schools where drugs were readily available were twice as likely to fear an attack at school. Also, students at schools characterized by presence of gangs were about twice as likely as students from schools without gangs to be afraid of attack, both at school and on the way to or from school.

In a survey in which data were collected to measure the presence of gangs throughout the state's public schools, the researcher's findings supported those of the above national survey. Even though data were collected from school administrators, i.e., superintendents and counselors, the findings were similar. For example, 18 percent of the public school superintendents reported the presence of gangs in schools in the superintendents' school districts while 13 percent of the high school counselors reported the presence of gangs in the high schools where the counselors worked (McConnell, 1993).

In a county-wide assessment of gangs in public schools, survey data were collected from teachers and 10th grade students from 19 high schools (Schwartz, 1989). Both students and faculty reported the presence of gangs in all the schools in the sample, however students and teachers differed in their perceptions about safety at school. Twenty percent of the students reported being anxious about their safety at school while 95 percent of the teachers indicated that they were afraid for the students. Eighty percent of the teachers reported that their classrooms and faculty rest rooms were the safer places on campus and that students were at risk in student rest rooms, empty classrooms, and parking lots.

Schwartz (1989) also asked teachers about their experiences with gangs, the effect of gangs on students, and school policies and practices regarding gangs. Some teachers (23%) reported that they had received verbal threats from gang members while other teachers (11%) reported that they had been physically assaulted by gang members. Generally teachers reported that gang members negatively impacted students in several ways. Seventy percent of the teachers indicated that gang members intimidate students at school while 57 percent reported personal confrontations between rival gangs on campus.

Fifty-nine percent of the teachers said that while at school, gang members pressure non-gang students to join the gangs. In terms of how teachers are impacted by gangs, about 20 percent of the teachers reported that "fear of gang members influences teachers in their treatment or evaluation of certain students" and that some teachers "use gang leaders to help control the behavior of gang members in class" (1989:328).

VICTIMIZATION OF YOUTHS

The rise in crime committed by youths and gangs has resulted in increased numbers of adolescent crime victims. Youths are more likely to become victims of theft and violence than adults (Wetzel, 1988). In fact, "one in six youths between the ages of 12 and 19 was the victim of a street crime during 1986 as compared to one in nine adults" (Wetzel, 1988:5). In addition, the young were less likely than adults to report crime. Victimized youths have been categorized as one of two types, (1) actual victims—people who have personally experienced a crime, or (2) vicarious victims—people who have witnessed or heard about a crime from friends. Floyd (1987) suggested that vicarious victims, because they are fearful of being attacked for reporting offenses, are the most reluctant of the two types of victims to report crimes.

Adolescent victims and offenders are often one and the same, especially in the case of gang-related crime. Gang members play both roles, they victimize fellow youth and are victimized themselves in altercations that involve rival gangs (McDermott, 1983). Little or no information is available about this type of victim/offender situation. This type of victimization is not reported unless witnessed by someone outside the gang or the victim sustains an injury so critical that authorities get involved.

The presence of gangs on school campuses and the escalation of crime rates among youths has had a negative impact on the learning process. Students who are fearful of being victimized find it difficult to focus on academics. Fearful youth might skip classes to avoid gang members, or they might not come to school at all on days when they are most fearful. And, even when students do attend class, one wonders about the quality of the educational process as the teaching ability of faculty who are fearful of attack by gang members is adversely affected (Toby, 1983).

Research on violence in school, sponsored by the National Institute of Justice, resulted in the following findings (Toby, 1983:2):

> Students were more frequently the victims of violent crime
> than were teachers; male students were more than twice as
> likely to be assaulted or robbed as female students.

Junior high school students were twice as likely to be victimized as senior high students.

Younger teachers were more likely to be attacked or robbed than older ones.

Minority students were more likely to be victimized than white students, perhaps because they were more likely to attend schools characterized by higher rates of violence.

Overwhelmingly, crimes were committed by students attending the schools rather than by intruders from the outside.

SCHOOL CRIME: A REFLECTION OF CRIME IN SOCIETY

Crime in schools is merely a symptom of what is happening in the rest of society, that is, crime does not occur in isolation from crime in the rest of society (Wilson, 1977). In fact, schools are strongly influenced by the surrounding environment. Put another way, crime in society affects the level of crime in society's schools (Zevitz & Takata, 1992). It was reported in the National Institute of Education's study of in-school crime that crimes, especially violent crimes, were increasing in schools, despite the fact that the number of students have decreased (Menacker, Weldon & Hurwitz, 1990). Researchers of in-school crime have often focused on school crime and violence, without much attention to the communities from which the children come. It has long been recognized that "socially disorganized, crime-ridden neighborhoods produce socially disorganized, crime-ridden schools" (Menacker, Weldon & Hurwitz, 1990). It was reported by a Senate Subcommittee on Juvenile Delinquency that "violence and vandalism in the nation's schools are a reflection of community delinquency problems and that 'in school conditions' may contribute to the level of disorder" (U.S. Senate, 1975). On the other hand, McDermott (1983) has stated that it is important to view 'in school conditions' as "a phenomenon that is separate from crime in the community." However, analyses of school crime studies revealed that teacher victimization rates were strongly related to the amount of poverty and unemployment in the community (Gottfredson & Daiger, 1979).

Hellman and Beaton (1986) studied community influences and in-school crime committed by students in middle and high schools. The researchers found that crime in middle schools was more a function of the school environment than the community, but that the community had some impact. As for high schools, crime was found to be more directly related to crime in the community. These results led Hellman and Beaton to conclude that, "the community exerts a strong, independent influence" on school crime.

Escalating violence in the schools is a reflection of its increase in society as a whole. It had been determined that several characteristics of the community enhance the degree of violence in schools: (1) availability of weapons, (2) gang activity and (3) availability of drugs.

Research by Gaustad (1991) provided some insight about the prevalence of guns in the United States. In this research it was determined that for every household in the United States, there are two guns owned by private citizens. Unfortunately, youths in American society have relatively easy access to weapons. Based on data collected through personal interviews with 67 gang members, it was determined that 77 percent of the gang members owned guns, in fact the most often reported number of guns owned by gang members was three (McConnell, 1994). Gang members further reported that they most often acquired their guns in one of three ways: (1) given to the gang member by a friend, (2) stolen by the gang member, and (3) purchased a stolen gun for a street vendor. These data leads one to question the effectiveness of gun control laws on gun-related crimes committed by gangs. It certainly does appear that gun control laws bear little relationship to the manner in which gang members acquire their guns.

Gang members also reported that a handgun was the most common type of weapon owned by the gang member, with shotguns being the second most common type. Semiautomatic and automatic weapons were preferred. Gang members owning multiple firearms usually owned a variety, i.e., handguns of the automatic and revolver type and long guns that consisted of shotguns and rifles. Gang members further reported that they carried their firearms on a daily basis (42%) and that they had used them in drive-by shootings (37%) or other gang confrontations (20%). Ninety-one percent of the gang members reported that they had carried their firearms to school, 63 percent reported that this was a weekly activity (McConnell, 1994).

Gang activity and drug trafficking have contributed to the rise in violent crime. It appears that gang members are carrying weapons to protect themselves from rival gangs as well as to protect their drug business. Drug dealing has become a dangerous occupation for many of today's youths. It is an activity in which many gang-connected youths engage, sometimes it is related to gang membership but not always. For instance, only 55 percent of the gang members interviewed, reported that selling drugs was a gang activity. In addition, most of the gang members, (73%), reported that one was not expected or required to sell drugs (McConnell, 1994).

Many gang members reported dealing drugs as an individual enterprise in which earnings were not expected to be shared with the gang. Most gang members reported that their connection with the gang provided them with opportunities to acquire drugs, either for resale or personal use. Drugs were also found to be a common feature of gang activity in that 80 percent of the gang members reported drug use as a common gang activity (McConnell, 1994).

Gang members also reported on the presence of drugs at school. Seventy percent of the gang members reported that drugs were sold at school but only 12 percent indicated that gangs were responsible for in-school drug sales. Sixty-four percent of the gang member sample indicated that drugs were sold and used at school on a daily basis and that marijuana was the most common type of drug sold (McConnell, 1994).

SCHOOL AS A CONTRIBUTOR TO CRIME

While a number of researchers have focused on the community's contribution to school crime, others studied the school itself as a contributor of crime, for example, see Cohen, 1955; Cloward & Ohlin, 1960; Hirschi, 1969; and Moore, 1985. Thornberry, Moore and Christenson (1985) found that negative school experiences affect delinquent behavior. They reported that most children are in school for eight hours a day, nine months a year for 12 years of their life. This considerable amount of time spent in the school environment no doubt affects their current and future behavior. According to Chernkovich and Giordano (1992:261), other researchers have found considerable support for school and school-related variables as causal explanations of delinquency. For example, cultural deviance theorists suggest that disorganized schools contribute to delinquency while strain theorists say that school environments frustrate student's goals and aspirations and leads to delinquent behavior. According to control theorists, a lack of attachment and commitment to the school results in delinquency. Conflict theorists propose that an educational system that provides an inferior education to poor and minority children contribute to their delinquency while social theorists say that the negative labeling of school failures and troublemakers increase the likelihood of delinquency. Although any one of these theories can explain situations of individual delinquency, they continue to leave many questions unanswered as to whether school causes crime.

Moore (1985:4) says that "youth gangs are particularly susceptible to labeling as deviants, regardless of their behavior." She goes on to say that in city after city, the youth gangs had been created or "is currently being created" through many processes, some of which are "media sensationalism and enhanced criminal justice system response" (1985:10). McConnell (1994) found support for this explanation when she asked gang members during personal interviews why they called themselves a gang. Nineteen of the 67 gang members responded that a gang is what the police and others in society call the group, so the gang members supposed that is why they called themselves a gang. In fact, one of the gang members explained how he and several of his buddies were out drinking on a Friday night and had gotten into a fight with several fellows from across town. Soon after the fight began, the police arrived, arrested the youths, and took them to the police station. During the booking process, the youths heard the police refer to them as the Diamond Rock Gang (a term for the area of town in which the youths lived). After that, reported the gang member, we began calling ourselves the Diamond Rock Gang, although we never had a name or considered ourselves a gang prior to the incident with the police.

One way that schools contribute to the self-fulfilling prophecies is through the use of educational tracks. One study concluded that it is a typical organizational and instructional practice of schools to employ a two trajectory system in the education of students. Low trajectory students are labeled and ill prepared for school success. These are the students who are more likely to become delinquent. The high trajectory students are encouraged to succeed in school and go on to college. This process constitutes the application of a negative label that some suggest results in the self-fulfilling prophecy of failure (Pink, 1984). Another researcher examined the effect of school bonding on delinquent behavior. Control theorists suggest that the greater degree of school bonding the lesser the chance of delinquency. For example, "the children who do not like school or do not care 'what teachers think' are likely to believe that the school has no right to control them" (Hirschi, 1969:27). In a recent study it was concluded that control theory is generally correct, and that increased school involvement decreases the likelihood of delinquency (Chernkovich & Giordano, 1992).

SCHOOL SAFETY PLANS

The escalation of violence in America's schools has forced educators and administrators to take various actions to control the situation. Running in the halls, chewing gum, and talking in class are no longer the primary problems that concern teachers and educational administrators. Weapons, drugs, and violence have replaced the seemingly simple problems of the past. Many do not realize the severity of the dilemma. A 1986 National Crime Survey reported 3 million incidents of attempted or completed street crime taking place inside schools or on school property (Wetzel, 1988). These crimes included robbery, assault, arson, extortion, gang warfare, and even murder (National School Safety Center, 1986). Protecting school children from harm has suddenly become a top priority in the educational system. In order to create a safe learning environment, schools are developing complex safety policies and procedures. Absence of written plans or guidelines has often resulted in school administrators relying on a reactionary approach. Many of the in-school crime problems are gang related; therefore, safety plans to curtail gang connected crime have been formulated to safeguard children in school.

Every school administrator needs to set down specific rules to address crime prevention on campus. First of all, educators should develop "a comprehensive written policy statement, including a disciplinary code, employee standards, security regulations and emergency procedures" (Okaty, 1991). In addition, they should develop a plan, not solely a product of the school, but one that is comprehensive, such that it includes input from all appropriate organizations and constituencies. For example, crisis plans that include police departments, fire departments, emergency medical personnel and facilities and crisis intervention specialists, such as counselors (Nichols, 1991).

The educational environment presents a unique situation that requires specific actions. Because there are several different classifications of people in the school, for example, teachers, students, administrators, staff and security personnel, it is important to implement policies and procedures that consider all the players. From time to time, local law enforcement officers and even federal agents could become involved with matters of school safety and security. As a result, it is essential for administrators to be prepared for any situation. Computerizing policies and procedures and networking with agencies that are part of a school's emergency plan is an excellent beginning.

Generic school crime is widespread, while serious crime in school is rising. Gang activity looms as the cause for much of the violence. "No school, small or large, urban or rural, is immune" (Nichols, 1991). Even so, many schools do not have written guidelines for dealing with these crises. According to McConnell (1993), only 31 of 371 public school district superintendents, responding to a statewide survey on gangs in school, indicated that they had a gang policy. Since 1985, 21 of those who reported that they had a gang policy indicated that the policies had been implemented.

A large number of schools are dealing with gang and crime problems by simply ignoring them or trying to change the atmosphere and environment of the school. It is widely believed that if school administrators can keep specific gang activity from occurring at their institutions, the gang problem will be solved. Some school administrators have tried to create an impression of neutrality, a habitat where all students can feel safe. In fact Schwartz (1989) found in his study of 19 high schools in Los Angeles County that one principal implemented gang control policies that defined the campus as "gang neutral, wherein members of traditional enemy gangs suspend animosities and gang members do not think of the school as belonging to any one gang, nor do they limit their social interactions to their own gang members" (1989:336).

One of the more popular strategies has been to limit access, by other gang members not enrolled at the school, to the campus. This is being tried through the use of fences, locked gates, and security guards and administrators that are watchful of strangers coming on school grounds. A common aspect of this strategy has been an open invitation to local police or sheriff's department deputies to come on campus at any time since their presence is regarded as discouraging disruptive behavior (Schwartz, 1989).

There are some schools that have policies for dealing with in-school crime. These policies typically focus solely on preventing delinquent behavior at the school campus. For example, school administrators in Eugene, Oregon obtained a court injunction to prevent several gang members from attending South Eugene High School. The county court barred the students permanently from the city's schools, "not on the basis of any specific actions, but because their mere presence at the school in clothing associated with gang membership constituted a danger to the health and safety of students" (Gaustad, 1991).

Because gang members were easily identified by their specific gang clothing and colors, many schools developed complex dress codes to prevent gang members from showing their gang affiliations at school. School officials were expected to be aware of the gangs that are active in their area, which distinguishing characteristics the gang members displayed, and the types of activities in which these youth engaged. It became increasingly difficult to classify gang dress and attributes. A few examples of clothing styles and colors that were prohibited included black, red or royal blue, clothing related to sports teams, any item with Disney characters or Looney Tunes characters, bandannas of various colors and numerous other styles of clothing. Almost every type of clothing imaginable has been shown at some time to be related to a particular gang. It has become so difficult to formulate dress codes that some school districts have considered going to uniforms to put some unity back into how students present themselves. Since gang clothing, symbols and gestures change continuously, school administrators need to rethink gang policies predicated on dress codes. By the time the policy is in print, the gang will very likely have changed its clothing, symbols, and gestures in order to circumvent the policy. If dress codes are used, they should be broad enough to provide administrators with latitude.

One cannot always depend on policies directed at visibly identifiable features. For instance some gangs go to great lengths to keep a low profile so that they can remain anonymous to authorities. During the course of a personal interview with a gang member from a highly organized drug and gun smuggling gang, the gang member reported that his gang did not have a name, a symbol, or a style of dress. In fact, the gang went to considerable efforts to have no distinguishing features, because to do so was to become identifiable to the police and therefore easier to arrest (McConnell, 1994).

Another activity common to gangs is graffiti. Gangs like to advertise their local affiliation by prominently displaying their names or symbols on school property, as well as on various businesses and buildings throughout the community. Gang graffiti has become trendy on clothing, and businesses are making a profit from gang popularity (Barber, 1993). According to the National School Safety Center (1986:26), "school principals who have the greatest success in limiting gang activities make sure graffiti is removed from school within a few hours after it appears." Schools could make an extreme effort to keep all signs of gang graffiti from their schools. Graffiti could be immediately painted over or cleaned from the schools. When the vandals are known, they could be involved in the cleanup. The crime should be reported to local law enforcement agencies and disciplinary action taken. The entire community can become involved in keeping graffiti from the area.

Gang members are taking weapons into the schools and using them with more regularity than most of us realize. Many students who are fearful are bringing weapons to school to protect themselves. Schools have enacted several policies to keep weapons out of the learning environment. Some educational institutions have installed metal detectors at the entrances to the schools and others have placed limitations on the type of book bag that students can bring into the school. For example, the bag must be made of transparent plastic or nylon mesh or some type of material that does not inhibit one from viewing objects inside the bag. Either of these approaches does little to control the throwing of objects over a perimeter fence to be picked up and used by someone inside the perimeter. At minimum, it has been recommended that administrators implement written policies concerning weapons. The policies should be written so that they are easy to understand and they should provide specific sanctions that administrators commit to employ.

Other schools have instituted a closed-campus policy. This means that students must stay on school property from the time they arrive in the morning until school is dismissed. Outside visitors are carefully monitored. Teachers and administrators watch the hallways, cafeterias and playgrounds to let students know they are watching (Stover, 1986). No loitering policies are implemented, so that only enrolled students are allowed on school grounds during the day.

Once schools have identified gang members and activities, the individual administrators have dealt with the problems in several ways. If the gang member commits a serious offense, the student is often transferred, suspended, or expelled. Often the transferred student, who is suspected of being a gang member, is not welcomed at the new school, either by the administration or the students. One of the more obvious difficulties with transferring students is that it only moves the problem from one place to another, and sometimes the gang leader recruits members at the new school. Transferring students is one means by which gang migration can occur. Some administrators believe that gangs in their schools are a result of migration, that is they move in from somewhere else. The problem remains, no one wants gang members in their schools; therefore, these students continue to be shifted around.

Some school administrators have addressed the gang problem by soliciting help from students, counselors, and parents. School personnel believe that it is crucial to identify children who are at-risk of joining a gang, and stop them before it is too late. One school in Santa Rosa, California gave parents a newsletter titled, "Is it a clique or a gang?" The school solicited parental involvement at the intervention level, so that youth would be discouraged from joining gangs (Nielson, 1992).

Another unique problem that affects gang behavior in school is the media. For the past several years, the press has been exploiting, and perhaps even glamorizing the gang situation. According to Zevitz and Takata (1992), media sensationalism about gangs abounds. An anti-gang program in Portland, Oregon has developed a strategy for dealing with the media. It is based on the belief that students do have a right to privacy in schools and that reporters cannot merely barge into a classroom without obtaining permission. The media does not have any special access to schools beyond what is normal for public facilities. Portland school districts also made an informal agreement with the media to not overplay or exploit gang-related activity (Prophet, 1990).

Many initiatives focus on prevention strategies at the school only, that is controlling the behavior of students at school. School administrators implemented these plans to keep the school grounds neutral. The enforcement of "behavior codes, graffiti removal, conflict prevention and crisis management" all focus on school-related behavior (National School Safety Center, 1988). "Their objective was not to change these youth, but to control their in-school behavior in the belief that it was too late to affect their development" (Schwartz, 1989). Policies that only address 'in school conditions' will not solve the gang problem. Gang members need added guidance from teachers, counselors, parents and other members of the community. Since the escalation of gangs and violence at school is a reflection of what is occurring throughout society, community wide prevention and intervention strategies are necessary.

ANTI-GANG PROGRAMS

Communities and schools have adopted anti-gang programs that reach beyond the 'in school' policies and procedures. These programs focus on changing the behavior of gang members, not merely on controlling it. According to Spergel, Curry, Ross and Chance (1989), schools and local officials, in a national survey, deal with the gang problems in one of five ways: suppression, including prevention and supervision; social intervention, including treatment for youth and their families; social opportunities, including education, training and jobs; community mobilization, including program development among justice agencies; and organizational development or change, including special youth agency crisis programs. Suppression was employed in 44 percent of the programs; followed by 31.5 percent using social intervention. Only 10.9 percent employed organizational development, 8.9 percent used community mobilization, and 4.8 percent provided social opportunities. These results demonstrated that the majority of schools are focusing on suppression and control. Since gang-related activity is increasing, it appears obvious that a more comprehensive plan is required to stop the gang problem and keep additional youths from becoming involved in gangs.

In order for any program to be successful, family, schools and communities need to be involved in the process (Clark, 1992). Several programs are in effect that have enjoyed degrees of success. The Tulsa Police Department and the city's East Central High School developed a unique Crime Stoppers Program to address the rising crime problem. This approach was aimed at the general prevention of crime, not just gang-related crime. School administrators, community leaders and students formulated a plan that allowed students to have easy access in reporting crime. An administrative liaison was appointed to act as a buffer between students and the school. Crimes beyond the school's jurisdiction were given to the police department. This program was successful in lowering crime because it actively involved the students and the community (Chance, 1990).

Granada High School in the San Fernando Valley developed a plan for action to stop gangs and related violence in their schools. The high school, characterized by an outstanding record for academic excellence, was also plagued by gang activity thus indicating that gang problems are not limited to only schools with poor academic records. Granada High School began creating a neutral safe environment by identifying the nature and actions of gangs. They implemented preventive policies and procedures that other schools were initiating, however, they went further than simply controlling student's 'in school' behavior. Policies went into effect to help students with academic tutoring and literacy skills. Teachers and administrators met with police to discuss gang motivation and how to stop additional youths from joining gangs. Students who were gang members or substance abusers were offered weekly counseling. The school staff also became informed about gang activity in the community, the staff worked with local officials in developing intervention strategies. This program has been successful because teachers, students, and the community worked together to create safe havens for at-risk youths (Rattay & Lewis, 1990).

In 1988, Del Mar High School in San Jose, California began to experience gang infiltration as a result of transfers, family mobility and growth of gangs in local communities. The problem grew rapidly, and soon gangs were prominently displaying their colors at school and disrupting the learning environment. Del Mar High School officials did not hesitate for long. They immediately developed an open line of communication between staff, students, parents, police, and the local community. The teachers began patrolling the school for signs of violence, and the San Jose Police visited the campus regularly. The school administration identified all gang members and began to monitor their activity. Members received counseling or were removed from the school. The school sought outside professional help, high visibility and open communication with the entire community. Their quick action kept the gang problem from escalating out of control. Police visits to Del Mar High School dropped from an average on 1.5 per day to one per week (Shaw, 1989).

Since the re-emergence of contemporary gangs in the United States, Los Angeles has been considered the "gang capital of the world" (Stover, 1986).

Los Angeles has an unusually high number of murders and other crimes as well. In 1987, 350 gang-related murders occurred in the city, an 80 percent increase since 1985 (Speirs, 1988). Therefore, many of the pinnacle anti-gang programs were initiated in the Los Angeles area. A five-point program was developed in 1989 to deal with some of the Latino gangs in Los Angeles; however, these ideas provide a good basis for stopping gang activity, regardless of race or ethnicity. First and foremost, the gang problem has be downplayed in the schools. Gangs should be ignored, except when essential to keep school order. Educators can concentrate on education and socialization, rather than simply on control. Second, educators need to be reoriented about gang youths. They need to realize that being a gang member is only one aspect of the youth's life, and that he or she has other individual characteristics. This step represents a major change from most anti-gang programs because it encourages one to ignore harmless gang customs and symbols. The elimination of rules surrounding gang behavior makes it easier for gangs to shed their deviant image. Third, teachers need to receive accurate information about gangs that sensitize teachers to youth. Students need to feel positive about student teacher relations, to not feel threatened or demeaned by teachers. Fourth, gang members need to realize that they are legitimate members of the school who are expected to perform academically and to participate in school activities. These students must have alternatives to gang life that allow for healthy interaction with other students. Finally, a guidance team, to deal with gang members, needs to be established. This team should consist of counselors, teachers, specialists, and parents. By following these five steps, some schools in the Los Angeles area have been successful in dealing with some of the gang problem (Schwartz, 1989).

Youth gangs are not just a metropolitan problem anymore. According to Stover (1986), "no one knows how quickly gang activity is spreading," but one federal study conducted by Needle indicates that one-third of the cities surveyed, with populations over 250,000, reported gang problems. Gangs and their related problems have surfaced in suburbs all over the country. Park Forest, a suburb of Chicago, has developed its own plan for dealing with local gangs. The gang members in these suburban schools often come from Chicago as their families, trying to escape the crime and poor schools associated with inner cities, move to the more peaceful suburbs. These students want to be accepted by their peers; but that is often difficult, and the youths revert to their old behavior. Therefore, Rich East High School in Park Forest has developed a 10-step gang prevention program that works effectively with suburban youth: (1) be honest and admit there are problems in the school, (2) get smart, become aware of gang behavior and banish all gang paraphernalia, (3) identify the school's leaders, get them on your side and reward good behavior, (4) do not close the doors at the end of the class day, (5) work with the police to solve the gang problem, (6) involve transfer students in activities, (7) educate the teaching staff on gang activity, (8) get parents on the side of the school and educate parents to signs of gang activity, (9) find role models to interact with at-risk youths and, (10) provide career counseling for marginal students. This program emphasizes extensive involvement with the school and the community (Moriarty & Fleming, 1990). It appears that the more successful prevention programs are those that emanate from the community, those based on a community coalition model.

All of these programs are targeted at alleviating the problems of gangs in schools, with some programs extending into alleviating the problem of gangs in the community. For any program to be a success, it must be comprehensive in scope, involving the school staff, teachers, students, parents and communities. It is essential that gang members and at-risk youths have alternatives to gang activity (Reum, 1992). After-school and community-wide activities can provide educational and emotional support. Improving the overall school environment can lead to less violence and disruption in the community (Hellman & Beaton, 1986). However, as stated previously, changes in the community are also necessary. Changing social conditions, such as unemployment, poverty, and discrimination would lessen gang and crime problems.

5

Addressing and Testing the Gang Migration Issue: A Summary of Recent Findings

George W. Knox
Chicago State University

James G. Houston
St. Ambrose University

Edward D. Tromanhauser
Chicago State University

Thomas F. McCurrie
Managing Editor, *The Gang Journal*

John L. Laskey
Morton College

INTRODUCTION

The purpose of this chapter is to clarify the language and theoretical concepts surrounding the issue of gang migration. Recent research findings on this issue are provided, and several competing hypotheses are discussed as well. A summary is offered of the current state of the art regarding what we know about gang migration and the direction that future research should take.

CLARIFYING THE LANGUAGE ABOUT GANG MIGRATION

Gang migration can mean many different things to different people. From a social scientific point of view, however, we must more precisely define the conceptual elements of gang migration.

Gang Proliferation

Gang proliferation simply means the recent modern proliferation of gangs and gang members throughout the United States. By whatever means, or from whatever cause, the fact remains that all states today have some gangs or gang members in their criminal justice system (i.e., jails, adult and juvenile correctional institutions, probation and parole, etc). Gang proliferation, therefore, means the rise and spread of the gang problem. Few would disagree with the assumption that gang proliferation—as a social phenomenon or crime phenomenon—has had much national impact in recent years. This means that while some larger urban areas (Chicago, Los Angeles, etc.) have pretty much had a long history of experience with gang problems, that many cities (large and small) in America have recently come to face some degree of the gang problem as well. The gang problem is no longer limited to large urban areas.

Gang Emulation, The Contagion Factor, and the "Copy Cat" Phenomenon

Some of the more rural areas of the United States, and those who only recently report some level of a gang problem in their jurisdiction, may often indicate that the gang members in their areas are simply "wannabe's." That is, such gang members may have the identity of such a larger or more well-known gang, and even use its symbols and gang argot, but these are basically what the gangs themselves call "renegades"—that is, independent operators having no recognized connection to or ongoing cooperation with the same gangs in other areas. Sometimes this happens to simply be a matter of social emulation; by gang movies and the youth subculture, the symbols and identity of a gang are simply adopted at a local level. Some also term this the contagion effect: where the colors and the symbols of the gang are readily adopted by any group of estranged or alienated youths in an area, and once they are up and running as an identifiable group, a rival group shortly there after emerges—or the concept of the law of natural group opposition formation: the appearance of a "Crip" gang will be followed shortly thereafter by the appearance of "Blood" gang, or "Peoples" and "Folks", etc. There are also the simple situations such as that reported by Waldorf (1993) where local kids decide they want to hook up with gangs in larger areas (i.e., Los Angeles), even though Waldorf (1993) questions the human ability of some gang members to function in areas outside of their own local turf.[1]

The Geographical Dispersion and Representation in New Areas of Individual Members

Gang members do travel, for a variety of reasons, and when they do they can spread the gang problem. How does this happen? In a variety of ways, as explained below.

Prison Transfers. One of the more popular techniques for dealing with prison gang leaders and other gang members who are disruptive behind bars or who represent a security threat is to give them "diesel treatment." It is an old concept in corrections going back many years, and simply means putting the inmate "on the circuit," which means transferring them to another institution in another area, perhaps another state. But such a gang member may simply start up a new chapter of the gang group or organization at the newly arrived location. Sending an active gang leader to a new facility may allow the exportation of the gang phenomenon or its reproduction or proliferation.

Correctional Institutions as an Exporting or Importing Phenomenon. Importation means the more police and prosecutors focus their resources to target gangs or gang members, their effectiveness means gangs and gang members are imported into the correctional system (Jacobs, 1974). There is also the matter of the difference, if any, between what has historically been meant by "prison gangs" and "street gangs." Today, these are pretty much the same phenomenon. A pure prison gang would be one that arose for the first time in prison and operates only there and not on the streets. The term "street gang" is used here to imply the source of origin for the gang was outside of the correctional environment.

Some believe that when gangs have a significant presence behind bars, which we call the matter of inmate gang density (the percentage within the inmate population who are gang members), that their visitors, family, and friends may sometimes move to the same area where the correctional institution is located and in this manner the gang presence arises in the same area as well—but outside the institution. Some believe that when inmates are released, some stay in the geographical area where the facility is located and start up new gang operations there.

Flight to Avoid Prosecution. There is nothing new about offenders who leave an area where they are wanted, they simply try to go underground, they often do cross state lines and international boundaries. Gang members do this too. It can also take the form of leaving an area of orientation, where one grew up or first operated in a gang, and setting up shop in a new area; such as when a gang member is individually targeted by rival gangs. In a new geographical area, not all will "drop their flag" (i.e., give up the gang identity or their allegiance to the gang, its code, and its life style). Some will simply carry on the same identity, and eventually attract new fellow-minded individuals who come to eventually be a new "set" of the same gang identity.

Individual Travel of Gang Members. Gang members do travel, like anyone else in normal behavior, for fun, profit, and adventure. And when they do, it is possible that they are able to rapidly penetrate the local subcultures and establish new ties to like-minded individuals. Thus, "wannabe's" become "gonnabe's" by learning the codified beliefs and doctrines of a gang group or organization (i.e., its prayers or oaths, symbols, history, perhaps its written constitution, etc.). For example, a number of Native American youths in a Oklahoma rural town near a Cherokee reservation, were using some of the stylistic behavior of Crips, but when an actual Crip gang member came through town and met with them and insisted they tattoo themselves with the Crip symbol, they apparently refused to get the tattoos.

There are a variety of ways individual gang members travel and it is important to understand the unique ways in which this contributes to gang proliferation. The matter of intentional travel to "spread the gospel" of the gang and to establish new "sets" does occur, as in the Latin Kings where an "ambassador" position is established in their written constitution and by-laws. Intentional spreading of the gang is called gang franchising and gang imperialism and is explained separately below under the matter of the spread of gang groups and organizations.

One common way individual gang members, in their travel, contribute to gang proliferation has been called the gang familial transplant phenomenon (Laskey, 1994). Here is how it works. A parent discovers a child is a gang member and, with good intentions, believes he/she can "salvage" the youth by simply moving out of the area to a new city, perhaps a smaller or suburban geographical area. But the change in residence is not accompanied by a change in values of the youth, the youth has the gang clothes, the tattoos, the knowledge of the gang, and a way to communicate with associates in the area of gang orientation. What happens? The youth starts a new set of the same gang, is visited by members of the same gang, and may start a new chapter; getting rank and a leadership position in the process.[2]

Some gangs do send their members on official missions across state lines. This happens, for example, when various "gang summit meetings" are held, often under the pretext of uniting for peace treaties. Such meetings have been held in Kansas City, Chicago, Minneapolis, and other cities in recent years. They attract gang members from across the United States; in fact the one held in Minneapolis was, in part, federally funded.

The Spread of Gang Groups and Organizations

The existence in diverse geographical areas of gang groups and gang organizations by the same name is not logically all a matter of gang migration, it is simply gang proliferation. The belief by some is that a major or significant proportion of gang proliferation is explained by gang migration. We do need to point out that this does not mean the entire gang migrates to a new area, even though under community policing this kind of "displacement effect" might be regarded as a measure of the success or effectiveness of community policing or local gang suppression initiatives. Thus, it is not simply a matter of the entire gang packing up and leaving.

There are some other systematic ways in which gangs spread geographically and these can be briefly explained below.

Gang Franchising. Gang franchising means exactly what it implies: an intentional extension of the gang by the same name, the development of a new "set" in a different or new geographical area. Some researchers point to the drug trade profits as the fuel in the engine of gang migration (Skolnick, Blumenthal, & Correl, 1990). Reuter (1989) in a RAND Corporation report had earlier dismissed this concept of drug gang franchising based on an anecdotal analysis. An example of this from Davenport, Iowa occurred when a drug dealer came to town a few years ago, with the presentation of self as a Vice Lord leader from Chicago and a large stash of drugs he needed to sell, and quickly tapped into the youth subculture. The result? A number of white Vice Lords suddenly appeared that were indigenous to Davenport. How did they get "up and running"? They were not simply "wannabes," in their own minds they were genuine members, enough so to be responsible for a rather gruesome torture killing of a 17-year-old girl. What appears to have actually happened is the man from Chicago presenting himself as a Vice Lord leader agreed to "bless" these new members into the organization with rank if they could help him sell his drugs. The drugs got sold, the Chicago man gave them some prayers and literature, had a party, gave them titles, and left town. Leaving behind a group that could be counted on to distribute illegal drugs for him. This is not an unusual phenomenon, and can be presumed to occur in other areas as well.

Gang Imperialism. Gang imperialism means what it implies: an effort to take over and gain representation in a new area. Sometimes this occurs in the context of routine travel of individual gang members in small groups of two or more who simply "spread the gospel." Gangs today have a definite ideology and belief system that is attractive to a diverse audience of alienated youths and other youths who, in every generation, have a resentment towards authority in general. It is a matter of simply proselytizing for the gang, and some gangs have been very adept at this kind of "image maintenance" work. For example, Gangster Disciples present themselves not as a gang, but as an organization dedicated to the growth and development of its members. Gangs like the Latin Kings have "goodwill ambassadors," whose job it is to travel and proselytize in the same fashion.

The Natural Phenomenon of the Ripple Effect in the Geographical Dispersion and Proliferation of Gangs and Gang Members Nationally. Similar in some regards to a larger version of the concentric zone theory, the "ripple effect" hypothesis advanced by Houston (1994a) holds that our largest gang density will be found in larger urban areas, and decreases outward progressively, from the suburban collar counties, into the rural areas where the lowest gang density is to be found. Like the splash effect, the ripples extend geographically outward, until the effect is minimal at the farthest distance from large urban areas. Short called this the diffusion of gangs from larger urban areas to smaller cities (1990). Gang density, of course, is measured by the percentage of persons in any given social context or system (i.e., school sample, jail sample, etc.) who are gang members. Houston (1994b) using recent data from a large sample of actual gang members (Knox, Houston, Laskey, Laske, McCurrie & Tromanhauser, 1994) was able to show a significant effect of this ripple effect from data in the midwest.[3]

RECENT LAW ENFORCEMENT RESEARCH FINDINGS

The research reported by Knox, Tromanhauser, Houston, Laskey, and McCurrie (1994) involved a mail questionnaire sent to all police chiefs and county sheriffs in the State of Illinois (N=752). The sample consists of N=289 law enforcement agencies, and thus includes 38.4 percent of all such law enforcement agencies in the State of Illinois. The data was collected in early 1994, and the preliminary results were first reported at the 1994 Annual Meeting of the Academy of Criminal Justice Sciences. The respondents in this case are typically the police chiefs or county sheriffs themselves.

This survey included a large number of variables about gangs and gang issues. In fact, it included 10 variables dealing specifically with gang migration. The basic overall findings are presented here without controlling for the existence, scope, or extent of the gang problem in the same cities.

The survey asked "have you seen gang influence from outside of your community or jurisdiction." Some 88.4 percent of the local police departments indicated that they had in fact seen gang influence from outside of their area. Only 11.6 percent of the Illinois law enforcement agencies responding to the survey reported they had not seen gang influence from outside of their area.

The survey asked "please estimate what percent of the crime in your community/jurisdiction is caused by gangs or gang members from outside of your same area." The results ranged from a low of zero percent to a high of 100 percent, with an overall mean of 12.8 percent. For about one-third of the law enforcement agencies in Illinois responding to the survey (34.2%) the estimate was that 10 percent or more of the crime in their jurisdictional areas was caused by gangs or gang members from outside of their same areas.

The survey asked "please estimate what percentage of the total gang population in your jurisdiction is attributable to families and individuals who have recently relocated to your jurisdiction." A previous question has established the number of total core and periphery gang members in their jurisdiction. The results for the estimate of what percentage of the local gang population is attributable to families and individuals who have recently moved there ranged from a low of zero percent to a high of 100 percent. One-half of the law enforcement agencies (49.1%) gave estimates of 20 percent or higher for this variable. About one-third of the law enforcement agencies (36.1%) felt that 50 percent or more of their local gang population was attributable to such recent relocations by families and individuals into their areas. The overall mean was 30.4 percent.

The survey asked "have gang members recently made even temporary visits (of at least a few days, for whatever reasons) to your community/jurisdiction." Just over two-thirds (69.4%) of the law enforcement agencies in Illinois responding to the survey indicated affirmatively that, in fact, gang members have made such temporary visits to their areas. A follow-up question asked, "if yes, when was your first experience with even temporary visits of gang members to your area? 19___." The results ranged from 1960 to 1994 when the survey was conducted. Only 24.3 percent indicated this first occurred prior to 1989 (1960-1988). The real action picked up in 1990 (19.5%), 1991 (17.2%), 1992 (17.2%), and 1993 (16%). Thus, regarding the year this phenomenon first appeared as reported by law enforcement agencies in Illinois, most of it (71%) occurred on or after 1990.

The survey asked "have you seen cases where a parent relocates to your area (knowing their child was involved with a gang and perhaps thinking they can move away from the problem), and basically transplants the gang problem to your area." Some 64.8 percent of the Illinois law enforcement agencies responding to the survey indicated that they had seen cases of this familial transplant phenomenon take place in their areas.

The survey asked "do you believe some gangs can migrate to jurisdictions such as your own." Only 3.1 percent of the law enforcement agencies responding to the survey did not believe this. The vast majority (96.9%) believed that some gangs can migrate to their own jurisdictions.

The survey asked "do you believe any of the gang problem in your jurisdiction is due to gang migration." Some 30.9 percent of the law enforcement agencies responding to the survey did not believe that any of their gang problem was due to gang migration. However, most of the respondents (69.1%) believed that some of their gang problem might be due to gang migration.

The survey asked "please estimate to what extent the gang problem in your area arose because of gang migration (i.e., outside gangs coming into your area to develop their own local chapters)." The response mode was a scale from a low of 0 (not a factor) to a high of 10 (major factor), and the results similarly ranged between 0 and 10. One-fifth of the respondents (20.4%) gave a rating of zero for an absolute low "not a factor" rating. The overall mean was 4.05 for this variable on a scale between 0 and 10.

The survey asked "please estimate to what extent the gang problem in your area arose because of the copycat phenomenon (i.e., youths who use names of national groups without really having ties to the same groups in other areas)." The same type of response mode was used: zero through 10, with zero being "not a factor," and 10 being "major factor, and the results ranged similarly between 0 and 10. Some 13.3 percent indicated a rating of zero, implying an absolute low value that this was not a factor. The overall mean was 5.02 for this variable on a scale between 0 and 10, somewhat higher than the impact estimate for gang migration alone given above.

These results can be easily summarized. In a survey that includes the results of N=289 law enforcement agencies in the State of Illinois during early 1994, most do believe gang migration can occur, and while the extent of this estimated impact varies, it is still of considerable interest to the law enforcement community.

SUMMARY, CONCLUSIONS, AND RECOMMENDATIONS FOR FUTURE RESEARCH

A gang may have something in its very name that implies migration, such as the Traveling Vice Lords (a.k.a., the Traveler Vice Lords), but that is no reason, *ipso facto*, to assume it has what Thrasher called "Wanderlust." The outlaw motorcycle club known as the Gypsy Jokers is not meant necessarily to imply they want to live the lifestyle of gypsies in a relentless meandering on two wheels.

Some gang members do hold real jobs, and do we call that migration when the youth works in another city? Consider the case of Oak Brook, IL, where the youth gang members come there to work only. Oak Brook is a wealthy, affluent community; 9,080 live there at night, but 70,000 are there during the day—shopping and working. It is too expensive for most gang members to live there. The cost of living is too high. Thus, their gang problem consists of gang members actually working in the community in various hotels and restaurants. There are, however, some organized crime mob members who do reside in the community.

The DEA hypothesis for gang migration, criticized by Malcolm Klein, was that gangs sprout up where interstate highways connect. This would seem one of the easiest hypotheses to actually empirically test. It is a belief widely held by law enforcement officials.

One plausible reason for gang migration would be the evasion motivation. In this scenario the gang member may be "wanted," and moves to a new chapter. Or the heat may be on in their home neighborhood, after a shooting, investigation, etc., so they move in with a girlfriend or associate who lives in the less-conspicuous suburban area, having less-intensive police surveillance.

However, one corollary hypothesis is this: Given residential segregation, it would may be easier for Latino gang members to migrate than for Black gang members; and this has not emerged yet in the migration research literature.

The gang's drug distribution potential provides the best motive for gang migration-eruption: the wannabe, after being moved to a new area, has some experience in the drug subculture of the gang, renews his "connect" to the gang, vows gang loyalty, and "sets up shop" in his new location. Another variation on this may be the small world phenomenon; two transplanted youths from the same city/neighborhood area, "homies" if they were in a national prison; bond by their residential propinquity, or their "hood" of orientation; they recall the gang images and symbols, adopt the same colors, and they are off and running as a wannabe gang by the same name, even though they may not have established reciprocal ties to the parent gang organization. In the small-world phenomenon, two or more such youths from the same area in a new location discover each other, and say to each other "ain't it a small world," bond, and start "kicking it," attracting others.

If an entire gang just packed up and left . . . that would be gang migration; but if it left because of gang suppression policy efforts, it would also be gang displacement: something considered desirable in community policing theory (that is: assuming the area of gang origin had implemented community policing).

Some of what might pass for gang migration may simply be a function of the criminal justice system itself. A gang appears in the correctional system of another state: a gang core member or leader gets on the "circuit;" he starts another gang chapter in the new prison location in a new state. Alternatively, inside a correctional facility, gang members visiting their confined colleague make a presence known in the largest city near the institution (e.g., Joliet, Marion, etc). They establish ties not only to their confined comrades, but to new contacts in the town they intermittently visit.

Then there is the interesting case of the Latin Kings on the East Coast: Gang Migration or Gang Reproduction? Evidence now shows that the Latin King chapters on the east coast have a totally different written constitution than the ALKN gang of origin based in Chicago. True, the east coast LK leader imprisoned in New York who organized there and who wrote the constitution, did have some association with the Chicago group; but he basically started his "own thang" on the east coast.

Recent prior research certainly reveals one thing: many people, particularly in law enforcement, believe that something called "gang migration" does occur. They also believe "gang emulation," the copycat syndrome, or the contagion effect also occurs. But these are, after all, "beliefs" about the problem, and not measures of the actual material and objective factors about the problem itself.

Having said this, it may also be that only an approximation may likely be gained by surveys of police because of the aggregation error.

The real problem, as we see it, is explaining "gang proliferation." Gang migration and gang immigration are only a part of this overall problem of gang proliferation. If we view the city containing gangs as an open-system, then our research methodology would probably need to focus on some systematic data archives on large numbers of actual gang members operating in any given city rather than on the judgments and opinions of those in criminal justice administrative or field positions—unless they can rely on the type of analysis you would prefer they report and unless they have the data you prefer to have analyzed.

Migration is an exogenous source of the gang proliferation problem for any given city. There are many variations on this particular exogenous source of the problem: (1) residential relocation to the new city, (2) temporary visits, and (3) regular visits for work *and* play, legitimate work and illegitimate work.

Among all of these variations there is still the possibility of intentional franchising as a way of creating "new chapters" of the gang. Finally, some "migration" could simply be accidental in nature: federal government agencies like DHHS, for example, have subsidized certain national "Gang Summit" meetings; and it is reasonable to at least hypothesize that in the movement of hundreds of such gang members across state lines, some will sense that the grass is greener elsewhere and may simply relocate. Further, the "familial transplant" phenomenon discussed by Laskey (1994) has several variations, evident in historical records (e.g., Jeff Fort's example[4]), case studies, and now some law enforcement data.

Indigenous sources of the gang proliferation problem must also be investigated before coming to any conclusion about the effects of "migration" as an exogenous source of impact. The copycat phenomenon is one of the leading candidates for indigenous, native, or homegrown gang proliferation. All of the above types of migratory behavior or migratory effects of gangs and gang members have their examples in the larger literature on gangs (Knox, 1995), but much more research is needed on this issue, because it ties into crime patterns.

How much of the variation in "gang proliferation" is therefore explained by "gang migration" is not yet fully known (Knox, 1995). We have only guestimates of this impact. A truly social scientific analysis of this problem cannot be solved solely with the use of agency opinions: it must be based on something we do not have yet—reliable and valid archival data systematically identifying all known gang members within cities being analyzed for this kind of assessment.

Opinions are better than nothing when that is the highest level of social scientific research yet achieved regarding issue as profound in its implications as that of "gang migration." Unfortunately, there is a trend for some gang authors to vastly overgeneralize from their data. The fact is, little hard data exists on this issue. Opinion surveys of those impacted by the problem (i.e., criminal justice practitioners) yield important information, and provide some approximation of the problem. But more detailed and rigorous research is going to be necessary to truly set the record straight about "gang migration."

Our first recommendation is to take a longitudinal approach to those communities in the USA that have not yet experienced any problem with gang proliferation.[5] These communities are now the exception to the rule in the USA. These communities represent the last few opportunities to study the gang proliferation issue before it actually impacts, and while it develops.

Our second recommendation is that government funding for this issue should go far beyond opinion research on criminal justice practitioners. Research should focus on the gang group or gang organization as a unit of analysis, ideally with a national focus. Thirdly, basic issues are not yet resolved: we do not even know the size of the gang population in America, which makes issues about such population research somewhat problematic. Thus, we have a long way to go until this issue is really resolved adequately.

NOTES

[1] Waldorf's (1993) findings are qualitative in nature and are therefore very mixed. Some evidence (verbal translations of interviews with gang members in San Francisco) suggests outside gangs did try to come in and develop franchises, and some evidence suggests simple emulation behavior. Basically, Waldorf states gang members "are often like fish out of water when they go elsewhere" (1993, p. 16) and thus feels they are less capable of intentional imperialism or franchising than some may believe.

[2] See Maxxson's (1993) conclusion that some well-intentioned actions by parents and judges to ship gang members elsewhere could potentially have reverse intended effects. Apparently, the findings here support that conclusion.

[3] This finding on the greater severity of the gang problem in urban areas, dissipating outward to a lower severity of the gang problem in rural areas, is consistent with the research by Quinn, Tobolowsky, and Downs (1994).

[4] Contrary to the claim by Hagedorn and Macon in *People and Folks* thatt there was little Chicago gang influence in Milwaukee, the fact remains that prior to Hagedorn's field work Jeff Fort had moved to Milwaukee and set up his gang operations there after release from prison. Chicago was too "hot" at the time for him. But Jeff Fort would eventually return to Chicago in the 1970's and build up his El Rukn gang organization.

[5] We are not aware of anyone other than ourselves who has been systematically tracking this information first hand and on a regular basis, that is other than federal agencies. The National Gang Crime Research Center has maintained an extensive file called the National Geographic Guide to Gangs and has been routinely updated continuously through national surveys for the last four years. Some of the best data has yet to be released on the gang migration issue, or it is confidential (i.e., the Illinois State Police Gang Intelligence report on gang migration, which tracks "hits" on the statewide gang computer file from routine "stops" where gang members are identified, and this data does suggest extensive travel by gang members in the State of Illinois across and between cities).

Section III

GANGS AND THE CRIMINAL JUSTICE SYSTEM

6

The Police Role in Dealing with Gangs

Jeffrey P. Rush
Jacksonville State University

"Failure to come to grips (with gangs) will cause the demise of our country" (Nichols, 1994). With this statement, Sergeant Mike Nichols of the St. Louis, Missouri, Police Department presents his assessment of the gang problem, and what it holds for the future of our society. Does he speak for all of law enforcement? When the community accepts and recognizes that a gang problem exists, it is law enforcement that they look to for solutions to, and obliteration of, the problem. Unfortunately, by that time, obliteration is all but impossible and solutions are difficult to come by. Sergeant Wes McBride says that by the time we know the gangs are here (through signs, graffiti, etc.) it is too late (1990). There are, however, many ways for police to respond to the gang problem. This chapter will discuss how law enforcement can and should respond to the problem of gangs, gang behavior, and gang violence.

Where gangs were once primarily an urban problem, that is no longer the case. Gangs exist or have the potential to exist in any city, town, or village. And where they exist, so too exists what Curtis Silwa refers to as the DID syndrome: Deny, Ignore, and Delay (1987). First we *deny* that there is a gang problem or that we even have gangs. Then we *ignore* the signs that appear (dress, graffiti, hand signs, admittance, etc.). Finally we *delay* our response to these signs. In some instances, law enforcement is simply responding to the directives of the city administration—this is bad enough. However, in other cases they are responding to the directives of their own command structure and directives. When those on the front lines refuse to, or are not allowed to, discuss gangs, how can the problem be confronted? How can it be addressed? How can prevention or intervention be accomplished?

One of the first things law enforcement must do in addressing the gang problem is to be in the forefront, to lead the charge against gangs. All too often, it is our police and our teachers who are the first to see the problem developing. Law enforcement must be aggressive in its response. They cannot sit around and wait. We expect law enforcement to be "out in front," we give them authority to protect us; they must exercise that authority. At a recent U.S. Senate subcommittee hearing on gang violence, it was agreed by all participants that the basic responsibility of law enforcement is to provide community safety. That is accomplished in many ways, including the identification of potential problems, and the communication of that potential to those who need to know. Such people include city leaders, community leaders, and the community itself. When law enforcement fails to exercise this responsibility, they are letting their community and themselves down, and are not living up to professional expectations.

It is law enforcement that is in the best position, among all of criminal justice, to appreciably deal with a gang problem focused on gang control through community improvement. This was identified as a viable function of law enforcement as early as 1983 (Needle & Stapleton, 1983). All too often, when gangs appear in a community, the residents retreat, often in fear. This leaves the police to do "battle" with the gangs. While the residents may have retreated, they are not disinterested. Under appropriate police leadership, community residents can take back their streets. Without it, they will lose their streets, and their sense of community, and perhaps the foreboding of Sergeant Nichols, will, in fact, come to pass.

It is clear, then, that law enforcement cannot solve the gang problem alone. In fact, the "typical police organization is not well structured to deal with (youth) gangs" (Huff & McBride, 1993:402). Huff (1989; 1990) identifies a typical law enforcement approach that I will call the DOO approach—Deny, Overreact, Overlabel. This is not unlike the DID syndrome, but it applies specifically to law enforcement's response to gangs.

As with DID, the first approach is *denial*. Again, sometimes the denial is lead by law enforcement, at other times, and law enforcement simply goes along with the community leaders. In any case, this is a dangerous stage, as it allows the gangs to obtain a foothold in the community.

Second is *overreaction*. Huff identifies this stage as one in which the gang problem is defined as one for the police to solve. This approach is easy for community leaders, as it absolves them of any responsibility for either the problem or its solution. Indeed, in many cases this approach allows them to blame the police. After all, they are the ones charged with protecting the community. They should have seen it coming. They should have done something about it. They should have informed us. It is their fault, it is their problem, it is their responsibility. They are the ones who should be held accountable.

Such rationale leads to the third stage, *overlabeling*. As law enforcement struggles to deal with gangs, often with few or scattered resources, they have a tendency to identify everyone interacting with a gangster or gang as being in that gang. It has even been suggested that this overlabeling actually influences individuals to join a gang when they might not otherwise do so (cf Hagedorn, 1988; Huff, 1989; 1990). This overlabeling, then, has the potential of escalating gang membership, recruitment, and conflict. These overestimates call into question the integrity of the agency and its officers, resulting in fewer resources and a less favorable impression.

Hagedorn (1988) identifies yet another problem in law enforcement's response to gangs, that is, a failure to understand gangs. He notes:

> The law enforcement paradigm defines gangs in a narrow and unchanging manner, which neglects the process of development that different age groups within gangs undergo, and ignores or undervalues variations of all sorts. Gangs are not seen as young people struggling to adapt, often destructively, to a specific economic and social environment. Rather, gangs are treated as a major criminal problem, and their members dehumanized as no more than aspiring "career criminals" (1988:106).

He goes on to suggest that racism contributes to this lack of understanding and "results in even greater hostility on the streets" (1988:106). It would appear that rather than explaining a failure on the part of law enforcement, Hagedorn is attempting to justify gang behavior. Gangsters are not criminals, but rather victims. And this victimization is enhanced by the response of law enforcement.

While it may be true that law enforcement overlabels individuals as gangsters, it is doubtful that gangsters are victims of anything other than their own choices. As for being a major criminal problem, most of those employed in criminal justice would agree that they are. Fagan's (1989) four gang types are all associated with criminal activity at some level. Even Hagedorn acknowledges the risk for violence, "All gangs we studied in Milwaukee were "fighting gangs" . . . (1988:100). This fighting apparently took place during their younger years. (Perhaps as they were establishing their presence?) As they matured, "their interests turned more to the fundamental problems of survival" (Hagedorn, 1988:100). Whether one commits criminal acts for "survival" or not, they are criminal acts nonetheless, resulting in the consequence Hagedorn himself notes, "the imposition of police patrols, vigilante justice and prisons" (1988:14).

Whether nonserious crime or serious crime, it is law enforcement that must respond, that must deal with the problem—a problem that is not only persistent, but continually growing. The recently held hearings on gang violence are instructive here. Three panels, composed of politicians, police officers, and correctional personnel indicated that gang violence was at epidemic levels and was responsible for a significant amount of violent crime (e.g., 20%

of all murders in St. Louis, Missouri) as well as property crime (frequently drug-related). One of the leading experts on gangs, Professor Irving Spergel, testified that the focus of criminal justice must be on "reducing gang violence and criminal activity" (1994), not necessarily on reducing gangs themselves. In fact, Los Angeles County Probation Officer Jim Galipeau indicated that you cannot get rid of gangs, but you can change their focus (1994). Similar comments have been made by Wes McBride of the Los Angeles County Sheriff's Office. Thus the "major crime problem" is real, and one that must be addressed, whether we understand the gangs or not. If the traditional responses of law enforcement have not worked, then what should the police do? That is what we will now examine.

While there is recognition that there must be more suppression and intervention (particularly on the part of the police), they cannot do this alone. The police response must be a part of a larger community-based strategy (Kramer, 1986; Spergel & Curry, 1990). Specific to the police, however, the law enforcement response must include the following:

1. Intelligence and information processing
2. Prevention
3. Enforcement
4. Follow-up investigation (Huff & McBride, 1993:402)

Unfortunately, even where it recognized that these are the proper purposes of law enforcement for dealing with gangs, all too often these responses are scattered throughout the police organization. When this scattering is coupled with the idea that every police agency sees their gang problem as unique to their jurisdiction, it is a wonder that as much is accomplished as there is.

For this reason, the above-identified responses must be consolidated into one unit (or one officer). This unit, however, cannot be seen as elitist or as the *only* unit in the department responsible for dealing with gangs. Clearly, every police officer is responsible for and will certainly deal with a gangster, or a gang or a gang crime. It must be remembered, however, that no two gangs are alike, and that gangsters and gang crime are, in many ways, substantially different from other criminals and crimes. The purpose of the centralized unit is to coordinate the department's approach and increase accountability for taking on the gang problem. The unit must also be responsible (in the absence of a statewide definition) for defining what a gang is, what a gangster is, and what constitutes a gang (or gang-related) crime. This specialized unit, then, becomes a resource for the officers in the department and the related criminal justice agencies. As much of their work will be on the streets in the gang community monitoring gang activity and talking with gangsters and "wannabees," this unit should be located organizationally within the patrol division. While a certain level of jealousy is to be expected between divisions, the unit being located in patrol should assist in interdepartmental communication and help reduce the idea that this is an elite unit.

This unit must establish a comprehensive procedure and database for data collection, analysis, planning, service delivery, and feedback, what Oxnard Police refer to as GO-CAP (Gang Offender Comprehensive Action Plan) (Owens & Wells, 1993:26). The "heart" of dealing with gangs is accurate and timely information concerning organizational structure, leadership, rituals, cultural beliefs, membership, etc. It seems that as soon as criminal justice identifies the graffiti, signs, dress, etc. the gangs change; they appear to always be one step ahead. Thus the importance of an accurate database is paramount. A hodgepodge of officers cannot provide this kind of accurate and timely information—a specialized unit can. The information collected and analyzed must include anything and everything even remotely believed to be gang related. Let the unit decide if it is or is not gang related, and then disseminate that information to patrol, investigations, etc. This centralized database will also assist in avoiding overlabeling or premature classification of gang members, which Huff and McBride indicates to be "particularly dangerous with respect to wannabees who often experiment with various gangs . . . and may or may not actually join one" (1993:407). This information can then be disseminated to the patrol division who can then be better informed and have their work (at least with respect to gangs) be better directed.

In addition to the collection, analysis, and dissemination of information, members of the gang unit need to be seen as part of the division. As such, they should be available for use as backups, and as members of multi-unit task forces. From time to time (as situations and crimes arise), members of the patrol division should likewise serve as part of the gang unit. For many, this could be a type of training or probationary period for future service, for all, it could help ease the jealousy as the (patrol) officers recognize that the gang unit does do important work and provide good information. Members of the unit should also serve as members of community task forces or other multi-agency criminal justice task forces geared toward gangs and gangsters. The information and expertise possessed by gang unit members can only serve to enhance the abilities and recommendations of such task forces. The specialized gang unit can help direct the department toward a balanced and comprehensive approach to gang control. As has been mentioned previously, law enforcement cannot do this alone. Dealing with gangs requires a comprehensive approach involving all members of the criminal justice community, schools, community leaders and the like. Led by the police, fundamental changes in the community structure can be accomplished, and it is only by making these fundamental changes can appropriate gang control measures be undertaken. Thus the community-oriented police (COP) approach appears to be the best model (at least for dealing with gangs and gang crime). Whether

COP is used throughout the department or not, it appears to be the most appropriate model for use in gang suppression.

It must be recognized, however that whatever model(s) is used, it must be appropriate to the individual department or jurisdictional's gang problem. All gangs are not alike, and all jurisdictions are not alike. While there are some similarities (most notably violence and drugs) there are substantial differences as well. The use of a centralized gang unit can be helpful in targeting (and leading) this balanced comprehensive approach. They can also be useful in staying abreast of current thinking and what is happening in other places. As Huff notes, ". . . officers who know a great deal about what is happening on their beats, do not necessarily know what is happening communitywide" (cited in Conly, 1993:53). Since part of their role is to serve as a departmental/community resource, the gang unit can more efficiently be aware of and disseminate information than can the individual officers.

Finally, the gang unit can work diligently (as individuals and in their role as a resource), to work and deal with current and potential gangsters in non-arrest situations. Such dealings helps to cultivate information and establish positive relationships. Members of gang units seem to recognize the importance of this more so than the average patrol officer, many of whom simply want to "kick ass." Huff (1989) has already noted that gangsters often cite individual officers as exerting a positive influence on them. How? By treating the gangster fairly, exhibiting a genuine concern for him/her or their family, and by constantly demonstrating professional behavior in their dealings with the gang. There seems to be a great paradox (Jackson & McBride, 1987) in dealing with gangs. Gangs/gangsters who view their treatment as fair and warranted will typically not retaliate against the officer or department. Behavior that is viewed as unwarranted or unfair results in an almost constant barrage of harassment and confrontation. The movie *Colors*, especially the character played by Sean Penn, is instructive here. As Jackson and McBride note, "there seems to be a perverted code of 'ethics' within gangs . . . it seems that a gang commits an act, passes judgement on itself, and then accepts punishment—as long as the punishment seems justified" (1987:109). By devoting their shift to working in, among, and with the gangs, the members of the gang unit can develop these positive relationships (without sacrificing the traditional police role) which result in an improvement in the investigation, prevention, and suppression of gang behavior. Gang unit members can then assist the "regular" patrol officers in developing their own relationships with the gangsters and, when necessary, serve as a buffer between the gang and the beat cop. While often resented by the beat cop, the lives saved by such an interaction are numerous.

Taking the lead among community and criminal justice agencies, law enforcement is involved with a variety of different prevention-type programs. Perhaps the most well-known of these is GREAT (Gang Resistance Education and Training). Following the DARE model; this program, a collaboration of local police, schools, and the BATF attempts to direct a structured anti-gang message to students. Initially focused toward seventh graders, GREAT now encompasses two programs focusing on four grades: third, fourth, seventh and eighth. The second program is a summer one, including education and participation in numerous recreational activities. Initially begun in Phoenix, Arizona, with the participation of FLETC in Glynco, Georgia, GREAT has now been expanded to over 250 agencies, in 39 states and the District of Columbia; reaching over 105,000 students during the 1993-94 school year (Humphrey & Baker, 1994). Unfortunately, an evaluation of its first year by Palumbo, Eskay and Hallet (1992) found that, "for the most part the training had very little impact" (p. 7). Part of this involved the students believing that gangs are not all bad, the gangs are helpful and provide an important outlet, and a disbelief of what the police officers were saying (Palumbo, et al., 1992). Its possible, indeed likely that GREAT will go the way of DARE—it looks good, sounds good, is relative inexpensive, but does very little.

As law enforcement undertakes the preventive aspect of gang work, it is incumbent upon them to pick and choose those programs that work, are effective, and are appropriate for their particular jurisdiction. To simply pick a program because its "sexy" or "politically correct" will more likely do more harm than good.

All of us, especially law enforcement must face the reality that the gang problem is not going away. In fact, many studies seem to indicate that the problem is worsening (cf Palumbo, et al.:1). Whether worsening or not, gangsters have become more bold in their criminality and other defiance of the law, demonstrating contempt for the public (and the police) believing they can violate the law with impunity (Huff & McBride, 1993).

A second reality is one that most law enforcement personnel should have no trouble grasping (or agreeing with). Gangs and gangsters are criminal enterprises, they are criminals—criminals who in many areas have banded together, criminals who have gone transnational. Perhaps, as Dart suggests, the time has come to "adopt a new approach—we must address the demise of these transnational organizations, not rehash their history and violence and endeavors" (1993:8). Let's treat them as the (organized) criminals they are, not some misguided, disenfranchised youth. They are misguided, they may be disenfranchised, poor, predominately one ethnic or racial group or whatever other spin the sociologists and social workers might want to take with (for) them—but they are also criminals, engaged in violent criminal activity, and should be dealt with accordingly.

A third reality is that we cannot obliterate gangs. Those who believe that (especially police officers) are faced with an insurmountable, unachieveable task. What can be accomplished is decreasing the rate of gang activity, and recruitment levels. This would serve to slowly remove the gang's existence by drying up the recruit pool. To do this requires a proactive approach on the part of law enforcement and the community, recognizing:

1. That street gangs are identifiable groups that inflict more heinous and tragic crimes on society than most other identifiable groups,

2. That street gangs are malignant entities that, like any other malignancy, *must not be ignored,* and

3. That while not obliterated, gang activity can be contained and managed, through *aggressive* interaction between the community and law enforcement agencies (Huff & McBride, 1993:411-412 emphasis added).

Understanding the above, and including in their response intelligence and information processing, prevention, enforcement and follow-up investigation, law enforcement can make a difference, and can provide the link with other criminal justice and community agencies necessary to effectively intervene, prevent, and in some cases suppress gangs and gang activity. To do so requires law enforcement to change their traditional thinking, be proactive in their enforcement efforts and in their efforts to include other individuals and agencies; and to understand and be wary of gangs. But not to give up their efforts, be fearful or, "in no way be alarmed by your opponents—which is a sign of destruction for them . . . (Philippians 1:28). That is what gangs hope for, what gives them their existence and we cannot and will not let them win.

7

Treating Youth Gangs Like Organized Crime Groups: An Innovative Strategy for Prosecuting Youth Gangs

Gregory P. Orvis
University of Alabama

INTRODUCTION

Youth gang membership in the past has always been treated as an unusual manifestation of juvenile delinquency that was a local problem particular to the biggest cities and, although occasionally violent, would not last as an ongoing pattern of crime in a youth's life beyond his or her teenage years. Today, there are more than 100,000 youth gangs with a combined membership of over one million juveniles and adults in the United States (Delattre, 1990). A 1992 police department survey revealed that all but 7 of 79 large cities and all but 5 of 43 small cities were troubled by gangs (Curry, Ball & Fox, 1994). Although many youth gang members do leave gangs as a passing phase of their lives, many stay with the gangs past their teens as "gangsters," or hardcore gang members in their twenties, and "OG"s, or original gangsters, who may be much older (Bureau of Alcohol, Tobacco and Firearms, 1989). Furthermore, gang violence and involvement in the lucrative illegal drug trade are prevalent and widespread in American communities as can be witnessed in the media's coverage of the problem every day. The black youth gangs, in particular the Bloods and the Crips, have expanded way beyond being a local problem, with a total membership of 15,000-20,000 and direct linkage to crack distribution in 46 states (Delattre, 1990).

As Dr. Carl S. Taylor (1990) notes, "The bottom line is that gangs in 1990 are not the same as gangs in 1950 or 1970—a fact that cannot be ignored." In fact, youth gangs today have much more in common with organized crime groups such as the mafia, the triads, the yakuza, and outlaw motorcycle clubs than they do with the youth gangs of the past. It is argued herein that since youth gangs are more like organized crime groups today than the loosely banded juvenile delinquents of yesteryear, then the criminal justice system, particularly prosecutorial organizations, should use the strategies developed to successfully battle other organized crime groups to fight the youth gang problem.

Crimes committed by youth gang members have traditionally been addressed singularly by prosecutorial organizations. Although certain types of crime have been used to monitor the magnitude of youth gang activity (Jackson & McBride, 1992), there has been no comprehensive plan to use the prosecutor's power to solve, or at least reduce, the youth gang problem. It is argued herein that youth gangs should be treated as organized crime groups by prosecutorial organizations. It may be argued that gangs are not structured enough to be considered as organized crime groups. However, when the definitional traits of organized crime groups are compared with those of youth gangs, such differences are minute and the prosecutorial strategies used against organized crime groups could be used against most youth gangs with equal success.

DEFINING YOUTH GANGS AS ORGANIZED CRIME GROUPS

Organized crime groups have been defined in many ways. Some definitions are very narrow and require a highly structured group to be an organized crime group. The President's Commission on Organized Crime (1986) defined organized crime as the collective result of three groups: (1) the criminal group, tied together by some bond and who use criminal acts to gain power and profit; (2) the protectors, who protect the criminal group's interests; and (3) the specialist support, who are on an ad hoc basis to further the criminal group's interests. Furthermore, they did not consider youth gangs as organized crime groups in their report (President's Commission on Organized Crime, 1986). However, Jay Albanese (1989) reviewed the definitions of organized crime scholars over a 15-year period to distill a definition of organized crime as "a continuing criminal enterprise that rationally works to profit from illicit activities that are in great public demand. Its continuing existence is maintained through the use of force, threats, and/or the corruption of public officials" (Albanese, 1989). Similarly, Howard Abadinsky (1990) notes that law enforcement officials and scholars found that there are eight characteristics that organized crime groups have in common. An organized crime group:

1. is nonideological;
2. is hierarchical;
3. has a limited or exclusive membership;
4. is perpetuitous;
5. uses illegal violence and bribery;
6. demonstrates specialization or division of labor;
7. is monopolistic; and
8. is governed by explicit rules and regulations (Abadinsky, 1990).

Each of these characteristics can be applied to youth gangs, although how close they fit may depend on the how far the individual gang is on the developmental continuum. Carl Taylor (1990) categorizes gangs by motivation: (1) "scavenger" gangs, whose behavior is impulsive and whose leadership can change on a day-by-day basis; (2) "territorial" gangs, who organize for a specific purpose, who have territorial turf, and who have clear leaders; and (3) "organized/corporate" gangs who are well-organized, who have managers rather than leaders, and whose criminal actions are strictly motivated by profit. Gangs may develop from loosely structured scavenger gangs who are not predominately motivated by economics to highly structured organized/corporate gangs with a high economic motive (Taylor, 1990). For the purpose of this chapter, the focus is on territorial and organized/corporate gangs because they are the major source for the growing violence and drug trade in gang-related activities.

These youth gangs are non-ideological in nature. In studies of how youths became gang members, most were drawn to the economic and social opportunities of gang membership (Fagan, 1990). Some juveniles join youth gangs because of peer pressure or to gain a "family" bond that is missing in their home life, while others join to gain a reputation and fortune (Weldon, 1990). As a gang becomes increasingly involved in the drug trade, so increases the economic opportunities from being a gang member. It is safe to say that economic and social rewards are what motivate gang members and not any gang "ideology."

Developed youth gangs range from having a highly structured hierarchy to a very loose leadership structure. Although most black gangs do not have a formal structure per se, older members who have earned their reputation are called "shot callers" and often control the younger members. Furthermore, a few black gangs that originated in the Chicago area have a formal chain of command, such as the Disciples who rank from foot soldier to King and whose hierarchy is reminiscent of the Mafia's organizational structure (Weldon, 1990). Hispanic gangs have ad hoc leaders with a "flat" organizational structure, whereas Asian gangs tend to have a stricter hierarchy bordering on bureaucratic structure (Jackson & McBride, 1992). The majority of the youth gangs have an organizational structure somewhere in between, but do have some type of structure.

Most developed youth gangs are perpetuitous. Walter Miller (1990) assures that, "Crime by gang members is largely a product of social and cultural learning." A characteristic of youth gangs is that many of their members are in their early teens, often called "wanna-be's," "pee wees," or "midgets," and they are influenced greatly by older gang members who act as role models (Miller, 1990). Some families promote their gang allegiances to their children , and this promotes the gang through generations. Often gangs are tied to a community, and the "OGs" promote the gang and socialize children in the community as "BGs," or baby gangsters (Bureau of Alcohol, Tobacco, and Firearms, 1989).

Although there is not much evidence supporting youth gangs bribing public officials, the use of violence by gangs is well documented. Gang members have been responsible for 2700 murders in Los Angeles County alone (Pace, 1991). In a recent National Institute of Justice study, one-half of all the recorded gang-related criminal incidents are homicides or other violent crimes (Curry, Ball & Fox, 1994). The potential violence of gangs was demonstrated in another National Institute of Justice study, wherein 75 percent of "structured" gang members and 72 percent of "unstructured" gang members informed that they had an automatic or semiautomatic handgun, and 53 percent of both groups reported owning military-style rifles (Sheley & Wright, 1993). In the study of Chicago gangs over a 26-year period, a gun was the weapon used in almost all gang-related homicides, with the use of automatic or semi-automatic weapons in such homicides increasing from 22 percent to 31 percent in the last three years (Block & Block, 1993). The Office of Juvenile Justice and Delinquency Prevention (1993) reports that gang violence has risen dramatically from the late 1970s and early 1980s, and that gang members are increasingly using gangs as a means to gain illegal money, particularly through street-level drug trafficking.

There is some specialization or division of labor even among those youth gangs with a "loose" hierarchy. Hispanic gangs often choose their leader for a particular activity depending on the nature of the activity and the individual's expertise as to that activity (Jackson & McBride, 1992). Gang members are often admired by their peers for their expertise as to a special crime, and gang leaders may consult them when such a crime is being planned.

Youth gangs are monopolistic, particularly as to their "turf." It is interesting to note that gang violence is more often related to turf that it is to the drug trade (Block & Block, 1993). Gangs have certain areas that are considered theirs, and that other gangs enter only at the risk of their lives. The gang's "turf" is usually marked with warning graffiti. Drug trade in a gang's turf is controlled by that gang, and encroachments by other drug dealers are often rewarded with violence.

There are explicit rules and regulations for youth gang members, although they may not be written as with some other organized crime groups. It is well documented that gangs have their own meanings for words, sign language, dress, and graffiti, with rules as to its use as well as rules concerning conduct, even when incarcerated (Jackson & McBride, 1992). In a manuscript compiled for an urban police department, the functions of gang slang are delineated as forming the gang culture, formulating a secret code to hide information from others, making hidden reference to drug deals and other crimes, and identifying gang members and associates to each other (Weldon, 1990). In many ways, informal gang slang serves the same purposes for youth gangs as the more formal "omerta" code of the mafia.

STRATEGIES FOR PROSECUTING YOUTH GANGS AS ORGANIZED CRIME GROUPS

In a survey of 254 respondents in 45 cities, the most common strategy in dealing with youth gang problems was "suppression" through the criminal justice process, although it was not generally associated with effectiveness (Spergel & Curry, 1990). The lack of success of a suppression policy may be because it was implemented by prosecuting crimes by gang members on an ad hoc basis rather than as a part of a comprehensive prosecution strategy to battle the youth gang problem.

Over 1,000 Mafia members and associates were convicted and sentenced to prison for federal crimes since 1981 due to the fact that U.S. attorneys and FBI agents followed a common strategy since that date: the enterprise theory of investigation. As the Federal Bureau of Investigation (1988) reports it, "Under the enterprise theory, investigative attention is directed at the hierarchy to penetrate the chain of command using conventional techniques such as informants and cooperating witnesses or extraordinary techniques such as undercover agents or court approved electronic surveillances" (1988:13). The prosecution's case is built in stages; within the first stage, law enforcement agents identifies an organized crime group's hierarchy and communication system. At the second stage, the criminal "enterprise" and individual criminal acts are initially identified and the laws providing sanctions for such activities dictate the progress of the investigation. At stage three, the leader of the organized crime group is targeted for prosecution along with any immediate associates in the criminal enterprise, thus disrupting the criminal group's activities. The illegal assets are then targeted under the civil and criminal forfeiture laws in stage four. Finally at stage five, the most severe sanctions are sought in both the criminal and civil courts to deter the criminal activities or "enterprise" from continuing (Federal Bureau of Investigation, 1988). Although it may be more difficult to identify and infiltrate a youth gang's hierarchy, a similar difficulty arose when the FBI tried the same techniques against the Chinese Triads, yet there has been growing success, albeit it slowly (Federal Bureau of Investigation, 1988). The enterprise theory of investigation, or some such comprehensive strategy for investigation and prosecution of youth gangs, must be implemented to address this growing organized crime problem. The targeting of youth gang leaders for prosecution under the enterprise theory of investigation is particularly significant in that police agencies in Los Angeles have noted that when a youth gang's leaders are incarcerated, the gang's criminal activities greatly decrease as well (Jackson & McBride, 1992).

Certain crimes have often been monitored to measure gang violence because they are consistently associated with gangs. Murder, assault with attempt to commit murder, assault with a deadly weapon, robbery, rape by force, kidnapping, arson, shooting into an inhabited dwelling, battery and assault with a deadly weapon on a police officer, extortion, and witness intimidation are monitored in some jurisdictions and compared with gang member lists compiled by police to determine if it is gang-related crime and thus measure gang violence (Jackson & McBride, 1992). A recent study found that national data on gangs is hard to obtain because jurisdictions differ in their definitions of what constitutes a gang-related crime (Curry, Ball & Fox, 1994). Constant definitions of such crimes are necessary to measure gang activity and facilitate prosecution (Jackson & McBride, 1992). Once such crimes are determined, a special division of a prosecutor's office could be created or a special prosecutor be designated to prosecute such crimes to the maximum penalty once they are identified as gang-related crimes during the screening process.

Some cities have had priority prosecution units for adult career criminals since the 1970s and for juvenile habitual offenders since the 1980s. These units include highly experienced prosecutors who engage in vertical prosecution (i.e., one prosecutor handles a case from the beginning to the end), case coalescence (i.e., one prosecutor handles all the cases pending against a defendant), increased use of pretrial detention, pursuit of conviction for the most serious crime, and close cooperation with the police in identifying those for priority prosecution. Once an offender is targeted for priority prosecution, it is more likely that the offender will be convicted, get a higher sentence with substantial time actually being served, and have intensive supervision in the correctional and aftercare services (Weiner, 1993). Such priority prosecution units can be established to target members of youth gangs for priority prosecution, and may pattern themselves after the organized crime task forces that operated successfully in the past against the Mafia in prosecutor's offices in New York and New Jersey. Special gang units in the police department with adequate support personnel and administrative control have also been suggested as necessary to the suppression of illegal gang activity (Jackson & McBride, 1992), and certainly would enhance the operations of corresponding priority prosecution units if communication and cooperation are maintained by proper liaisons.

Some jurisdictions lobby for legislation that targets gangs (Spergel & Curry, 1990). Prosecutorial organizations could lobby state legislatures for heavier penalties for crimes determined to be gang-related crimes, or crimes that are associated with gang activities. Some jurisdictions have successfully lobbied to make it easier to prosecute minor gang members as adults as part of their gang "suppression" strategy, and prosecutorial organizations should lobby for this as well. Some prosecutorial organizations have enough resources to hire their own full-time lobbyist, such as the Dallas prosecutor's office in the 1980s. Other prosecutorial organizations lobby on an ad hoc basis. Because the problem of youth gang crimes is a constant one and laws are the tools for fighting the problem, local prosecutorial organizations should pool their resources to hire a full-time lobbyist to the state capital so that prosecutors have the tools that they need to address the youth gang crime problem in a comprehensive manner.

EXISTING LAWS AS TOOLS FOR PROSECUTING YOUTH GANGS AS ORGANIZED CRIME GROUPS

Prosecutors should also use those statutes that were developed by Congress and state legislatures to specifically target organized crime groups against youth gangs. The Bureau of Alcohol, Tobacco, and Firearms (1989) suggests the Anti-Drug Abuse Act of 1986, the Comprehensive Crime Control Act of 1984, and the Gun Control Act of 1968 as significant tools in the prosecution of gang members, and which are often used against more traditional organized crime groups. The Organized Crime Control Act of 1970 in general and its provisions governing witness immunity and the witness protection program have been useful in combating traditional organized crime groups (Albanese, 1989), and could be used with equal success against youth gangs that cross state boundaries. Howard Abadinsky (1990), the renowned expert on organized crime, notes several federal statutes that have been successfully used against organized crime groups, including the Bank Secrecy Act of 1970 (i.e., money laundering), the Hobbes Act (i.e., making it a federal crime to engage in crimes that interfere with interstate commerce), the Internal Revenue Code, Controlled Substances statutes, Consumer Credit Protection Act of 1968 (i.e., loansharking or extortion), and the Comprehensive Forfeiture Act of 1984. These federal laws could be useful tools against youth gangs' criminal activites, although some are more applicable to highly developed youth gangs or to their adult members or to crimes that cross state boundaries.

In particular, the Racketeer Influenced and Corrupt Organizations (1970) statute, commonly called RICO, has been described as "the most important single piece of legislation ever enacted against organized crime" (Abadinsky, 1990:422). RICO was designed specifically to target the overall and ongoing operations of an organized crime group by prohibiting racketeering activities, which include drug trafficking, murder, and many crimes not normally considered under federal law, or its profits from being used to acquire or maintain the business of an existing organization such as an organized crime group (Bureau of Justice Statistics, 1988). RICO has been used quite successfully against the Mafia and could be used with equal success against those youth gangs with criminal ties across state borders. Because of the flexibility of RICO's provisions generally, and specifically its forfeiture provisions, RICO has been referred to as the "new darling of the prosecutor's nursery" and is so broad that any criminal transaction that uses the mail, telephone, or interstate wire communications opens the door to a possible criminal prosecution under RICO (Gardner & Anderson, 1992).

The President's Commission on Organized Crime (1986) recommended that states develop similar statutes, or "Little RICOs." As of 1989, 26 states have passed similar legislation (Abadinsky, 1990). However, in the absence of a "little RICO," other states, such as Alabama (Criminal Conspiracy statutes, 1993), have convicted members of organized crime groups for similar criminal activities by prosecuting under traditional conspiracy statutes. Building a conspiracy case is time and resource consuming for a prosecutorial organization, but important for deterring other youths from joining even the planning of the illegal activites of a youth gang (Jackson & McBride, 1992). Other states, such as Texas, passed legislation (Organized Crime statute, 1994) aimed at criminal activities often engaged in by organized crime groups and youth gang members have been charged with these crimes (Avera, 1994). These practices should continue in all states if youth gang crimes are to be successfully prosecuted as organized crime.

PROBLEMS IN PROSECUTING YOUTH GANGS AS ORGANIZED CRIME GROUPS

The foremost problem in prosecuting youth gang crimes is admitting that a youth gang problem exists. This reluctance of elected and law enforcement officials to recognize a youth gang problem in their jurisdiction makes it difficult to categorize gang crime and fragments law enforcement efforts to control gang activities (Connors, 1991). The President of the Institute of Law and Justice noted several problems in the criminal justice system's handling of youth gang crimes, including a lack of cooperation between police and prosecutors and a lack of a national reporting system on gang crime that hinders communication (Connors, 1991). Assuming that a gang problem exists in a jurisdiction by prosecutors, developing a uniform reporting system of gang crimes, and creating a police liaison as to gang activities are necessary prerequisites to a comprehensive anti-gang prosecutorial strategy. All of these factors relate to the communication problem that must be overcome if such a strategy is to be successfully implemented.

Several problems are inherent in the prosecution of youth gang members like members of traditional organized crime groups. The presence and intensity of such problems may differ somewhat with the community and the origin of the youth gang. One problem is that leadership in youth gangs is not as structured as organized crime groups, and hence harder to target for prosecution. It is argued that acquiring a target for such prosecution is difficult, but it is not impossible if the nature of the youth gang is taken into account. Strategies for identifying the leaders and prosecutorial targets may depend on the ethnic nature of the youth gang. Asian gangs tend to be more organized with a clear leadership, whereas Hispanic gangs have no formally recognized leaders, but have ad hoc leaders, depending on the situation and whose talents are needed at the time (Jackson & McBride, 1992). Other youth gangs' leadership structure fit between these two extremes, often depending on their cultural background and how "evolved" a youth gang is on the developmental continuum. Different strategies in identifying youth gang leaders will have to be developed for different ethnic youth gangs.

A second problem is the growing mobility of gang members. Some gang members are mobile to avoid local law enforcement, while others are mobile to escape the violence of conflicts with rival gangs. Others are purposefully mobile in order to establish drug trafficking in other parts of the country than their normal turf. This has been found to be common of "Crips" and "Bloods" gang members originating from Los Angeles (Bureau of Justice Statistics, 1992). Asian ethnic groups are highly mobile, having family members or friends in various locations, thus creating convenient hideouts across the country for Asian gang members fleeing the law or violent rivals (Keene, 1987). However, this may be a benefit in that federal prosecutorial organizations and their greater resources may become involved when gang activities cross state lines.

A third problem is the exclusive nature of gang membership that makes it nearly impossible for investigators to infiltrate youth gangs like other organized crime groups. Other, perhaps more expensive and technological, investigative techniques will have to be relied on if successful prosecution of youth gangs is to be maintained in the future. It is even harder to get informers from within the group when prosecutors have not been able to implement witness protection programs for such cases (Connors, 1991).

A fourth problem is that the vast majority of gang members are juveniles and family court punishments are slight if at all. In response to increasing levels of violent crimes by juveniles, many states are changing their juvenile justice system as a whole from a rehabilitative model to a crime control model, such as by Washington' s and Texas' determinate sentencing for juveniles

(Forst & Blomquist, 1992). Statutory reform of juvenile punishments and special laws targeting gang activity must be called for a the state level, where most substantive and procedural criminal law is located.

A fifth problem is that there may be a lack of cooperation with law enforcement from the community in which the youth gang operates. Some community members may still view the problem as a mere juvenile delinquency problem, with a "boys will be boys" attitude, rather than as the organized crime problem that really exists. Other community members may distrust the police. Language differences can also cause difficulties in ethnic communities. These latter two problems have been particularly distressful in Asian ethnic communities (Keene, 1987).

Special training of prosecutors may be necessary to implement any comprehensive prosecutorial strategy aimed at gang activity. Prosecutors on an anti-gang task force in Los Angeles are trained on how to prosecute gang cases at the police academy (Genelin, 1991). If a comprehensive anti-gang strategy is adopted, all of the prosecutors in a prosecutorial organization should be specially trained in its implementation.

SUMMARY AND CONCLUSION

Several points have been made in this chapter. First, the most developed, and usually most violent, youth gangs are organized crime groups and therefore pose a significant crime problem to the public that should be treated as such by prosecutorial organizations. Second, prosecutorial organizations must create special youth gang prosecution units and must work with police organizations to develop a comprehensive "suppression" strategy to combat the youth gang problem. Prosecutorial organizations may look to the enterprise theory of investigation for guidance because its application to other organized crime groups, such as the Mafia and Triads, has been successful. Third, prosecutorial organizations should use federal and state laws that have been used to successfully combat other organized crime groups to attack youth gangs; in particular, the RICO and little RICO statutes. Furthermore, prosecutorial organizations should lobby for new laws that specifically target gang-related crimes for harsher sanctions. Fourth, although the nature of the youth gang and the community in which it operates may cause problems for the prosecutorial organization, they are problems that prosecutors have dealt with before in fighting more traditional organized crime groups. Problems of a community's reluctance to admit an organized crime problem, targeting the group's leaders, the group members' mobility, difficult group infiltration, inadequate sanctions for criminal behavior, and community resistance to law enforcement have confronted prosecutors of traditional organized crime groups in the past as they confront prosecutors of youth gangs today. Such problems were then and are today exacerbated by a lack of cooperation, communication, and specialization of law enforcement units investigating an organized crime group's activities. These problems were overcome then as to the Mafia and the Triads and can be overcome now as to youth gangs with the proper legislative tools, a comprehensive prosecutorial strategy, special units, interagency cooperation and communication, and perseverance.

8

Prison Gang Dynamics:
A Research Update

Robert S. Fong
California State University—Bakersfield

Ronald E. Vogel
California State University—Long Beach

Salvador Buentello
Texas Department of Criminal Justice

INTRODUCTION

For more than two decades, the proliferation of prison gangs has severely disrupted many American correctional institutions. In a pioneer nationwide study, Camp and Camp (1985) identified the presence of 114 gangs with a total membership of 12,634 in 33 prison systems, including the Federal Bureau of Prisons. While prison gangs accounted for only three percent of the U.S. prison population, they were believed to be responsible for 50 percent of all prison management problems (Camp & Camp, 1988). A classic example of the disruptive, violent and destructive nature of prison gangs is demonstrated by the recent history of the Texas Department of Criminal Justice (TDCJ), formerly Texas Department of Corrections. In that system, prison officials nearly lost control of their prisons as a result of the sudden surge of prison gangs during the mid-1980s (Beaird, 1986; Fong, 1990). In other jurisdictions, it was not uncommon for gang members inside and outside of prison to routinely make death threats against prison officials (Daniel, 1987). Despite these facts, many prison administrators have adopted a public policy of categorically denying the presence of prison gangs (Camp & Camp, 1985; Fong, 1990; American

Correctional Association, 1993). However, this lack of official recognition has not led to the disappearance of prison gangs, but has only served to mask their existence. As Fong, Vogel and Buentello (1992) noted:

> Not only have prison gangs not vanished, they have grown to become the most dangerous crime syndicates in America. The economic reality of organized crime dictates that prison gangs are here to stay (p.72).

In a subsequent study, Knox (1991) estimated that there were as many as 100,000 inmates that belong to prison gangs. However, a study conducted by the American Correctional Association (1993) revealed less than one-half that number.

In the years following the Camp and Camp (1985) study, the interest in prison gangs generated a number of empirical investigations by practitioners and scholars. Initially, the study of prison gangs was hampered by several factors. First, many prison administrators, in line with their denial approach to the problem, were reluctant to permit prison gang research. Second, the lack of a gang-tracking system (recording-keeping and monitoring) in most jurisdictions made it difficult to study such groups. Third, the strict code of silence required of all gang members helped block access to the best information source, namely gang members themselves (Fong & Buentello, 1991a).

Despite these problems, a few researchers have managed to gain significant insights into these groups. Their empirical investigations have focused on organizational structure (Camp & Camp, 1985; Beaird, 1986; Fong, 1990); recruitment methods (Fong, 1990); methods of communication (Fong, 1990); code of conduct (Fong, 1990; Buentello, Fong & Vogel, 1991); and the nature and extent of criminal activities (Camp & Camp, 1985,, 1988; Crist, 1986; Fong, 1990; Ralph & Marquart, 1991). Other findings of important policy implications include strategies for the detection of prison gang development (Fong & Buentello, 1991b); and management strategies for combatting prison gang violence (Daniel, 1987; Camp & Camp, 1988; Knox, 1991; Fong & Buentello, 1991b; *Management Strategies in Disturbances and with Gangs/Disruptive Groups,* 1991; *Gang Manual,* 1994).

Although measurable progress has been made toward understanding the development, structure, operation, and growth of prison gangs, more research is necessary. Because prison gangs continuously change to minimize official scrutiny, researchers as well as practitioners are constantly challenged to maintain up-to-date information. This chapter provides the reader with data concerning the latest developments of prison gang dynamics since the publication of the Camp and Camp (1985) study. It addresses such issues as a theoretical model of prison gang development, the creation of a new name for prison gangs, the extent of prison gang expansion, the magnitude of prison gang violence, new strategies for managing prison gang problems, and the latest trends in the evolution of prison gangs.

PRISON GANG DEVELOPMENT: A THEORETICAL MODEL

According to Buentello, Fong, and Vogel (1991), prison gangs evolve through a five-stage process.

Figure 8.1
Prison Gang Development: A Theoretical Model

Copy appears

INMATE (Stage 1)	• Feeling fearful of new setting • Sensing danger • Feeling isolated • Feeling lonely
CLIQUE (Stage 2)	• Sense of belonging • No rules for acceptance • No commitment to group • No rules of conduct • Members can come and go • No formal or informal leadership exercised • No involvement in criminal activity
PROTECTION GROUP (Stage 3)	• Self-identity • Existence of simple general rules • Existence recognized by inmates and staff • No involvement in criminal activity • Does not initiate violence unless provoked • Informal leadership based on charisma • No formal code of conduct
PREDATOR GROUP (Stage 4)	• Discussion of formalizing rules of conduct • Beginning to realize strength • Exclusion of "undesirable" or "unwilling" members • Involvement in inmate/staff intimidation • Involvement in retaliation and assaults • Initial entry as a group into illegal activity • Emergence of strong leadership, although informal • Existence and activity limited to inside penal setting
PRISON GANG (Stage 5)	• Formal rules and constitution • Well-defined goals and philosophy • Hierarchy of formal leadership with clearly defined authority and responsibility • Membership for life • Members wear gang tattoos • Wholesale involvement in criminal activity both inside and outside the penal setting • Ongoing criminal enterprise

In **Stage 1,** the offender realizes that he has entered a volatile world where one must adapt quickly. For many inmates, the initial stage brings feelings of loneliness, isolation, and fear. To overcome these feelings, the prisoner moves into **Stage 2,** which is characterized by the development of relationships within the prison environment. The associations that begin with cellmates, homeboys, and classmates may lead to cliques that satisfy the need for belonging and survival. These loosely formed groups do not have rules, and individuals are free to come and go as they please. While some of these cliques break down over time, some develop into self-protection groups—**Stage 3.** The primary purpose of the self-protection group is for survival and protection from attacks by others. Group members do not abide by a strict code of conduct or participate in illegal activities. The leadership in this stage is informal and members enjoy increased recognition within the institution. **Stage 4** emerges as a predator group when the charismatic leaders begin to cement the cohesiveness of the group. Formal rules are established, members are expected to hold similar viewpoints, and group loyalty is considered extremely important. Weaker individuals are forced from the group as their illegal activities expand into such arenas as extortion, gambling, and prostitution. A predator group exhibits significant power over other inmates and they are generally feared. Predator groups also pave the way for full-blown prison gangs, **Stage 5,** which are characterized by a creed of blood-in-blood-out. Prison gang members are involved with contract murder, drug trafficking, extortion, gambling, and homosexual prostitution. If a member of a prison gang does not abide by the rules, his death is imminent. Unlike predator groups, some prison gangs have expanded their base of operations to the streets and have a formal leadership hierarchy, which is discussed later in this chapter. Prison gang members also wear tattoos (see Figure 8.2), which signify gang pride and serve as a warning to other inmates that they are dangerous and must be respected.

PRISON GANGS OR SECURITY THREAT GROUPS: A NEW DEFINITION

Recognizing the major impact of prison gang disruptiveness in correctional institutions, the National Institute of Justice, in October 1991, awarded the American Correctional Association (ACA) an 18-month grant to conduct a nationwide study on prison gangs. This project was the first nationwide effort to study prison gangs since the Camp and Camp (1985) study. To ensure the successful completion of the project, eight experts with experience combatting prison gangs were invited to serve on the advisory board. In December 1991, at the first board meeting, the members decided that the term "prison gangs" needed to be changed to "security threat groups" (STG).[1] It was believed that this change would facilitate participation in the study because many prison administrators were uneasy with the term "prison gangs" (American Correctional Association, 1993). According to the ACA advisory board, a security threat group is defined as:

> Two (2) or more inmates, acting together, who pose a threat to the security or safety of staff/inmates and/or are disruptive to programs and/or to the orderly management of the facility/system (1993:1).

To label an inmate group as a security threat group, the following criteria must be considered:

1. intent and purpose of the group

2. organizational structure of the group

3. specific violent acts or intended acts of violence that can be attributed to the group (e.g., assaults, murders, conspiracy to commit murder, etc.)

4. specific illegal acts, to include the intention or conspiracy to commit such acts that can be associated with the group (e.g., extortion, protection, racketeering, etc.)

5. demographics of the group to include size, location, patterns of expansion or declining group membership

6. propensity for violence by the group

7. the degree of threat to the facility/system security (American Correctional Association, 1993:27-28).

Once a group is confirmed to be a security threat group, the following checklist is used to identify inmates as group members:

1. self-admission

2. identified STG tattoo

3. possession of STG paraphernalia

4. information from outside law enforcement agencies

5. information from internal investigations

6. inmate correspondence or outside contacts

7. individual or group STG pictures (American Correctional Association, 1993:28).

THE EXTENT OF PRISON GANG EXPANSION

The ACA (1993) study surveyed 125 correctional systems, which included all 50 state prison systems, the Federal Bureau of Prisons, the District of Columbia, and 73 jail systems. Their findings revealed that security threat groups were present in 40 prison systems, as compared with 33 in the Camp and Camp (1985) study.[2] Nationwide, 1,153 security threat groups, including all religious groups (e.g., Nation of Islam), were identified by the ACA (1993) study.[3] Overall, 46,190 group members were reported by survey participants, which accounts for 5.9 percent of the U.S. prison population (American Correctional Association, 1993).

Table 8.1
Survey Comparison of 1985 Study* to 1992 Survey

State	Inmate Pop 1985	# STGS	# STG Members	% Mem	Inmate Pop 1992	# STGS	# STG Members	% Mem
Alabama	NA	no gangs	NA	NA	17,000	15	275	1.6
Alaska	NA	no gangs	NA	NA	2,298	no gangs	NA	NA
Arizona	6,889	3	413	6.0	16,200	8	200	1.2
Arkansas	4,089	3	184	4.5	7,731	11	213	2.7
California	38,075	6	2,050	5.4	105,602	491	3,384	3.2
Colorado	no data	NA	NA	NA	7,300	37	508	6.9
Connecticut	5,042	2	NA	NA	10,832	19	1,070	9.8
Delaware	NA	no gangs	NA	NA	1,649	9	56	3.4
D.C.	no return	NA	NA	NA	10,500	13	125	1.2
Florida	26,260	3	NA	NA	47,300	18	1,101	2.3
Georgia	15,232	6	63	0.4	24,561	no gangs	NA	NA
Hawaii	no data	na	NA	NA	2,774	16	NA	NA
Idaho	1,095	3	NA	NA	2,140	12	268	12.5
Illinois	15,232	14	5,300	34.3	31,000	25	14,900	48.1
Indiana	9,360	3	50	0.5	13,500	35	215	1.6
Iowa	2,814	5	49	1.7	4,476	9	357	8.0
Kansas	NA	no gangs	NA	NA	6,054	13	NA	NA
Kentucky	4,754	4	82	1.7	9,787	no gangs	NA	NA
Louisiana	NA	no gangs	NA	NA	15,000	no gangs	NA	NA
Maine	no data	NA	NA	NA	1,000	no gangs	NA	NA
Maryland	12,003	1	100	0.8	NAR	NAR	NAR	NAR
Massachusetts	4,609	1	3	0.1	9,000	10	465	5.2
Michigan	14,972	2	250	1.7	34,383	20	1,500	4.4
Minnesota	2,228	2	87	3.9	3,777	38	686	18.2
Mississippi	NA	no gangs	NA	NA	6,195	8	379	6.1
Missouri	8,212	2	550	6.7	15,240	7	300	2.0
Montana	NA	no gangs	NA	NA	1,217	no gangs	NA	NA

Table 8.1, *continued*

State	Inmate Pop 1985	# STGS	# STG Members	% Mem	Inmate Pop 1992	# STGS	# STG Members	% Mem
Nebraska	NA	no gangs	ANA	NA	3,173	9	98	3.1
Nevada	3,192	4	120	3.8	6,069	5	272	4.5
New Hampshire	NA	no gangs	NA	NA	1,500	6	36	2.4
New Jersey	no return	NA	NA	NA	23,600	13	6,000	24.4
New Mexico	no data	NA	NA	NA	3,229	26	100	3.1
New York	30,955	3	NA	NA	61,000	no gangs	NA	NA
N. Carolina	15,485	1	14	0.1	20,000	no gangs	NA	NA
N. Dakota	NA	no gangs	NA	NA	560	no gangs	NA	NA
Ohio	17,766	2	NA	NA	33,469	17	1,200	3.6
Oklahoma	7,076	5	NA	NA	13,660	16	675	4.9
Oregon	NA	no gangs	NA	NA	6,500	20	300	4.6
Pennsylvania	11,798	15	2,400	20.3	22,175	11	2,181	9.8
Rhode Island	NA	no gangs	NA	NA	3,000	2	20	0.7
S. Carolina	NA	no gangs	NA	NA	16,500	5	800	4.9
S. Dakota	NA	no gangs	NA	NA	1,500	8	43	2.7
Tennessee	no return	NA	NA	NA	8,889	19	724	8.1
Texas	32,256	6	322	0.9	51,609	7	2,720	5.3
Utah	1,328	5	90	6.8	3,024	6	NA	NA
Vermont	NA	no gangs	NA	NA	1,175	no gangs	NA	NA
Virginia	10,093	2	65	0.6	16,876	10	894	5.3
Washington	6,700	2	114	1.7	10,032	13	275	2.7
West Virginia	1,628	1	50	3.1	1,867	1	47	6.9
Wisconsin	4,894	3	60	1.2	8,040	96	1,369	17.0
Wyoming	NA	no gangs	NA	NA	723	no gangs	NA	NA
SUB-TOTAL	NA	109	12,416	NA	724,696	1,104	43,756	6.0
FBOP	30,147	5	218	0.7	66,144	49	2,434	3.7
TOTAL	NA	114	12,634	3.0	790,840	1,153	46,190	5.9

*Camp, George M., and Camille Graham Camp (1985). *Prison Gangs: Their Extent, Nature, and Impact on Prisons.* Washington, DC: U.S. Department of Justice, pp. 11, 19.

NOTES
Inmate Pop 1985: This is inmate population as reported by the Camp and Camp study
Inmate Pop 1992: This is inmate population as reported by survey respondents
STGS: Number of security threat groups
#STG Members: Number of security threat groups identified
% MEM: Percentage of security threat group members in system
no data: Agency reported gangs, but provided no data
no gangs: Agency did not respond to survey
NA: Information not available
NAR: Information not authorized for release

Source: American Correctional Association (1993). *Gangs in Correctional Facilities: A National Assessment* (Grant No. 91-IJ-CX-0026). U.S. Department of Justice, Office of Justice Programs, National Institute of Justice, pp. 8-9.

In 1985, California, Illinois, and Pennsylvania were recognized as the states with the largest populations of prison gang members in the United States. In 1992, Illinois, New Jersey, and California were at the top of the list. In 1985 and 1992, Illinois reported more prison gang members than any other state and in 1992 had more prison gang members than all the states put together in 1985. Almost one-half of all inmates incarcerated in Illinois were affiliated with prison gangs, followed by New Jersey, where almost a one-quarter of their prisoners were prison gang members.

Among the 52 prison systems that responded to the ACA questionnaire, 40 prison gangs were identified as being most active, most violent, and national in scope. Table 8.2 shows a list of all these groups and the number of prison systems that experience their presence. In reviewing this table, the reader should be mindful of the fact that even though a particular gang is reported to be present in several prison systems, it does not necessarily mean that they are all related. For example, the presence of the Aryan Brotherhood was reported by 29 of the 52 prison systems. This is not to be interpreted to mean that all 29 Aryan Brotherhood groups are under the command of a single leadership. In fact, there may be no connection between these groups. In most cases, a gang adopts a particular name for its prominance. The name of Aryan Brotherhood can generate instant recognition and fear by other gangs or individuals.

In addition to the major security threats that are identified in Table 8.2, all 52 prison systems were asked to name those less active and less violent security threat groups that were present in their particular systems but were not national in scope. Table 8.3 reveals a total of 282 such groups.

EXTENT OF VIOLENCE BY SECURITY THREAT GROUPS

Even though prison gangs have been given a new name, they continue to function as a powerful and destructive force behind prison walls. According to the ACA (1993) study, security threat groups are believed to be responsible for approximately 20 percent of the violence toward prison staff and 40 percent toward prisoners. In jurisdictions such as Texas, prison intelligence reveals that prison gangs are responsible for nearly 90 percent of the prison violence. Heading the ACA list of violent security threat groups is Brothers of Struggle (classified as 'high-violence only'), followed by the Aryan Brotherhood, Crips, Nation of Islam (classified as both 'high and low violence' groups), Bloods, Five Percenters, Hells Angels, Jamaican Posse, Ku Klux Klan, Pagans, Skinheads, and Vice Lords (classified as 'low-violence only').

While violence and prison gangs usually go hand in hand, there has been an increase in violence and a growth in nontraditional prison gangs (e.g. KKK). A possible explanation for this phenomenon may be found in a study conducted by Hunt, Riegel, Morales, and Waldorf (1993). Their study, which was based on interviews with 39 released street and prison gang members

Table 8.2
Prevalence of Security Threat Groups

(NAME)	Prison Systems (N=52)		
	No.	%	Rank
Aryan Brotherhood	29	57	1.5
Crips	29	57	1.5
Skinheads	26	51	3.5
Bloods	26	51	3.5
White Supremacy Group	24	47	5.0
Ku Klux Klan	20	39	6.0
Nation of Islam	19	37	7.0
Black Disciples	18	35	8.5
Latin Kings	18	35	8.5
Hells Angels	17	33	10.0
Vice Lords	16	31	11.0
Jamaican Posse	13	26	12.5
Pagans	13	26	12.5
Brothers of Struggle	12	24	14.0
Organized Crime	11	22	16.0
Outlaws	11	22	16.0
Mexican Mafia	11	22	16.0
Five Percenters	10	20	17.5
El Rukns	10	20	19.0
Texas Syndicate	8	17	20.5
La Nuestra Familia	8	17	20.5
Black Guerilla Family	7	14	22.5
Mariel Cuban	7	14	22.5
Dirty White Boys	6	12	24.5
SE Asian Organized Crime	6	12	24.5
American Indian Movement	5	10	27.0
Bandidos	5	10	27.0
Black Panthers	5	10	27.0
Yahwehs	4	8	29.0
Diablos MG	3	6	32.5
International Terror.	3	6	32.5
Miami Boys	3	6	32.5
Misfits MG	3	6	32.5
Mongols MG	3	6	32.5
Vagos MG	3	6	32.5
Domestic Terrorists	2	4	37.0
Jewish Def. League	2	4	37.0
Mexikanemi	2	4	37.0
Silent Brotherhood	1	2	39.0

Source: American Correctional Association (1993). *Gangs in Correctional Facilities: A National Assessment* (Grant No. 91-IJ-CX-0026). United States Department of Justice, Office of Justice Programs, National Institute of Justice, p. 22.

Table 8.3
Additional Active Security Threat Groups Not Included in Table 8.2

18th Streeters	Dream Team	Kensington Street
20 Love	Drifters MC	International
27's	Drug Cartel	King Cobras
4 Corner Hustler	East Omaha Rats	La Familia-Milwaukee
4th-Reich MG	East Side Crushers	La Blancas
5-N-O Street Crew	East Side Guadalupes	Lamphom Park Knockouts
58th & Blaine NE Crew	East Side Kings	Latin Counts
8-Ball Posse	East Side Motherfuckers	Latin Disciples
A-Key-She-TA	East Side White Pride	Latin Lords
African Kingdom Alliance	Eastside Connection	Latin Locos
Afrikan National Ujamaa	Eastside Mafioso	LeDroit Crew
(ANU)	Egyptian Pimps	Lorton Norton Crew
Afro-American Council	El Paso Tip	Los Carnales
Arizona Aryan Brotherhood	Elm Street Gang	Los Home Boys
Aryan Nation Church	Exiles MG	Los Tresas
Aryan Warriors	Family	Lost Race MC (2)
Avengers MG	Fila Boys	Macvilles
Banshee MG	First & O Street NW Crew	Mad Black Souls (2)
Barbarian MG	Floral Kings	Mandingo Warriors
Best Friends (Hit team for	Folks	Maniac Latin Disciples
YBI)	G.O.D.S. (Bikers)	Melanic Islamic Palace of
Black Dragons	Galloping Goose MG	the Rising Sun
Black Gangster	German Outlaw	Metro East
Black Gangster Disciples (2)	Ghost Riders	Metro Boys
Black Souls	Ghost Riders MC (2)	Mexican Posse
Black Stones	Gypsy Jokers (3)	Mickey Cobra Stones
Black Stone Rangers (3)	H.P.B. MC	Mickey Cobras
Blackstones	Hawaiian Brothers	Montana Crew
Bones Gang	(Philipino)	Moorish Science Temple of
Booze Runners MC	Hebrew Israelites	America (MST of A)
Border Riders MC	Helter Shelter	Moorish—Temple-Science
Breed MG	Hermanos de Pistoleros	Nation
Brick City Outlaws	Hesh-Kes (want-to-be's)	Nations Against Violence
Brother Speed	Hessian MG	(NAV)
Brothers of Unity	Hessians	Naturals (2)
CC Riders MC	Hi Riders MC	Netas (2)
Chaldeans/Iraqi s	Highland Court Bloods	New Aryan Empire
Cleveland Park Kings	Highwaymen MC	New Mexican Mafia
Clubsters	H.O.B.Z.	New Mexico Syndicate
Cobra Stones (2)	Home Boys	New Street Crew
Cobras	Huns MG	New Style Crew
COTC-Church of the Creator	Imperial Gangster Disciples	New World
Cretin Street Gang	Inland Empire Mob	Ninja Crew
Cuban Corporation	Insane	Nip Boys
Cultists	Insane Gangster Disciples	Nomads MC
Cycle Groups	(IGD)	North Ender 14
DC Eagles MG	Insectos	Northsiders
De Eagles MC	Irish Republican Army	Nuestra Carnales
Death Warriors	Iron Horsemen MG	Old Mexican Mafia
Death Dealing Deltas	Jackonsville Boys	One Way Posse
Deviants MG	Jaguars MC	Orange Street Crew
Devil s Disciples	Juaritos	Original Gangster Posse
Dirty Dozen MG	Jungle Boys	(OGP)
Down South Boys	Kappa Phi Si Nasty	Original White Gangster

Table 8.3, *continued*

Outcast MC	Shorty Folks	Union Correctional
P Street Crew	Silent Brotherhood (want-to-	Institution Posse
P.M.B.(Pimps Taking Over)	be's)	United CRIP Gang (UCG)
Pharoahs MG	Simon City Royals	United Prison Bikers
Peace Stone Rangers	Skinhead (crue)	Varrio Norwalk
Pee Wee Stones	Society of Resurrected	V Boys
Penthouse Kings	Brothers	Vice Dice
Polynesian Club	Solid Gold Boys	Vietnam MG
Posse Committatus	Solidos	Vipers
Prison Mortorcycle	Sons of Satan MC	W.A.R.
Brotherhood-PMB(3)	South East Boot Boys	War Lords
Prison Brotherhood	South Side Locos	Warlocks MG
Proponents of Ritualistics	Southside Wrecking Crew	Warrior Society (Native
Activity	Spanish Cobra's (2)	American Prison Gang)
Puerto Rico Stones	Spanish Gangster Disciples	Warriors
R Street Crew	Street Boys	Weatherman
Raza Unida	Sundowners MC	West Helena Posse
Red Cobras	Syndicato Nuevo Mexico	Westside Warriors
Renegades MG	Texas Mafia	Wheelmen MC
Road Kings MG	Texas Aryan Brotherhood	White Aryan Resistance La
Rock Lords	The Albany Boys	Florencia
Rude Boys	The Association	White Aryan Resistance
S.W.P.	The Atlanta Boys	White Gangster Disciples
Sacred Order of Norseman	The Boyz (TBZ)	White Odinists
(SOON)	The Brownz	White Opel Gang
Satan Disciples MG	The Edgewood Crew	WICCA
Satanic Groups	The Family	WSPMA
Satanist	The La Familia	Young and Wasted
Satans Dragons MC	The Lynch Mob	Youg Boys Incorported
Satans Slaves MCScorpians	The Warlords	(YBI)
MG	Time Boys	Zodiac MC
Seven Sons MG	Treys MG	
Sharks		

Note: Numbers beside names indicate how many times that STG was identified.

In addition to the major security threat groups that are identified in Table 8.2, all 52 prison systems were asked to name those less active and less violent security threat groups that were present in their particular systems but were not national in scope. Table 8.3 reveals a total of 208 such groups.

In addition to 12 STGs included in the 39 STGs listed on the survey, California identified 479 STGs that are not included in the above list (76 Blood sets, 172 Crip sets, 231 other groups).

39	STGs identified and listed on the survey
244	Individual STGs listed above
479	California STGs not listed above or included with the 39 listed on the survey
762	Total STGs identified

The survey identified 46,190 inmates as STG members or 5.9 percept of the inmate population. Additionally, 11 states indicated they did not have any STGs, 3 states reporting authorize release of its statistical information.

Source: American Correctional Association (1993). *Gangs in Correctional Facilities: A National Assessment* (Grant No. 91-IJ-CX-0026). United States Department of Justice, Office of Justice Programs, National Institute of Justice.

from the California Department of Corrections, concluded that when prison officials segregate members of traditional prison gangs, a vacuum is created within the prison population and new groupings develop. Among these groups is a new breed of inmates known as the "pepsi generation" who go "around wearing their pants down below their ass and showing absolutely no respect for anyone or anything" (1993:403). The implication is that more violence can be expected in prison.

STRATEGIES FOR MANAGING
SECURITY THREAT GROUPS

In the Camp and Camp (1985) study, it was reported that only a few correctional jurisdictions had established policies to deal with the problems caused by prison gangs. In the years following, several empirical studies have suggested various strategies for the management of prison gangs (Daniel, 1987; Camp & Camp, 1988; Fong & Buentello, 1991b). Despite these efforts, the ACA (1993) study revealed that only 15 of the 52 prison systems reported having operating procedures for controlling security threat group activities. Their strategies can be divided into two categories: policy-oriented and programmatic. There are four policy-oriented control strategies. The first strategy is the designation of a central monitoring unit. Under this system, prison officials use a separate prison unit (e.g., Pelican Bay prison in California) for the confinement of all confirmed security threat group inmates. The second policy-oriented control strategy is the creation of policies and procedures for managing security threat groups. The third strategy involves the development of policies and procedures to validate the existence of security threat groups and their members. The final strategy provides for the development of policies and procedures to prohibit STG activities. Table 8.4 shows that the majority respondents favored the central monitoring (separate unit) approach and the development of policies and procedures to curtail STG activities.

Programmatic control of security threat groups consists of 12 strategies.

1. Segregation: placing all confirmed STG members in a housing unit or prison apart from general population inmates;

2. Disciplinary sanction: removing good time from or placing STG members in solitary confinement for violating institutional rules;

3. Within-state transfer: STG members are transferred among prison units within the same jurisdiction;

4. Custody upgrade: reclassifying STG members to a high security level so that they can be housed in high security prison units;

5. Mail monitoring: monitoring incoming and outgoing inmate mail for communications concerning STG activity;

Table 8.4
Use of Policy-Oriented Control Strategies

	Prison Systems (N=51)*	
	No.	%
Central Monitoring Unit	28	55
Policy & Procedure for STGs	15	29
STG Validation Policy & Procedure	27	53
STG Prohibition Policy & Procedure	28	55
*The Federal Bureau of Prisons was not included in these calculations.		

Source: American Correctional Association (1993). *Gangs in Correctional Facilities: A National Assessment* (Grant No. 91-IJ-CX-0026). United States Department of Justice, Office of Justice Programs, National Institute of Justice, p.17.

6. Criminal prosecution: prosecuting any STG member for any STG-related criminal offenses;

7. Telephone monitoring: monitoring any outgoing calls made by STG members;

8. Out-of-state transfer: transferring certain STG members, including influential leaders or defected members to other jurisdictions;

9. Urinalysis: performing urine tests on STG members for possible drug consumption;

10. Protective custody: placing defected STG members or other informants in protective custody;

11. No contact visits: prohibiting STG members from receiving contact visits;

12. No furlough privileges: denying furlough requests submitted by STG members (American Correctional Association, 1993).

Table 8.5 shows that the most widely used strategy is segregation, which is implemented by 40 prison systems. The least preferred strategy is the denial of furlough privileges, which has been adopted by only eight jurisdictions.

PRISON GANGS: THE LATEST TRENDS

The ACA study has provided vital information on several aspects of prison gang development. There are, however, other areas of prison gang operations that were not included in the study. This section presents an up-to-date review of such dynamics as organizational structure, recruitment methods, use

Table 8.5
Program Control Methods Used

	Prisons Systems (N=51)*		
	No.	%	Rank
Segregation	40	78	1
Disciplinary Sanction	39	76	2
Within-in-state Transfer	37	73	3
Custody Upgrade	36	71	4
Mail Monitoring	35	69	5
Criminal Prosecution	32	63	6
Telephone Monitoring	27	53	7
Out-of-state Transfer	24	47	9
Urinalysis	24	47	9
Protective Custody	24	47	9
No Contact Visits	15	29	11
No Furlough Privileges	9	18	12

* The Federal Bureau of Prisons was not included in these calculations.

Source: American Correctional Association (1993). *Gangs in Correctional Facilities: A National Assessment.* (Grant No. 91-IJ-CX-0026). United Stated Department of Justice, Office of Justice Programs, National Institute of Justice, p. 19.

of tattoos, and methods of communication. These topics have not been addressed since the study of Texas prison gangs by Fong (1990). The findings in this section are based on intelligence information collected from law enforcement and correctional experts across the United States. Access to this information was secured by one of the co-authors who is a leading prison gang expert and a member of both the ACA study advisory board and the National Major Gang Task Force, which was created in 1993. This task force is comprised of more than 100 law enforcement and correctional gang experts from across the country. Their mission is to disseminate information to prison officials in their efforts to combat the growth of prison gangs. Due to the sensitive nature of this information (internal police and prison communications and confiscated gang documents), citations are not included in the following sections.

Organizational Structure

As noted in earlier studies (Camp & Camp, 1985; Buentello, 1986), prison gangs organize themselves along ethnic and paramilitary lines. The organizational structures of today's prison gangs are based on three general models: paramilitary, hierarchical, and steering committee. Chart 8.1 depicts the paramilitary model, which has been adopted, in part, by the Texas Syndicate.

Chart 8.1
Paramilitary Structure

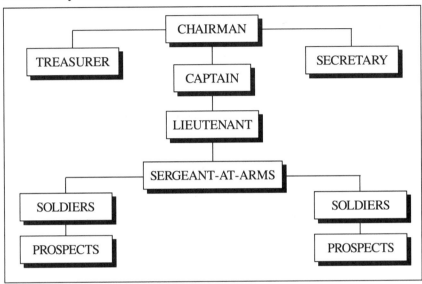

Chart 8.2 shows the hierarchical style of leadership, which has been found in use by the Mexican Mafia.

Chart 8.2
Hierarchy Structure

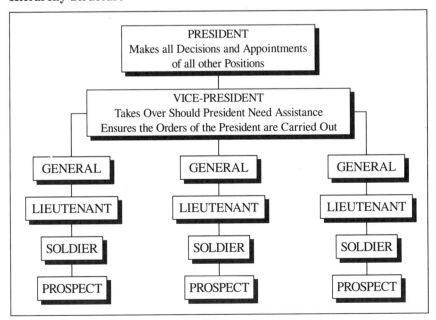

Finally, the steering committee structure, as shown in Chart 8.3, reveals the organizational framework preferred by the Aryan Brotherhood.[4]

Chart 8.3
Steering Committee Structure

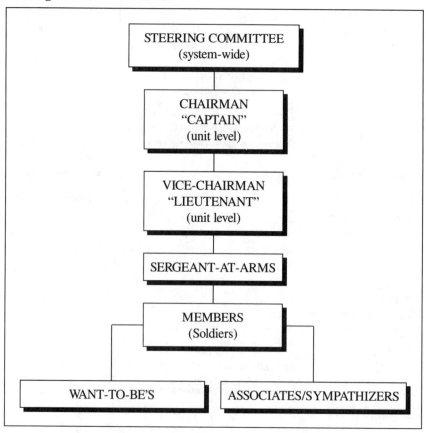

Although the paramilitary and hierarchy models are self-explanatory, further explanation is needed for the steering committee model. As shown in Chart 8.3, the steering committee acts as the primary head of this organizational model. With no exceptions, the committee is always comprised of an odd number of members (e.g., three, five, seven, nine, etc.). The main reason for this arrangement is the avoidance of a tied vote. Unlike the other two organizational structures, where leaders are elected by the membership, members of a steering committee are normally the founding members of the gang and their leadership is not subject to question or vote. When one member is released from prison or dies, the committee fills the vacancy by appointing anyone they wish.

As the ruling authority of the gang, the steering committee appoints leaders for each prison unit. Depending on the size of the gang, unit leadership may include such ranks as chairman or captain, vice chairman or lieutenant, sergeant-at-arms, and members or soldiers. In addition to appointing unit leaders, the steering committee issues orders for all major gang activities.

One important point about all prison gang organizational structures is that the prison is the center of power. All orders, including those for illegal acts to be committed on the streets, are issued from inside the prison. The rationale is the avoidance of police harassment and surveillance, which makes it easier for prison gangs to conduct criminal activities on the streets.

Prison Gangs As Religious Groups?

Even though prison gangs have been classified as crime syndicates, prison intelligence reveals that some gangs are beginning a movement to petition the courts for recognition as religious groups. In order to achieve this status, prison gangs must meet the guidelines specified in *Cooper v. Pate*, 378 U.S. 546 (1964). Basically, those who petition the court for legal recognition must be able to demonstrate that:

1.   the individual or group is sincere in his/her or its belief; and

2.   the religion is indeed a religion in that the belief system:

     a.   teaches such fundamental values as right and wrong, good and evil;

     b.   teaches the ultimate concept of faith; and

     c.   is based on established rituals such as organizational hierarchy, worship requirements, etc.

The impetus for prison gangs to seek religious recognition has developed from the passage of the Religious Freedom Restoration Act (RFRA) of 1993 (Title 42 U.S. Code, Section 2000bb) by the United States Congress. Specifically, this act states that ". . . governments should not substantially burden religious exercise without compelling justification" (Section 2.a.3). The act further states:

> A person whose religious exercise has been burdened in violation of this (act) may assert that violation as a claim or defense in a judicial proceeding and obtain appropriate relief against a government. Standing to assert a claim or defense under this (act) shall be governed by the general rules of standing under article III of the Constitution (Section 3.c).

The implication is that many court-approved restrictions that have curtailed religious practices in prison may not survive legal challenge under this act (National Institute of Corrections, 1993). However, there are no indications that prison gangs will succeed in their quest for religious recognition.

Recruitment Methods

In earlier studies (Buentello, 1986; Fong, 1990), it was reported that prison gangs utilize the "homeboy connection" as a technique for recruiting new members. Each new member has to be sponsored by someone who is already in the gang. The sponsor is required to investigate the background of potential recruits and is responsible for any of their misconduct, even when they become members. This also includes carrying out a "hit" on the new member if he violates the code of conduct, also known as the "constitution." While this method of recruitment continues, official scrutiny has necessitated the addition of new methods. One such method has been to use nonmembers known as associates, want-to-be's and sympathizers both inside and outside prison (see Fong & Buentello, 1991b). Associates are unorganized individuals (e.g., street criminals such as drug dealers) who agree to carry out gang activities for monetary compensation or drugs. Want-to-be's are "homeboys" who share similar beliefs as the gang and would like to become members. Sympathizers are unorganized individuals who do not wish to join the gang but share the beliefs of the gang. These individuals perform certain gang functions with or without compensation.

In those prison systems where only confirmed gang leaders are confined in administrative segregation, the recruitment of regular members continues in the general populations.

New Operational Strategy

Recent police intelligence indicates that prison gangs are intensifying their efforts to carry out criminal activities on the streets by using juvenile street gangs. There are several reasons for this new development. First, juvenile street gangs are more organized when compared to individual associates, want-to-be's and sympathizers, thus, enabling them to carry out their activities more effectively. In one recent incident in Houston, a juvenile street gang was ordered by the Texas Syndicate to burn down the house of a person on a gang hit list. The fire killed the target as well as four other innocent victims (TDCJ intelligence record). Second, prison gang members are aware that juveniles are more likely to be sanctioned by juvenile courts or, if bound over to adult courts, may receive more lenient sentences. Third, law enforcement officials do not scrutinize juvenile gang activities as closely as adult gangs. Fourth, juvenile gangs provide an abundant resource base upon which prison gangs can recruit their future members.

Tattoos

Gang tattoos serve three important purposes in that they identify one's membership in the gang, symbolize one's commitment to the gang, signify status for members, and generate fear and respect by nonmembers (see Fong, 1990). The use of tattoos has evolved through several stages since the Camp and Camp (1985) study. To avoid permanent confinement in administrative segregation (lockup), prison gang members had, at one time, changed from openly displaying their gang tattoos (forearms, chests, back of body) to putting them in places not easily detected (e.g., on the scalp under the hair). Other prison gangs, such as those in Texas, eliminated tattoos entirely. However, as a result of the high costs of confining prison gang members in administrative segregation, many prison systems have mixed gang members with general population inmates. In those jurisdictions, prison gangs openly display their tattoos.

For unknown reasons, prison gang tattoos are rarely exhibited in the prison gang literature. The following diagram shows samples of tattoos worn by four Texas prison gangs: the Texas Syndicate, Mexican Mafia, Mandingo Warriors, and Texas Mafia.

Methods of Communication

The constant scrutiny imposed by police and prison authorities dictates that prison gangs be innovative in the methods by which they communicate with their members both inside and outside prison. In earlier studies, prison gangs were found to practice three common methods of communication: number code messages, tic-tac-toe, and chain-bus delivery (Fong, 1990). To bring the reader up-to-date on these strategies, the following illustrations are provided. The number code message system hides messages in letters. An example of this method can be seen in this letter.

Dear Bro,

Heard nothin from ya'll for 3 weeks. What's goin on? Got a visit from my old lady yesterday. She gotten fat since July 4th. Gained at least 20 pounds. Said just joined the Weight Watcher Program. Said has to eat them diet food three times a week. Wants to lose 1 pound a day for eight weeks. Said wants to look pretty when I go on furlough the weekend of November 10.

Kinda happy about it. My boy is fixin to turn 15. Can't wait to give him half a dozen hugs and kisses. He'll be in 12 grade when I get out this joint in one year.

Well, gonna to put the brakes on for now. Give my best to the best and f... the rest.

Your bro till death

Figure 8.2
Prison Gang Tattoos

Texas Syndicate

Mexican Mafia

Mandigo Warriors

Texas Mafia

To interpret this coded message, the receiving inmate will first look at the first number of the letter. In the above example, it is three. This lets the reader know they should use alphabet numbering code number 3 to decipher the message. There are several numbering codes that correspond to the alphabet and the third set appears below:

A	B	C	D	E	F	G	H	I	J	K	L	M	N
6	2	22	5	1	9	12	7	4	14	16	3	23	13

O	P	Q	R	S	T	U	V	W	X	Y	Z
11	15	25	8	24	20	18	19	21	17	10	26

With the number code in hand, the inmate then reads the letter and extracts all number and dates in the order in which they appear. For example, in the third sentence of the first paragraph, July 4th is mentioned. This date corresponds with numbers 7 and 4. The next number, 20, appears in the fourth sentence, etc. Overall, the letter reveals the following sequence of numbers: 7, 4, 20, 3, 1, 8, 11, 10, 15, 6, 12, 1. Notice that each paragraph has its own set of numbers. This is because when the message is finally decoded, each paragraph forms one word.

> Paragraph 1—7, 4, 20
> Paragraph 2—3, 1, 8, 11, 10
> Paragraph 3—15, 6, 12, 1

Applying these numbers to the letter designations will reveal the following message:

7	4	20		
H	I	T		

3	1	8	11	10
L	E	R	O	Y

15	6	12	1
P	A	G	E

Obviously, the decoded message is to hit or kill Leroy Page.

The above example illustrates the simplicity and surreptitious nature of secret codes. Coded messages were part of the "cat and mouse" game that easily evaded official scrutiny and were constantly changed to ensure that they were not broken by prison authorities.

The "Tic-Tac-Toe" strategy relayed messages through the use of a matrix code.

Figure 8.3
Tic-Tac-Toe Matrix

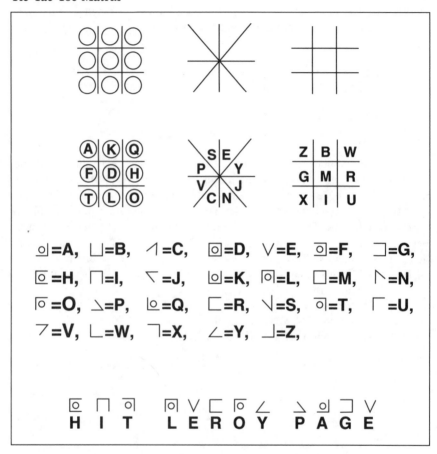

Unlike the coded message approach, the tic-tac-toe method easily raised official suspicion because of the drawings. Still, this was a method widely used by the Mexican Mafia in the Texas Department of Corrections during the mid-1980s.

The chain-bus delivery method utilized inmates (members and non-members) to carry verbal messages to intended members at units to which they were being transferred by chain buses. Non-gang members agreed to perform this service to avoid being physically assaulted by gang members at the new unit.

Recently, prison intelligence revealed that four new methods of communication are being practiced by prison gangs across the country. The first involves the use of a bench warrant. This method can be illustrated in the following example. Member A of the Mexican Mafia needs to convey a message to Members B, C, and D, who are assigned to three separated prison units. Member A will file a lawsuit (e.g., brutality) against a prison official and petition the court for a bench warrant, which identifies the other three inmates as witnesses. The bench warrant allows witnesses to meet with litigant A to prepare for his case. Prison officials have no choice but to obey the court order and legal visits are exempt from official audio monitoring.

The second method of communication occurs by having gang members work as legal aides to attorneys both inside and outside prison. Such status affords legal aides the opportunity to meet with members of his gang under the pretense of conducting legal interviews.

The third method uses spiritual advisors (outside religious leaders—e.g., church pastors), who are involved in providing church service and counseling to prison inmates, to serve as unknowing messengers. For example, a gang member may complain to a religious advisor that his religious freedom has been infringed upon because he is not being allowed to disseminate religious material to other inmates. The gang member will then manipulate the advisor into delivering a letter, supposedly containing religious literature, to another member at another institution.

The fourth method involves getting female family members, of those in prison gangs, to work in local law firms as clerical workers. Because legal mail is not subject to mail censorship, gang information can be freely sent back and forth. Upon receipt, the clerical worker places it in official law firm stationary and sends it to the gang member for whom the message is intended.

CONCLUSION

This chapter provides a brief summary on the progress that has been made on gang research since the Camp and Camp (1985) study. Although a great deal of knowledge has been acquired since that time, much remains to be explored. Regardless of what we call them, prison gangs are here to stay, grow, and disrupt. Unless correctional officials take a proactive approach to this problem, the ability to curtail their growth and activities seems bleak. Nothing can be accomplished by denying their existence, growth and development. Correctional officials should be encouraged to communicate with one another, support research, and develop sound policies and procedures to control the prison gang phenomenon. Below is a summary list of the suggestions provided in the ACA (1993) report regarding future research on prison gangs:

1.   Jail Study: a more comprehensive study of the problem of security threat groups in local jails and official responses to the problem be conducted.

2.   Street Gangs versus Prison STGs: a study of the impact of street gangs on STG management, to include the acceptance of street gangs by STGs or vice versa, be conducted.

3. Funding National Gang Training and/or Technical Assistance: a study of the feasibility of establishing a national symposium to be attended by gang coordinators be conducted. This symposium is to be followed by a series of seminars designed to provide more indepth in-service to police, prison and jail staff. These seminars should be held in different regions of the country.

4. Study the Relevance of a Central Depository for STG Intelligence: a study of the feasibility of establishing a national clearinghouse for gang information be conducted.

5. Study the Role of Cooperative Networking Among Criminal Justice Agencies on the Issue of STG Intelligence: such a study would enhance the effort of all involved in combatting STG problems.

NOTES

[1] In this chapter, the terms security threat group and prison gang will be used interchangeably.

[2] The figures for the ACA (1993) and Camp and Camp (1985) studies include the Federal Bureau of Prisons but do not include jail systems.

[3] In the Camp and Camp (1985) study, religious security threat groups were excluded.

[4] These examples were selected from prison gangs in the Texas Deppartment of Corrections (see Fong, 1990, Buentello, Fong & Vogel, 1991).

Section IV

SETTING GANG POLICY

9

A National Gang Strategy

Finn-Aage Esbensen
University of Nebraska, Omaha

INTRODUCTION

In this essay, it is my intent to place the current "gang problem" in historical and criminological perspective prior to presenting suggestions for a national
gang strategy. Given the current concern about gangs and youth violence, it
would be easy to conclude that both of these phenomena are recent developments in American society. The facts, however, reveal otherwise. Both have
been prevalent for centuries, but during the past 100 years, juvenile crime,
especially youth violence, has come under increasingly closer societal scrutiny.

The current attention accorded youth gangs is but the latest phase in the
public's concern with juvenile misbehavior. Much of this concern can be
attributed to media presentations on the topic. For a discussion of the role of
this media coverage with regard to juvenile delinquency, consult Bernard
(1992). Many commentators have suggested that youth gangs are a twentieth-
century phenomenon. This position ignores volumes of historical documents in
which the vagaries of youth have been described. Distress about juvenile indis-
cretions can be found in the writings of Socrates as well as in the Old
Testament. Even discussion of *group* adolescent misdeeds is nothing new. With
respect to late twentieth-century youth gangs, two aspects do distinguish them
from earlier youth collectives: (1) the increasing lethality of their group violence; and (2) the media and public attention bestowed upon youth gangs.

Historically, violent crime has represented a greater percentage of all
crime than it does today. Interpersonal violence was far greater during the
middle ages than it is today. Some estimates presented in the literature indicate
that approximately 80 percent of all crime consisted of crimes against persons
(e.g., Hagan, 1994; Messner & Rosenfeld, 1994; Shelley, 1981). What percent

131

of this violent crime was committed by juveniles is unknown. Current data reveal crimes against persons comprise less than 15 percent of the UCR Index offenses and, of these, only 13 percent are committed by juveniles (U.S. Department of Justice, 1993). While little evidence exists with regard to historical offending patterns of youth, there is little reason to believe that it differed much from the general crime pattern. Thus, while youth have traditionally been involved in larceny, vandalism, and disorderly conduct, they also have participated in assaults, rapes, robberies, and murders. Their involvement in these behaviors is not new. Some might argue that the apparent recent increase in violent juvenile crime is responsible for the public attention, but data suggest that the media attention preceded the violent juvenile crime increase. Why, then, have youth violence and juvenile gangs come to the forefront of the "war on crime?"

Prior to developing any coherent national gang strategy, it clearly is necessary to consider the extant literature in the gang arena. Several comprehensive reviews can be found in Covey et al., (1992) and Spergel (1990). For the purposes of this essay, let it suffice to touch on the main characteristics of the rich historical documentation of gangs.

The vast majority of gang research and subsequent policy suggestions maintain that gang behavior is a consequence of poverty, economic marginality, lack of legitimate opportunities, social disorganization, or some combination of the these social structural conditions (e.g., Curry & Thomas, 1992; Fagan, 1990; Hagedorn, 1988; 1992; Huff, 1990; Miller, 1990; Vigil, 1988). However, there is also a caveat extended by these researchers indicating that the social structural conditions by themselves cannot account for the presence of gangs. Fagan (1990:207), for instance, comments that "inner-city youths in this study live in areas where social controls have weakened and opportunities for success in legitimate activities are limited. Nevertheless, participation in gangs is selective, and most youths avoid gang life." Similarly, Miller (1990) notes that it is inadequate to assume that gangs develop as a result of lower-class life. "It is almost always true that where you find youth gangs you will find lower-class communities, but the obverse does not obtain. . . . there are numerous lower-class communities that do not have gangs" (Miller, 1990:280-281). Thus, while gangs do not develop in every community exhibiting the above characteristics, it is implicitly assumed that social structural conditions, from poverty to rapid changes in population characteristics brought about by migration, are closely intertwined with gang formation.

In their recent work, Maxson and Klein (1994) suggest that gangs are not exclusively an urban phenomenon, as is often suggested. They report that gangs also exist in communities with populations of less than 25,000. The fact that gang researchers have generally limited their studies to traditional gang cities may have contributed to the creation of very biased estimates of the distribution of gangs in the United States. Even Spergel and Curry's (1990) national study failed to investigate gangs in small towns and rural communities. Does this finding by Maxson and Klein suggest a change in the gang situation or does it simply signify the "discovery" of an old problem?

Juvenile crime has been studied extensively by American criminologists during the twentieth century and it is important to examine gangs within the more general framework of criminology. Much of the theoretical and empirical research found in criminology, in fact, has its origins in research on juvenile behavior. The works of social strain theorists (e.g., Cohen, 1955; Cloward & Ohlin, 1960), control theorists (e.g., Hirschi, 1969), labeling theorists (e.g., Schur, 1973), learning theorists (e.g., Akers, 1985; Miller, 1958), and advocates of theoretical integration (e.g., Elliott et al., 1985; Thornberry, 1987) all focus on delinquency. This body of knowledge has provided numerous, often contradictory, explanations for the causes of delinquency, and a comparable number of recommendations for prevention of delinquency or intervention in the lives of delinquents.

How do gangs fit into this general paradigm? How do they differ from juvenile delinquency in general? Are specific prevention and intervention programs necessary for gang members? These are vital questions that have been asked all too infrequently in the history of gang behavior. The trend has been to study gangs as a phenomenon distinct from the general study of delinquency. Despite the recent emphasis on gangs and calls from the Department of Justice (e.g., the 1995 OJJDP Program Plan which calls for the creation of a National Gang Assessment Center, Evaluation of Spergel's Comprehensive Community-Wide Approach to Gang Prevention, Intervention, and Suppression Program, and several other gang specific initiatives), there is reason to believe that gangs should be studied within the overall context of juvenile delinquency. The recent works of Esbensen and Huizinga (1993) and Thornberry et al. (1993), for example, suggest that while the gang environment does enhance delinquency, gang members are already delinquent prior to joining the gang. Furthermore, the recent work of Esbensen et al. (1993), which compared gang members to self-reported serious offenders that were not in gangs, found these two groups to be quite similar on a number of theoretically relevant measures. It appears that gang members may not be that different from other youth. This, in conjunction with the finding that delinquency generally precedes ganging, suggests that prevention and intervention strategies should NOT be limited to gang intervention or suppression. The level of delinquent behavior within the gang, however, does warrant further attention. While research shows that delinquency precedes gang affiliation, the same body of research also reveals that rates of delinquency are exceptionally high during periods of gang membership (e.g., Esbensen & Huizinga, 1993; Esbensen et al., 1993; Thornberry et al., 1993; Winfree et al., 1994).

GANG STRATEGIES

For an excellent review of past programmatic approaches to the gang problem, consult Spergel et al. (1991). The past 60 years have seen a wide array of gang intervention strategies, including: efforts focused on environmental factors and provision of improved opportunities (e.g., the Chicago Area Project (CAP) developed by Shaw and McKay, the Mid-City Project evaluated by Miller (1962), and the Mobilization for Youth program (Bibb, 1967)); programs with a distinct social work orientation (e.g., most notably the detached worker approach reported by Klein (1971) and Spergel (1966)); and the more traditional gang suppression strategy. The majority of these programs have experienced short lifespans due to the absence of any immediately noticeable effect or due to a change in administrative priorities.

According to Covey and his colleagues (1992), two criteria should underlie any program or suggested change. First, what are the causes of the phenomenon? Second, which of those causes can be manipulated to achieve the desired outcome? As current gang suppression and intervention strategies are discussed in the following section, it is important to assess the programs with these two questions in mind. Three recent anti-gang programs are described to illustrate the diversity of programs and to underscore the perceived severity/uniqueness of the gang problem.

Several Recently Developed Programs

A number of new programs emerged in the late 1980s and early 1990s to address the gang problem. While police departments appear to be assuming the leadership role in the anti-gang movement, many of the new programs transcend the traditional suppression approach. Three relatively new police programs representative of suppression, intervention, and prevention approaches are described below.

Representative of the suppression approach, the Chicago Police Department has implemented the "Flying Squad," a special unit composed of carefully selected young officers from Chicago's three gang units. According to Dart (1992), Chicago has an especially chronic gang problem with residents feeling intimidated and harassed. Citizens "fear not only for their own safety but for the welfare of their children, who are often trained in immediate action drills to the sound of gun shots" (Dart, 1992:100). In response to this situation, the Chicago Police Department decided to give the impression of an "omnipresent police force." To achieve this, an additional 100 officers were assigned to the Gang Crime Section and the Flying Squad was designed to saturate a small area of approximately five square blocks each evening. It is interesting to note that while this tactic is intended to hold gangs accountable to the "fullest measure of the law," the author acknowledges that "To win the war. . . . there must be a marriage of intervention, prevention, and suppression strategies aimed at deterring and containing gang activity" Dart, 1993:104).

The Reno, Nevada Police Department implemented an intervention strategy in response to a deteriorating youth and gang crime problem. A series of violent juvenile crimes in the mid 1980s prompted the Reno police to "get tough" on juveniles. Their suppression efforts included constant scrutiny of gang members and arrests for a variety of offenses. Results of this approach included increased media fascination with gang-related crimes, heightened citizen fears of victimization, and declining satisfaction with police performance. To address this decaying situation, the police chief implemented a number of new approaches based on a community policing philosophy. The gang suppression approach was abandoned and substituted with the Community Action Team (CAT) which was "designed to work with the community to address a wide range of youth gang issues" (Weston, 1993:80). Officers received cultural diversity training to enable them to better interact with gang members on the street. An intervention program (e.g., a jobs program for gang members) to deter gang activity replaced the earlier suppression approach. Neighborhood advisory groups were established to foster closer collaboration between the police and community members. Although the program has not been formally evaluated, Weston (1993:84) states that "it would appear that limited violence and limited growth in gang membership is related to the many success stories resulting from intervention efforts."

Representative of prevention efforts, the Phoenix Police Department introduced a school-based program in 1991 that seeks to provide "students with real tools to resist the lure and trap of gangs" (Humphrey & Baker, 1994:2). The nine-week program introduces students to conflict resolution skills, cultural sensitivity, and the negative aspects of gang life. Modeled after the DARE (Drug Abuse Resistance Education) program, GREAT (Gang Resistance and Education Training) has proliferated throughout the country during its short history and by the end of 1994 had been incorporated into school curricula in 38 states. In 1992 the Bureau of Alcohol, Tobacco, and Firearms (ATF) joined forces with the Phoenix Police Department by promoting and funding the program and in 1994 the National Institute of Justice (NIJ) funded a national evaluation of the program (Esbensen, 1995).

Previous Recommendations for a Gang Policy

In addition to specific anti-gang programs such as those just described, a number of recommendations for combatting crime in general and gangs in particular have appeared in the academic literature. Given the complexity of the topic and the diversity of opinions expressed in the popular press, it is indeed surprising to find a high degree of agreement among gang researchers concerning policy recommendations. I must admit that the proposals advanced at the conclusion of this essay mirror those of previous commentators. Perhaps with adequate repetition, those in a position to implement policy will do so.

In 1989, Elliott Currie called for a broad approach to the generic crime problem in the United States. Among his proposed recommendations were: intensive early education programs; expansion of health and mental health services; commitment to family support programs; reduction in social and economic inequality; and more constructive rehabilitative programs in the correction system. These proposals are based on the assumption that social structural factors are the underlying causes of crime and that significant social and economic changes are required to address the crime problem. Given the results of the 1994 national, state, and local elections, and the apparent movement to retribution and social Darwinism, these recommendations are even more unlikely to be implemented than they were when first proposed. Despite the low probability of implementation, Currie's suggestions need to be considered.

Huff (1990) maintains that gangs should be viewed as a manifestation of other problems endemic in our socioeconomic structure and in certain ecological areas of cities. Research shows that most gang members are drawn primarily from the urban poor and culturally marginal youth. However, it is important to note that the majority of such youth do NOT become gang members. Intervention strategies, he argues, need to involve community participants to counteract the decay of local institutions (e.g., families, churches, schools, recreational, and job opportunities). Similar to Currie, Huff concludes that "Whether one believes that gangs are a result of individual pathology or structural inequality, we should be able to agree that the provision of social justice, including an adequate quality of life, is the most efficient investment we can make" (1990:316).

As an example of the need to address the quality-of-life issue raised by Huff and alluded to by Currie, I would like to present the following. A single person working full-time at minimum wage ($4.25 per hour) would barely surpass the federal poverty level ($7,537.00 in 1993—$4.25/hr X 40 hours = $170/week X 52 weeks = $8,840 per year with no benefits, health care, nor vacation). Such conditions of economic marginality are generally acknowledged as contributing to the crime and gang problem.

In one of the more recent and far-reaching attempts to examine the gang problem and programmatic response, Spergel & Curry (1990) surveyed 45 cities. They were interested specifically in assessing the extent to which different agencies within these cities cooperated to address the gang issue. They concluded that:

> Policy recommendations emanating from these findings
> would not necessarily require a new war on poverty, but
> rather a series of programs targeted specifically at the youth
> gang problem addressing not only issues of economic depri-
> vation and lack of opportunities but social disorganization
> and the mobilization of community institutions in a con-
> certed attack on the problem (Spergel & Curry, 1990:309).

Another commentator on the gang situation observed that while considerable attention has been paid to gangs during the past century, it is somewhat disconcerting that so little progress has been made in dealing with the gang problem (Miller, 1990). He commented that it is not because of a lack of effort—there have been numerous programmatic attempts to combat youth gangs. However, "the great majority of programs could be described as pedestrian and unimaginative" and that "A central reason for the failure of the United States to deal effectively with youth gang problems lies in its failure to develop a comprehensive national gang control strategy" (Miller, 1990:267-268).

While a comprehensive national gang strategy may not be THE answer, it may prevent the continual vacillation between retribution and rehabilitation that is so counterproductive to an effective policy. American crime policy can be considered a dismal failure. During the past 25 years, we have experienced the full range of approaches, from the President's 1967 Crime Commission promoting rehabilitation and an improvement in social programs to the War on Crime popularized by Presidents Nixon, Reagan, and Bush. The sad reality is that there is no "quick-fix" to the crime problem or the gang problem. To adequately address the gang phenomenon, a long-term commitment to a consistent policy is required. Policymakers need to address the underlying causes of gangs and seek to remedy these situations. (Considerable controversy surrounds this issue, but a "best guess" needs to be made and then adhered to unless overwhelming evidence suggests that the best guess is wrong.) We cannot continue to shift direction every two to four years as the political winds change. To develop this national policy, attention should be paid to other nations and their experiences with gangs and juvenile delinquency.

While a national strategy is required, this is only part of the solution. Gangs remain a local problem and each locality presents a slightly different set of circumstances. Thus, local solutions must also be developed. With regard to a national strategy, if we look at the correlates of delinquency and gang behavior, then there are certain factors that surface. First, youth gangs are by definition largely confined to the adolescent life-stage. Adolescence, especially in urban industrialized societies is characterized by stress, uncertainty, and turmoil. Any gang policy needs to be shaped within the adolescent reality—not adult reality. Second, gangs are most pronounced in urban areas—or more importantly—in areas in which substantial economic and/or social disparity exists. Third, most delinquents mature out of delinquency, and so do gang members (e.g.,

Esbensen & Huizinga, 1993; Thornberry et al., 1993). Fourth, youth gangs are found in rural areas and upper-class suburban areas, they are peer group adaptations to adolescent situations. The shape of this peer group behavior is largely conditioned by the local community and the opportunities found there.

A gang strategy, therefore, must involve knowledge and familiarity with the life cycle and adolescent developmental issues. Certainly, family, school, religion, polity, and other social institutions are important in regulating youth gang activity. But, the question remains, how? Will parenting classes help? How about outlawing single-parent families? What about demanding that people have a license before being allowed to give birth? After all, people are not allowed to drive without training, and child-rearing certainly is more complex than driving a car? What about mandatory instruction in religion and ethics?

Covey et al. (1992) reinforce the need to examine the dynamics that shape the adolescent experience. They concluded their review of the gang intervention literature by focusing on the importance of addressing micro-level interactional patterns and stating that:

> There appears to be little we can do to directly alter patterns of interaction with relatives and friends. There do appear to be some interventions at the micro-social level that hold promise for improving the relationships between adolescents and their families and schools . . . but these are likely to affect gang delinquency only indirectly, by affecting patterns of association with gang members and non-members. . . . (1992:248).

Drawing from the more general delinquency and drug use literature (e.g., Hawkins & Catalano, 1993; Huizinga et al., 1994), support is found for a comprehensive prevention and intervention approach to the gang problem. The three projects of the Causes and Correlates Program funded by the Office of Juvenile Justice and Delinquency Prevention (OJJDP) conducted longitudinal research beginning with cohorts as young as seven (Huizinga et al., 1994). Among their major findings were: (1) contrary to popular perception that delinquency is an adolescent problem, there were indications that problem behaviors have an early onset, and the earlier the onset of these problem behaviors, the more serious and extensive the delinquent career; (2) while delinquency is often seen as a result of a number of other factors, delinquent behavior also affects these presumed causes (e.g., parental attachment, commitment to school, and peer associations); (3) peer group association is of central importance for not only delinquency but also such other phenomena as gang affiliation and gun ownership; and (4) the existence of multiple pathways to delinquency.

These findings are instructive for gang intervention and prevention efforts. First, as Huizinga and his colleagues suggest, prevention programs need to start early in the life cycle. "Waiting until the high school years may be far too late for many serious offenders. By that time, juveniles' characters are already well formed, and they are often resistant to change and able to thwart efforts by others to change their behavior for the better" (Huizinga et al., 1994:22-23). Second, intervention programs need to be comprehensive. "There is no single cause of delinquency. Factors such as family, school, peers, and neighborhoods are all related to delinquency" (Huizinga et al., 1994:23).

SUMMARY

The national gang strategy proposed in this summary section should be viewed with two caveats in mind. First and foremost, it must be acknowledged that juvenile delinquency in general and gang behavior in particular are not new nor unique to contemporary twentieth-century America. Collective youth violence has existed throughout the human life cycle in all cultures. The transition from childhood to adulthood has become increasingly complex with modernization and industrialization, contributing to the uncertainty of adolescence. Within this context, society needs to evaluate the manner in which adolescent exploration can best be channeled without destroying the creativity associated with adolescence.

Second, it is imperative that the role of the media in promoting public perception be taken into consideration. The mass hysteria surrounding the gang phenomenon in contemporary America is largely unfounded. For example, while the national press focused on the car-jackings and deaths of several tourists in Miami, creating a state of siege mentality among residents and a fear of travel among tourists, the homicide rate in Miami was actually declining! The current youth gang problem is to a considerable extent a media creation. As such it is difficult to suggest prevention, intervention, or suppression programs without these caveats in mind. In this light, let us consider a potential national gang strategy.

The Department of Justice has recently initiated a comprehensive strategy for the study and prevention of gangs. Within the OJJDP money has been allocated for the creation of a National Gang Assessment Center. The purpose of this center is to collect comprehensive data from multiple sources on the nature and distribution of gangs in America. One objective of this initiative is to encourage the adoption of common definitions of gangs and gang-related incidents. Given the array of definition, this should be a major accomplishment. To date, consensus has been lacking (see, for example, Covey et al., 1992). In spite of long-standing definitional problems, it does appear that a shared definition is being developed and a National Gang Center might help to promote widespread acceptance of a common definition. At this point, Spergel (1991:163) indicates growing agreement that the term "gang" refers to "juvenile and young adults associating together for serious, especially violent, criminal behavior with special concerns for turf and criminal-enterprise interests" (Spergel, 1991:163).

Two other promising programs that may lead to better understanding of gangs and possible intervention strategies have been initiated by OJJDP and NIJ. In response to the research conducted by Irving Spergel and his colleagues at the University of Chicago, OJJDP has proposed funding to implement and evaluate Spergel's Comprehensive Community-Wide Approach to Gang Prevention, Intervention, and Suppression Program. Such federal action hopefully will result in greater knowledge of and assessment of strategies for addressing the youth gang situation. The NIJ has also funded a national evaluation of the GREAT program. This experimental design with longitudinal followup will provide assessment of this school-based prevention program with regard to both juvenile violence and gang involvement. These program descriptions are not intended to summarize the anti-gang prevention and intervention programs, but simply to illustrate the types of positive programmatic attempts that are being initiated to address the gang problem. Numerous other laudatory programs have been developed and should be evaluated.

In addition to these types of program initiatives, it is also imperative that we begin to address the factors that have been repeatedly found to be associated with the emergence and proliferation of youth gangs and crime in general. In her address to the American Society of Criminology (1994), U.S. Attorney General Janet Reno acknowledged the importance of nonlegal factors such as early childhood development and family environmental factors in the production of crime. Accordingly, a national gang strategy must consider increased funding of prenatal and postnatal care, sex education to delay pregnancy and parenthood, parent training, preschool programs with adequate pay for child care providers and preschool teachers, after-school and summer programs for youth—especially for youth living in situations in which adult caretakers are absent. While the 1994 U.S. national elections do not bode well for such initiatives, it is imperative that attention be paid to the precursors and causes of gang behavior. For far too long America has relied upon post hoc band-aid approaches, while neglecting prevention efforts. We can no longer afford to waste billions of dollars dealing with the problem AFTER it has manifested itself. It is past time to invest our time and money in efforts to reduce the problem PRIOR to its emergence. Just as the reactive policing model has been replaced by a proactive community policing model, so must the gang reaction model be replaced with a comprehensive prevention model. Dollar for dollar, prevention monies are better spent.

Gangs are, and have been, both a national and a local problem. While a national gang strategy can focus and direct the gang response, local communities need to address their own particular circumstances. From what we know about gang development, the following initiatives are recommended:

1. the mass media should strive to present more balanced coverage of crime and delinquency;

2. educational opportunities need to be improved and expanded;

3. meaningful employment opportunities, including adequate paying jobs, need to be developed;

4. adequate health care must be made available to all members of society;

5. communities should place greater emphasis on the activities of youth, including increased involvement of parents, guardians, and other adults in the lives of youth;

6. local communities need to develop more activities for youth, including athletic and service activities such as midnight basketball leagues (this, incidently was referred to as "fluff" by opponents to the 1994 Crime Bill); and

7. local and national leaders must make a commitment to create an overall supportive environment for child and adolescent development.

These suggestions are by no stretch of the imagination new or original. They are, however, a call for a reversal of the "get tough" and retributive trend currently being witnessed throughout the United States in general and within the juvenile justice system in particular.

10

The Policy Analysis of Gang Violence*

Ira Sharkansky
Hebrew University

INTRODUCTION

There is no doubt that gang violence is a hot topic. Local newspapers proclaim the spread of gangs, and the violence associated with them, like a plague from Los Angeles and other urban centers. Scholars describe, differentiate, categorize, and analyze gangs and their affiliates. Media commentators, politicians, and scholars offer their proposals for dealing with gangs, and criticize each other's proposals (Huff, 1990a; Padilla, 1992; Knox, 1991; Jankowski, 1991; Cummings & Monti, 1993; McKinney, 1988; Prothrow-Stith & Weissman, 1991; Sampson, 1993).

What seems to be a flurry of recent work is actually an issue that has been on the research agenda of American social science for several decades (Thrasher, 1927; Whyte, 1943). A popular fascination with gangs, not always one of condemnation, extends backward in time much further. It has attached to Al Capone, Jesse James, Robin Hood, and the biblical David. During the period when he was fleeing from the unstable Saul, David was said to have gathered

> every one that was in distress, and every one that was in debt, and every one that was discontented. . . and he became a captain over them: and there were with him about four hundred men. (I Samuel 22:2)

* Thanks to Professors Susan Olson and Jeffrey Ian Ross for helpful comments on an earlier draft.

The story of Nabal describes a landowner who would not pay David and his men for the protection of his shepherds and flocks. Nabal made a righteous speech about not giving in to David's gang. When the story is over, Nabal is dead, and his widow has become David's wife (I Samuel 25). There is hardly any doubt as to who is the hero of this story. The Hebrew word that the Bible uses as the name of the landowner (Nabal) translates as "fool," or "clown." David had already been anointed as the chosen of God by the prophet Samuel, and he was not to lose that designation even though his behavior was puzzling or sinful on several occasions[1].

The tendency to view gangs in positive terms is not restricted to those of history. Studies of contemporary groups whose violence is recorded in the FBI Uniform Crime Reports describe symbiotic relationships with their surroundings. Gangs provide their members with status as well as protection and economic benefits that they are unlikely to achieve outside the gang. Gangs enjoy at least some support from their neighborhoods. Police officers charged with enforcing the laws that gangs violate, and politicians who stand for safe streets have recognized the gangs as well established within their communities, and have dealt with them in patron-client relationships. Gangs may control enough resources to buy protection from some agencies of law enforcement. Gang populations together with their family members and those who identify with them vicariously may be large enough to qualify as a constituency that elected officials must deal with circumspectly (Padilla, 1992; Knox, 1991; Cummings & Monti, 1993). The positive side of gangs is a sign of an underlying ambivalence about them, which joins a number of other features in making them difficult subjects for policy analysis.

ASPIRATIONS AND PROBLEMS OF POLICY ANALYSIS

"Policy analysis" is a label with a wide sweep. It includes the assessment of social problems with an eye to formulating policies; benefit-cost analysis of proposed policies or programs; the evaluation of ongoing programs; and the contemplation about the ways in which policy analysis occurs in academic research, think tanks, and government agencies (Dror, 1968; Wildavsky, 1979). Thus, policy analysis encompasses discrete activities found under the heading of social and economic analysis, program evaluation, and "meta policy analysis" (i.e., analyses about policy analysis). Each of these activities are relevant to the topic of gang violence, and each will show itself in the following sections.

The aspirations and limitations of policy analysis are well known. Numerous scholars and policymakers advocate the systematic assessment of social problems and policy options. In order to be "rational," according to common formulations, policymakers should be explicit in identifying the problem they wish to solve; specify all of their goals; rank goals according to their priorities; measure the costs and benefits associated with each policy option that can be chosen in order to achieve each of the goals; and select the package of goals and policy options that offers the greatest benefits and the least costs (Dror, 1968; Quade & Carter, 1989).

Rational policymaking sounds good, but has been disparaged by numerous social scientists. There are usually contrary ways of defining the problem(s) that underlie the symptoms of social or economic difficulties that are perceived, and several further ways of deciding what may be contributing to the underlying problem. Additional factors complicate an issue beyond the capacity of rational calculations to define and rank all the possible policy goals and program options, and to measure their costs and benefits. The enormous number and great range of options that can be conceived for dealing with problems confounds any aspirations to take everything into consideration, and to assess all the costs and benefits associated with alternative conceptions of each problem that is perceived, and the full list of potential policies and programs that creative analysts can put on the agenda. Numerous social values are imponderable, and do not lend themselves to systematic analysis. The long-range benefits of undertaking a social program can only be guessed about once it is recognized that numerous other factors will also influence the developments of individuals and communities over the years.

Policy analysis can aid in decisions that seem to be mostly economic in their character, and amenable to calculations of benefits and costs: e.g., the design of prisons or the choice of civil service positions or contracted service for prison personnel. Yet even on such matters, policy analysis can run afoul of intense feelings. Unions of government employees are likely to campaign against contracted services. Emotions concerned with the use of private companies to operate prisons, or the location of undesirable facilities like prisons or halfway houses (not in my backyard!) provoke arguments about how to conceive and measure items that intense political advocacy renders imponderable (Piller, 1991).

The ideological and political implications of policy choices mean that policy analysis is not a profession for those who are innocent and trusting. Policymakers have perceptions of long standing that limit their capacity to make calculations objectively. They are conditioned by previous experience as they interpret events in their surroundings. They approach their tasks with some options already ruled out, and others destined to be highly favored. Policymakers and advocates use all the tricks of politics in order to advance favored options and defeat those which they oppose. Politicking is likely to occur not only within legislative arenas, but also among the technocrats who examine proposals or evaluate programs. Politically astute individuals know the implications attached to particular definitions of the problem at stake, the choice of discrete policies and programs to be analyzed, and deciding how to define and measure variables for purposes of benefit-cost analysis or program evaluations. Among the concepts used to depict what interferes in rational policymaking are ideology, partisan loyalties, group think, and the self-interest of individual agencies and professions (Allison, 1971; Dery, 1984, 1990; Janis, 1983; Quade & Carter, 1989; Stone, 1988; Lindblom, 1965; Wildavsky, 1964).

THE POLICY ANALYSIS OF GANG VIOLENCE

The policy analysis of gangs should be placed at the outer edges of difficult issues. It is affected by conflicting conceptions of the issue at hand, and contrasting postures with high political intensity. Some analysts conceive gang problems to be issues of criminal behavior while others see them as manifestations of economic and social pathologies in inner cities or the society at large. With such wide differences in the starting points of analysis, the end points are also likely to be far apart. A perception of gangs as groups of criminals tends to be associated with recommendations that they be dealt with by a strict enforcement of existing laws. An economic or social perception tends to be associated with proposals that gang violence be addressed via social programs or structural changes in urban economies.

WHAT IS A GANG?

One problem of a fundamental sort that affects the policy analysis of gang violence concerns the central phenomenon. The key term (i.e., gang) is not defined clearly. A dictionary definition of gang is, "a band or company of persons who go about together or act in concert.[2]" This fits a range of groups from those which seem to be led by psychopaths and terrorize neighborhoods to those which organize pastoral outings and charitable activities under the auspices of a church or school. A popular connotation of "gang" is negative, and associated with criminal activities. Even within this conception, however, gangs differ on a number of traits. The earlier research dealt with Irish or Italian gangs. There are still white ethnic and punk gangs (Lukas, 1985), but now the more prominent colors are black and brown. African American, Hispanic, Samoan, and Asian gangs are prominent in the recent literature. Compared to the earlier work, this continues the theme that gangs are likely to form in communities that are poor and marginal, whose youth are limited with respect to education, income, and opportunities for well-paid or high-status employment.

The gangs described in the mass media and the scholarly literature are multifaceted, and differ greatly from one another. While some are loosely articulated, fluid groups that appear sporadically at street corners or video game parlors (which replace the pool halls or bowling alleys of earlier generations), other gangs are institutionalized to impressive degrees. They have distinctive clothing and ritualized handshakes, and persist for years with programs of recruitment, training, the advancement of members from junior to leadership ranks, and the retirement of senior members.

Some gangs provide their members with little more than an identity and self-proclaimed status, including a veneer of machismo or womanhood. They appeal to young members of marginal social groups, who are likely to experience a heightening of the insecurities that affect teenagers generally. Gangs provide for the poor what Boy Scouts and Girl Scouts, high school athletic teams, and church youth groups provide in mainstream communities.

Delinquency is likely to characterize some gangs more than others, and is found among teenagers not affiliated with gangs (Jankowski, 1991; Cummings & Monti, 1993b, Preface). The illegal activities of delinquent gangs range upward from low-level theft, vandalism or violence, to organized drug-dealing, protection, and prostitution. While the violence of some gangs is sporadic, others conduct paramilitary campaigns of defense or preemptive strikes to protect or enlarge their territory and economic monopolies against rivals. Scholars have described gangs with a variety of labels that suggest a range of behaviors from the benign, to those which pose a serious threat to public safety: "social," "retreatist," "party," "hedonistic, " "serious delinquents," "instrumental," "wilding," and " predatory." Gangs labeled "corporate" or "moneymaking" provide members with substantial incomes from illegal activities.

The "members" of a gang may vary from those who participate full time, to those with only sporadic affiliation. There are leaders and followers. In order to describe different qualities of affiliation, the literature uses terms like "chiefs," "Indians," "hardcore," "affiliates," "peripheral," "cliques," "core," "fringe," "regulars," "leaders," "soldiers," "associates," "sympathizers," "marginal," "topdogs," "maingroup," and "wanna be's." Ages range from preteens to the late twenties and even beyond (Knox, 1991; Cummings, 1993).

We are left with the message that we should know a gang prone to criminality when we see it. However, we may not agree on what a gang is, if a particular group is a gang or not, or whether it represents a serious threat to its members and the public! Nonetheless, enforcement may proceed according to policy-influencing criminal stereotypes.

WHAT TO MEASURE? HOW TO MEASURE IT?

A second problem that affects the policy analysis of gang violence concerns issues of measurement and analysis. This is related to the first problem (i.e., what is a gang), but goes beyond it. Even if researchers accept a negative conception of gang (e.g., a group of toughs up to no good), there is still a problem of identifying gangs and associating them with actions in ways that can be systematically recorded and analyzed.

It is common to assert that increasing gang violence is threatening American communities. But perceptions might be running ahead of what is actually happening on the streets. It would not be the first time that images of disorder and violence linked to foreign, poor, and/or nonwhite populations created fear in more affluent neighborhoods. The concerns of previous generations with drunkenness, opium smoking, and white slavery were associated with mass immigrations from eastern and southern Europe, and China. The current concern with gangs may be linked to a spurt of Hispanic and Asian immigrations, and the worsening of social conditions among inner-city African Americans who have not benefited from opportunities to advance into the middle class (Kappeler et al., 1993; Scheingold, 1991; Mann, 1993).[3]

The problems of data that are generally present in the criminal justice field are especially severe with respect to gangs. The FBI Uniform Crime Reports are known to be problematic, but at least they provide a basis of analysis for those crimes they have recorded over the years. A policy analysis of gangs is made difficult by the lack of the label "gang" in systematic official reports about crime that are collected according to standard categories (Bureau of Justice Statistics, 1991). There are no reliable indicators that can be used to show increases or decreases in violence or other phenomena associated with gangs across the United States, or to allow the systematic analysis of gang activity with respect to social or economic variables. Efforts to avoid this problem by assuming that gang activities are somehow related to recorded crimes of violence are risky. There is no firm indication about the proportion of violence associated with gangs, and whether that incidence is increasing or decreasing. Moreover, the evidence is mixed as to whether crimes of violence overall are increasing, remaining stable, or actually decreasing.

Newspaper reports concede that rates of violent crime may actually be decreasing even while the reports describe increased fears of gang activity[4]. Such reports may add to the fears that they describe, even though they are qualified by mentioning ambiguities in the data.

Annual rates of violent crimes reported by the FBI show an increase of about 40 percent from the 1970s, and increased virtually every year from 1983 through 1991: from 538 to 758 incidences per 100,000 population (*U.S. Statistical Abstract, 1993*:Table 300). Victimization surveys typically show crime rates substantially higher than the police reports compiled by the FBI. It is common to assert that most crimes are not reported to the police, and that victimization surveys are more accurate than the FBI data. However, victimization surveys have moved up and down within a range of 2,800 and 3,500 cases of violence per 100,000 persons since the early 1970s. In a recent period, the rates have gone down from 3,500 in 1981 to 3,100 in 1991 (*U.S. Statistical Abstract, 1993*:Table 309; Biderman & Lynch, 1991).

The absence of gangs from centrally collected, official records produces a situation where researchers work with different perspectives, definitions, techniques for gathering data, and research sites. It should come as no surprise that their findings differ and even contrast one with another. Thus, the epidemiology of gang violence is hindered by measurement issues that confuse realities.

Scholars who write about gang research distinguish between field observation of active gang members and "courthouse research" that relies on local records, plus interviews with local officials and incarcerated gang members. Neither courthouse research nor field observation may perceive the true extent of gang violence and other activities, the extent to which they are changing over time, or vary from one place to another. Insofar as there are no centrally defined indicators for gang-related criminality and no central clearinghouse with responsibility for monitoring data collection, locally collected records about gangs vary in character and quality from one place to another. The informants relied on by courthouse researchers have incentives to distort what they report in one direction or another. Local officials may be inclined to inflate or lessen their descriptions of gang activity, with an eye to increasing budgets for enforcement, or gaining credit for having minimized crime. Incarcerated gang members may maximize their stories in a spirit of bravado, or minimize them in order to curry favor with someone who could help them gain an early release or some other benefit.

Field observation has its own dangers. Some researchers have been assaulted by members of their subject gang or its rivals. Even when scholars emerge whole from their research site, they cannot generalize rates of gang affiliation or violence beyond their own locale, or explain what they have found by means of systematic comparisons between gang traits and indicators for community variables (Hagedorn, 1990; Miller, 1990).

GANG ANALYSES AND PROPOSALS

A third problem that confounds the policy analysis of gang violence appears in the proposals for action. Without clear conceptions of what gangs are, or to what extent the objective threat is changing, gang scholars and other commentators are free to see what they are prepared to see, and propose what they are inclined to support.

A falling off of resources for studying the problems of the poor may be weakening the capacity for intelligent social policymaking just as the problems of gang violence are becoming more severe. Several factors have occurred since the 1960s that may be responsible for this situation: a frustration with social programming that derives, in part, from exaggerated promises that the "War on Poverty" would deal with poverty once and for all times; the success of social programs and assaults on racial discrimination that have allowed upwardly mobile African Americans to leave the ghettos for middle-class education, occupations, and housing; and the indifference to social programming identified with the Reagan and Bush administrations (Wilson, 1987; Cummings

& Monti, 1993b). This combination of events may deprive ghetto youths of accessible role models within the mainstreams of education and occupation, and heighten the frustration of those whose families have not moved upward. It may also leave inner-city youth to stew in their own juice, with a minimum of research funding directed at gang issues.

> Gang control is a low national priority in large part because those with good access to resources put a low priority on gang problems and those who put a high priority on gang problems have poor access to resources (Miller, 1990).

Without clearly agreed upon definitions of gangs or firm data about the violence associated with them, scholars and political activists have staked out sharply different postures with respect to public policy. Some proposals read more like a reflex to popular sentiment or the idealogy of the proposer than the result of serious research and reflection.

On the one hand is an *enforcement posture* (Jackson & Rudman, 1993; Hearings, 1990; McKinney, 1988). By this view the task of the police and courts is to enforce the laws against violence, intimidation, drug-dealing, prostitution, and protection that have been associated with gangs. The enforcement view may also lead to the enactment of additional measures directed at the practices associated with gangs. These include curfews, as well as school regulations against carrying weapons or the wearing of gang "colors" by students.

An enforcement posture appears to be most widespread among policy-makers and commentators in the popular media, but has numerous critics among criminal justice academics. Critics of the enforcement perspective express a number of views. They cannot be described as "anti-enforcement," because many include a component of enforcing criminal laws against gang members. What these alternative perspectives have in common is a perception that enforcement deals only with part of the gang phenomena, and perhaps not the part that is most important. Indeed, an emphasis on enforcement may actually strengthen the atmosphere of *establishment vs. underdog* that is part of gangs' appeal to potential recruits, and thus contribute to gang activities (Jankowski, 1991; Spergel & Curry, 1990; Huff, 1990b).

One multifaceted cluster of recommendations would pursue enforcement activities against youth who have committed acts of violence. However, this multifaceted approach would allocate much greater resources than at present to "treating" the members of low-income, marginal communities who might be turned from affiliation with violence-prone gangs. The ingredients of this treatment are alternate activities for young people (e.g., sports and social clubs), programs that teach how to deal with anger nonviolently that are offered in schools and community centers, and greater attention to job-creation and job training in poor communities (Prothrow-Stith & Weissman, 1991; Cummings & Monti, 1993b).

Related to the views that prevention activities may be more efficient than enforcement activities in dealing with gangs are dismal perspectives on the efficacy of enforcement with respect to the future of those who are imprisoned, and the failures of enforcement in protecting society from criminals. Supporting these perspectives are high rates of recidivism, and the incapacity of an enforcement strategy to clear the streets of criminals when jails and penitentiaries are so crowded that they cannot accept or retain all who qualify. About one-half of releasees return to prison, most of them in the first three years after release. Prison populations grew by 52 percent between 1980 and 1985, while prison space grew by only 29 percent in roughly the same period (Bureau of Justice Statistics, 1988:108, 111). *"The criminal was out of jail before the victim was out of the hospital"* is an epigram that has been politically useful to those who promote an enforcement emphasis for dealing with urban violence. It also reflects a condition where procedural rights, crowded courts and jails, and high caseloads for judges, public defenders, and probation officers create a situation where criminality seems to have overwhelmed the system of criminal justice.

A simple preoccupation with enforcement may lead police authorities to waste resources that are not capable of supporting full coverage for all their responsibilities. A view that its proponents call "problem-oriented policing" is skeptical about the conventional practice of chasing down every infraction or responding immediately to every call for help (i.e., the 911 syndrome). According to problem-oriented policing, authorities can become more efficient by deciding in advance which crimes have high priority in their communities. They can then decide what proportion of their resources to allocate for citizen calls, and what proportions for community education about crime prevention, neighborhood patrols, and intelligence activities directed against high-priority crimes. Against the danger that a death or injury may result from a delayed response to a citizen's call, problem-oriented policing claims to offer greater overall security for community residents and their property (Goldstein, 1990).

DEMAGOGUERY

The issue of gangs, like other topics related to crime, has no shortage of demagoguery. A recently published history of criminal justice in the United States concludes that bombastic proposals are most likely to come from political arenas that are furthest removed from those that deal directly with crime (Friedman, 1993). Elected officials and candidates at state and national levels can proclaim their opposition to gangs and other perpetrators of crime, while leaving it to local politicians, judges, and other criminal justice personnel to deal with the difficult questions of implementation. Among the messiest problems are which criminals to actually incarcerate in overcrowded institutions, and how to maintain rapport with ethnic and racial communities whose social and economic conditions provide the breeding grounds of gangs and violence?

> The irony is that recent conservative presidents, who have long mouthed slogans about states' rights and local government, have been more zealous than the liberals in denouncing crime, drug use, and the like. They have thus helped keep alive the myth that the federal government can actually do something about the problem. In fact, there is not much the federal government *can* do, at least under present laws and jurisdictional arrangements. Of course, the federal government could *pay* state and local governments . . . But the federal government is loath to put its money where its mouth is (Friedman, 1993, 275-6).

There is also demagoguery from the left, and in the professional literature as well as the mass media. Some argue that nothing less than a total reform of urban economies can alter the infrastructures of poverty, marginal status and hopelessness that provide the explanations of gang violence. In certain formulations this reform may consist of massive budget additions for job training and other social programs. For others, it entails the tearing down of capitalism and the reconstruction of the economic system in which the cities exist. Some of those who oppose an enforcement perspective on gangs identify with ethnic or racial communities that have the highest incidence of gangs. They assert that white social scientists and policymakers cannot deal effectively with gang issues because of bias or ignorance about nonwhite cultures. One black scholar has condemned the entire criminal justice system on account of what is perceived as pervasive racism:

> . . . racial minorities are still predominantly unequal in this country, and . . . the legal structure, primarily the criminal law, by design and implementation is maintained to keep them in that status (Mann, 1993:ix).

IS THE POLICY ANALYSIS OF GANGS DIFFERENT FROM OTHER DIFFICULT ISSUES?

To this point, the argument is that multiple concepts, diverse and unreliable data, and contrasting perspectives on the policies appropriate to gangs render gang violence a poor candidate for policy analysis. Gang violence represents much that is horrible in the inner cities of the United States, but gangs are also viewed with understanding or even praise by some social scientists and the residents of the neighborhoods where gangs prevail. Against the calls for harsh law enforcement are arguments that campaigns of enforcement may make violent gangs more attractive to potential recruits. Some alternative remedies demand thoroughgoing change in economics and social services in order to do away with poverty, joblessness, and hopelessness. Other alternatives to enforcement are modest in advocating more money for teenage sports and social centers, plus family-centered training programs in how to deal with conflict and anger nonviolently.

It is appropriate to ask if gang violence is different with respect to their suitability for policy analysis from other cumbersome issues that have been high on the public agenda. Drug use, teenage pregnancies, and abortion are likewise affected by competing values and conceptions of how the underlying problems should be defined, as well as by competing moral values and intense feelings. For these issues, like gang violence, there are no lists of policy options with agreed upon assessments of their benefits and costs.

The problems in rendering unambiguous policy analyses about difficult issues does not take them off the policy agenda. As we have seen in the case of gang violence, the limited utility of policy analysis may actually free advocates from intellectual discipline, and allow free reign to demagoguery.

There has been no shortage of policy follies in ancient and modern times. Although it is common to teach children that they cannot eat their cake *and* save it for another day, policymakers are not prevented from pursuing goals that run counter to one another. A book on the Reagan administration written by its early Budget Director is filled with stories of how the President of the United States, sitting at the center of the world's greatest array of policy analysts, could not be led to grasp elementary facts. He could not reduce taxes by 25 percent, refuse to cut the large item of Social Security expenditures, increase the even larger item of defense expenditures, and avoid budget deficits of unprecedented proportions (Stockman, 1987).

These obvious contradictions between wanting to eat one's cake *and* save it provide textbook examples for the persistence of policymaking that is resistant to policy analysis. The contradictions between other goals are more subtle. Difficulties in perceiving contradictions may reflect a lack of clarity in policymakers' purposes. Policymakers can travel a long way down a costly road before they realize that they cannot achieve their objectives. Politics assures that optimists will focus on brief signs of success in their efforts. However, frustration will be the more prominent and lasting result of pursuing goals that cannot exist with one another.

"Victimless crimes" such as gambling, prostitution, and drug use resemble the issue of gang violence. They offer examples of impossible dreams or conundrums, i.e., problems without solutions. They are conundrums insofar as policymakers strive to eradicate activities that address the needs of substantial populations. While some policymakers strive to enforce laws against gangs or the use of illegal gambling, drugs and prostitution, the target activities thrive.

In the case of drug use or illicit sex, for example, actual enforcement is likely to fall far short of public rhetoric. Ten to eighteen percent of individuals in different age and ethnic categories reported using various illegal drugs in 1991 (Statistical Abstract, 1993, Table 209). There is no shortage of key elected officials and their aides, plus ranking law enforcement personnel who have been caught sampling the forbidden pleasures of drug use or illicit sex. A nominee to the United States Supreme Court was derailed on account of previous drug use, and President Bill Clinton admitted to drug experimentation during his youth.

Enforcement activities against illegal gambling rank especially high on society's hypocrisies, insofar as an increasing number of state and local governments have legalized lotteries and casinos in order to cash in on what is illegal if operated privately. Thirty-seven states reported revenues from pari-mutuel betting or lotteries in a recent year (Statistical Abstract, 1993, Table 485). Perhaps reflecting the spread of state-sponsored gambling, only 12,000 persons were arrested in 1991 for gambling. By comparison, the numbers arrested for the victimless crimes of prostitution and commercial vice were 79,000 and for the use of illicit drugs were 763,000 (Statistical Abstract, 1993, Table 313).

Strongly held attitudes seem to contribute more than objective science to the choice of which activities to make illegal on account of the real or potential harm they threaten to users. There appears to be no other explanation for the legality of alcohol and tobacco, but the prohibition of marijuana. How leaders read the tolerance of their constituencies can render their policy goals manageable or unattainable. If drugs or prostitution are undesirable from some perspectives, but craved from another perspective, why not make them legal, but regulated? Or make them legal, but organized for the benefit of the public, like state-operated gambling? The answer is likely to reflect policymakers' views of public tolerance, or the policymakers' own views of what is right and wrong. "Symbolic politics" refers to the great weight of labels and beliefs in policy discourse. The reputations attached to symbols grant advantages to some policy options, while rendering others unfit for consideration (Edelman, 1964).

It is not only the policy analysis of victimless crimes and gang violence where temptations for dramatic, heroic, and thorough treatments of problems come up against complex issues that foil simple analysis and policymaking. The prospect of complete solution entices sophisticated policymakers and analysts at all levels of government. An example that appears to be outside the realm of this chapter, but nonetheless has a lesson for the policy analysis of gang violence, comes from the posture taken by the White House during the run-up to the 1991 Gulf War.

Some of the writing about gangs suggests that if only the goals of a policymaker could be defined clearly, the tasks of assessing alternatives and producing recommendations would fall into place (Knox, 1991). One theme in the writing about the Gulf War praises President George Bush for defining his goals clearly, and recruiting political support from key domestic and international constituencies (Summers, 1992). Thus, if a president could define national goals and do effective policymaking in foreign affairs, why not in a domestic issue like gangs?

The complications in the President's analysis of his options began to be apparent even before the applause from his supporters died down. Critics accused President Bush for making a shallow comparison of his confrontation against Saddam Hussein with that between Winston Churchill and Adolf Hitler. Hitler's activities made those of Saddam Hussein seem mild by comparison, and the closely balanced power ratios of Hitler's Germany and Churchill's Britain were in sharp contrast to the uneven tilt between the armed forces of the United States, Great Britain, France, and others against those of Iraq. Critics also questioned Bush's savvy in ending the war with the Iraqi leader still in control of a sizable military force (Graubard, 1992). Commentators who sought to avoid outright criticism or praise emphasized the difficult choices facing Bush. While they avoided great praise, they also did not condemn him. Rather, they defined the dilemmas of competing options: pursuing the war more completely (perhaps to the streets of Baghdad), as opposed to preserving the unity of domestic support and the international coalition that would have been threatened by the bloodletting involved in a more complete victory (Hilsman, 1992).

The message for gang violence in this writing on the Gulf War is that the simplicity of options and policy choice perceived by some observers is likely to be more imagined than real. A powerful group of countries could strike an impressive blow to a single, much weaker country, but serious problems remained. The Gulf War was not an ideal model of policy analysis and implementation. It is more useful as a case of policy analysis that seemed deceptively ideal. It suggests that a simplistic enforcement strategy with respect to gangs may also be deceptively appealing. Tough-talking authorities may achieve short-term success in a locality with strong enforcement measures. However, the success might not be applicable over the wide range of situations that are described in the literature dealing with gangs, or have a lasting effect against the economic and social infrastructure that produces gangs and their violence.

GUN CONTROL AND GANG CONTROL

A profound handicap in the policy analysis of gang violence in the American context is the *a priori* elimination of one policy option (i.e., far-reaching gun control) that is strongly related to-violence. Guns figured in 66 percent of the murders recorded by the FBI for 1991, and in no less than 58 percent for every year since 1980 (*U.S. Statistical Abstract, 1993*:Table 304). Where guns are less freely available, rates of violence are dramatically lower than in the United States. Homicide rates in Canada and Finland are one-seventh those in the United States, while those of Germany and Japan are one-twentieth and one-fortieth those of the United States (Friedman, 1993:461; Prothrow-Stith & Weissman, 1991). The problems in enacting even anemic gun control against new-weapons purchases are well known. Twelve years of entrenched opposition to any gun control legislation elapsed between the assassination attempt on President Ronald Reagan and the passage of the "Brady Bill" to regulate the purchase of firearms. As yet there is no indication as to how the required screening of gun purchasers will be implemented, much less whether it will prove significant in reducing gun ownership or violence. Attaining serious control equivalent to that in Canada, Europe, or Japan will involve more far-reaching federal enactments, as well as campaigns to induce or force current holders of pistols and rifles to give up their weapons. One can only imagine the scenario of gun-searching sweeps of inner-city neighborhoods, suburbs, and rural areas!

To be sure, a thoroughgoing program of gun control is not the only viable option in a serious effort against gang violence. Gang violence would not disappear even with extensive gun controls. However, posing the issue suggests that gang violence is lower than gun privileges on the policy agenda. The message conveyed to policy analysts is that gang violence is not of supreme importance. Killings in the inner city are part of the price that Americans pay for their unwillingness to dispose of gun freedoms. To put the issue another way: without significantly greater gun control, the prospects for controlling gang violence may be too small to be worth the effort.

Gang violence shares some traits of other insoluble problems. Like prostitution and drug use, gang violence is distasteful to large segments of the population, and is a favorite topic of mainline media and politicians. On the other hand, the eradication of gangs would seem to demand too much in terms of money and legal enactments, as well as changes in attitudes widely held among one group or another. Saturation patrols of ethnic neighborhoods would be expensive and threaten the sensitivities of civil libertarians and leaders of the communities where gangs operate. Without far-reaching controls over firearms, the effort might not prove worthwhile. Without the legalization of currently banned substances, gang profits from drug dealing offer an economic activity that poor youth cannot resist. Thorough-going reform of the capitalist system, or even greatly increased outlays for conventional social programs, do not appear high on the agendas of contemporary policymakers. For the foreseeable future, ethnic and racial neighborhoods of inner cities seem destined to remain economically marginal with high levels of school dropouts and dismal prospects for income or status. There is unlikely to be a shortage of recruits for each generation of gang leaders.

COPING

Alongside the frustrations for policy analysts and the weight of problems that can be described as insoluble, several routines have been described that policymakers employ in such settings. The aspirations are moderate: to keep problems from getting worse; and to avoid options that do more harm than good (Wildavsky, 1979). A number of political scientists have used the term "coping" to convey the encounter with serious problems via *adapting, managing, dealing with, judgment,* and *satisfying* (Moynihan, 1975; Simon, 1976). *Coping* implies something less than *solutions.* It implies decisions that are "good enough," even if they are not what any of the participants really want.

Psychologists have sharpened the concept of coping in ways that make it useful for this discussion of gang violence. They define coping as responding to stress, and have described different ways of coping. Formulations for what some term "engagement" as opposed to "avoidance" coping are similar to what others call "active" as opposed to "passive" coping, or "hardiness" as opposed to "helplessness." Engagement coping (i.e., active coping or hardiness) responds to stressful situations with control, challenge, commitment, creativity, objective information seeking, goal definition, organization, and discipline. It includes surveying options and recruiting support; efforts to salvage something from a difficult situation; changing expectations in the face of conditions that are not likely to change in the short range; or ranking priorities in order to achieve or preserve the more important at the expense of the less important.

Avoidance coping (i.e., passive coping or helplessness) responds to stress with a lack of control, hopelessness, confusion, rigidity, distortion, disorganization, anxiety, avoidance, withdrawal, flight, or submission. It exhibits pointless emoting that involves loss of control and direction for oneself and potential allies; quixotic choice of options in an effort to *do something!* without taking account of likely costs and benefits; or frittering away resources in efforts that do not produce significant accomplishments (Coelho et al., 1974; Folkman, 1984; Tapp, 1985; Moos & Schaefer, 1986).

Engagement coping by policy analysts concerned with gang violence would entail an explicit recognition of diverse perspectives, values, and interests, and the impossibility of producing a single analysis or prescription that is widely accepted as legitimate. Implied in this is a continuation of present lines of research, with social scientists of different perspectives describing and analyzing the numerous aspects of gangs and their members. If the result is to convince policymakers that there is no one best way to conceive or treat gang-related problems, then the work will not be wasted.

Coping options may also address the plight of citizens as potential victims or community residents obsessed with the issue of personal safety. The muddied concepts and data concerned with gang violence offer slim chance that policy analysts will discover a solution for these stresses. Yet it is known to social scientists and to many urban residents where gang violence, like other crime, is likely to occur in the urban space. The American city resembles Disraeli's England in being two nations of the desperately poor and frequently violent, and more fortunate others (Disraeli, 1845/1926). Those who can afford to avoid the inner city do so, and thereby minimize their exposure to what is unpleasant and unsafe. This is not a prescription that is morally attractive for a society that concerns itself with equality and justice, but it is advice that many learn from their parents, and teach to their children.

CONCLUSIONS

The discussion of this chapter has ranged widely, drawing on materials from the gang of biblical David to the Gulf War of 1991. It is not the purpose to make light of the suffering that predatory gangs cause for susceptible teenagers or innocent bystanders in American cities. Nor is it the purpose to conclude that policy analysis has nothing to contribute to those who would deal with violent gangs. Rather, the concern has been to caution that gang violence is not a simple issue. Gang behavior has proved vexatious for the rational assessment of good and bad. Gangs have been associated with difficult analytical issues at least from the time when ancient rabbis began pondering David's favor in the eyes of the Almighty, against the stories of Nabal, Bathsheba, and Uriah. Policy analysis is not a rigorous science, especially when it encounters issues that are complicated by contending points of ideology and a lack of hard data.

Both an aggressive policy of enforcing existing laws, and a thoroughgoing reform of the economic conditions that breed violent gangs do not seem to be credible solutions for gang violence. A strict enforcement posture seems likely to fail in the long run, due in part to financial costs and concerns for civil liberties, a refusal to get rid of the guns that make such a direct contribution to violence, and the contributions that strict enforcement may offer to gangs that recruit young people who consider themselves to be marginalized. Thoroughgoing economic reform seems beyond the probable responses of the contemporary American society. This is especially so insofar as the communities that produce gang violence, and suffer most of its consequences, are rendered outside of the mainstream by traits of race, ethnicity, social class, and lifestyle.

Policymakers may pursue the widely described routine of incrementalism by allocating more money than they have previously to gang-related issues, taking care to deal with concerns of prevention as well as enforcement. This means supporting more benign options to potential gang recruits (e.g., youth clubs and sports facilities), to allocate more resources than at present for the economic needs of the communities associated with gang violence, to invest in programs for teaching nonviolent ways of dealing with frustration, and to upgrade the quality of police forces, all the while avoiding the illusion that any of these holds the key to urban peace.

Luck may play a part in keeping down the tendency for political demagoguery, and thus allowing reasoned analysis to play a part in shaping policy toward gang violence. It will be helpful if those indicators that suggest a lessening of violence are more persistent than those that suggest an increase. Policy analysts should hope for a waning rather than a waxing of media preoccupation with gangs, and that few horrendous incidents occur on their watch.

NOTES

[1]   Waldorf's (1993) findings are qualitative in nature and are therefore very mixed. Some evidence (verbal translations of interviews with gang members in San Francisco) suggests outside gangs did try to come in and develop franchises, and some evidence suggests simple emulation behavior. Basically, Waldorf states gang members "are often like fish out of water when they go elsewhere" (1993:16) and thus feels they are less capable of intentional imperialism or franchising than some may believe.

[2]   See Maxxson's (1993) conclusion that some well-intentioned actions by parents and judges to ship gang members elsewhere could potentially have reverse intended effects. Apparently, the findings here support that conclusion.

[3]   This finding on the greater severity of the gang problem in urban areas, dissipating outward to a lower severity of the gang problem in rural areas, is consistent with the research by Quinn, Tobolowsky, and Downs (1994).

[4]   Contrary to the claim by Hagedorn and Macon in *People and Folks* that there was little Chicago gang influence in Milwaukee, the fact remains that prior to Hagedorn's field work Jeff Fort had moved to Milwaukee and set up his gang operations there after release from prison. Chicago was too "hot" at the time for him. But Jeff Fort would eventually return to Chicago in the 1970s and build up his El Rukn gang organization.

[5]   We are not aware of anyone other than ourselves who has been systematically tracking this information firsthand and on a regular basis, that is other than federal agencies. The National Gang Crime Research Center has maintained an extensive file called the National Geographic Guide to Gangs and has been routinely updated continuously through national surveys for the last four years. Some of the best data has yet to be released on the gang migration issue, or it is confidential (i.e., the Illinois State Police Gang Intelligence report on gang migration, which tracks "hits" on the statewide gang computer file from routine "stops" where gang members are identified, and this data does suggest extensive travel by gang members in the State of Illinois across and between cities).

6   For example, his offer to fight alongside the Philistine King Achish against the Israelites (I Samuel 27-29); his adultery with Bathsheba and his arrangement of the death of Uriah, her husband (II Samuel 11).

7   *Oxford English Dictionary, 2nd Edition, on CD-ROM.*

8   Immigration rates have increased in each decade since the 1930s (*U.S. Statistical Abstract, 1993*: Table 5).

9   *Salt Lake Tribune,* February 27, 1995.

Bibliography

Abadinsky, H. (1990). *Organized Crime* (3rd ed.). Chicago, IL: Nelson-Hall, Inc.

Akers, R.L. (1985). *Deviant Behavior: A Social Learning Approach* (3rd ed.) Belmont, CA: Wadsworth.

Akers, R.L., M.D. Krohn, L. Lanza-Kaduce & M. Radosevich (1979). "Social Learning and Deviant Behavior: A Specific Test of a General Theory." *American Sociological Review*, 44(4):635-655.

Albanese, J. (1996). *Organized Crime in America* (3rd ed.). Cincinnati, OH: Anderson Publishing Co.

Allison, G.T. (1971). *Essence of Decision: Explaining the Cuban Missile Crisis.* Boston, MA: Little, Brown and Company.

American Correctional Association (1993). *Gangs in Correctional Facilities: A National Assessment* (Grant No. 91-IJ-CX-0026). U.S. Department of Justice, Office of Justice Programs, National Institute of Justice.

Anderson, E. (1990). *Streetwise: Race, Class, and Change in an Urban Community.* Chicago, IL: University of Chicago Press.

Armstrong, G. & M. Wilson (1973). "City Politics and Deviance Amplification." In I. Taylor & L. Taylor (eds.) *Politics and Deviance.* New York, NY: Penguin Books.

Asbury, H. (1927). *The Gangs of New York.* New York, NY: Alfred A. Knopf.

Aultman, M.G. & C.F. Wellford (1978). "Towards and Integrated Model of Delinquency Causation." *Sociology and Social Research*, 63:316-325.

Aver, M. (1994, October 30) "2 Jailed After Drive-By Shooting," Police Chase. *Tyler Courier-Times-Telegraph*, pp. 1, 9.

Babbie, E. (1992). *The Practice of Social Research.* Belmont, CA: Wadsworth Pub. Co.

Barber, M. (1993). "Lack of School Safety Related to Growth of Gang Activity on Campus." *California Journal*, 24(6):27-29.

Bartol, C.R. (1980). *Criminal Behavior: A Psychosocial Approach.* Englewood Cliffs, NJ: Prentice-Hall.

Bastain, L. & B. Taylor (1991). *School Crime: A National Crime Victimization Survey Report*. Bureau of Justice Statistics, Washington, DC.

Beaird, L.H. (1986) "Prison Gangs: Texas." *Corrections Today,* 18:22.

Berger, A.S. & W. Simon (1974). "Black Families and the Moynihan Report: A Research Evaluation." *Social Problems,* 22:145-161.

Bernard, T.J. (1992). *The Cycle of Juvenile Justice*. New York, NY: Oxford University Press.

Bibb, M. (1967). "Gang Related Services of Mobilization for Youth." In M. Klein (ed.) *Juvenile Gangs in Context: Theory, Research, and Action*. Englewood Cliffs, NJ: Prentice-Hall.

Biderman, A.D. & J.P. Lynch (1991). *Understanding Crime Incidence Statistics: Why the UCR Diverges From the NCS*. New York, NY: Springer-Verlag.

Bjerregaard, B. & C. Smith (1993). "Gender Differences in Gang Participation, Delinquency and Substance Use." *Journal of Quantitative Criminology,* 9(4):329-351.

Bloch, H.A. & A. Niederhoffer (1958). *The Gang: A Study in Adolescent Behavior*. New York, NY: Philosophical Library.

Block, C.R. & R. Block (1993). *Research in Brief: Street Gang Crime in Chicago* (Report No. NCJ-144782). Washington, DC: National Institute of Justice.

Bolitho, W. (1930). "The Psychosis of the Gang." *Survey,* 1:501-506.

Bookin, H. (1980). "The Gangs That Didn't Go Straight." Presentation to the Society for the Study of Social Problems, New York.

Bookin-Weiner, H. & R. Horowitz (1983). "The End of the Youth Gang: Fad or Fact?" *Criminology,* 21:585-602.

Bowker, L.H., H.S. Gross & M.W. Klein (1980). "Female Participation in Delinquent Gang Activity." *Adolescence,* 15:509-519.

Branham, V.C. & S.B. Kutash (1949). *Encyclopedia of Criminology*. New York, NY: Philosophical Library.

Buentello, S. (1986). "Texas Syndicate: A Review of Its Inception, Growth in Violence and Continued Threat to The Texas Department of Corrections." Unpublished manuscript, Texas Department of Corrections, Huntsville, Texas.

Buentello, S., R.S. Fong & R.E. Vogel (1991). "Prison Gang Development: A Theoretical Model." *The Prison Journal,* LXXI(2):3-14.

Bureau of Alcohol, Tobacco & Firearms (1989, March). *Crips and Bloods Street Gangs: Volume I-II*. (Limited distribution). Washington, DC: U.S. Government Printing Office.

Bureau of Justice Statistics (1988). *Report to the Nation on Crime and Justice* (Report No. NCJ-105506). Washington, DC: U.S. Department of Justice.

Bureau of Justice Statistics (1991). *Sourcebook of Criminal Justice Statistics—1991*. Washington, DC: U.S. Department of Justice, Office of Justice Statistics,

Bureau of Justice Statistics (1992). Drugs, Crime, and the Justice System: A National Report. (Report No. NCJ-133652). Washington, DC: U.S. Government Printing Office.

Burkett, S.M. & G.F. Jensen (1975). "Conventional Ties, Peer Influences, and the Fear of Apprehension: A Study of Adolescent Marijuana Use." *Sociological Quarterly*, 16:523-533.

Burkett, S.M., G.F. Jensen, C.S. Sellers & D.L. Clason (1993). "Social Learning and Adolescent Deviance Abstention: Toward Understanding the Reasons for Initiating, Quitting, and Avoiding Drugs." *Journal of Quantitative Criminology*, 9(1):101-125.

Camp, G.M. & C.G. Camp (1985). *Prison Gangs: Their Extent, Nature and Impact on Prisons* (Grant No. 84-NI-AX-0001). U.S. Department of Justice, Office of Legal Policy. Washington, DC: U.S. Government Printing Office.

_____ (1988). *Management Strategies for Combatting Prison Gang Violence*. South Salem, NY: Criminal Justice Institute.

Campbell, A. (1987). "Self-Definitions by Rejection: The Case of Gang Girls." *Social Problems*, 34:451-464.

_____ (1987). *Girls in the Gang*. New York, NY: Basil Blackwell.

_____ (1990). "Female Participation in Gangs." In C.R. Huff (ed.) *Gangs in America*. Newbury Park, CA: Sage.

Chambliss, W.J. (1973). "The Saints and the Roughnecks." *Society*, 11:24-31.

Chance, B. (1990). "School Crime Stoppers." *FBI Law Enforcement Bulletin*, 59:7-9.

Chernkovich, S. & P. Giordano (1992). "School Bonding, Race and Delinquency." *Criminology*, 30(2):261-291.

Chin, K.L. (1990). "Chinese Gangs and Extortion." In C.R. Huff (ed.) *Gangs in America*. Newbury Park, CA: Sage.

_____ (1993). "Gang Violence in Chinatown." Paper Presented at the annual meetings of the American Society of Criminology, New Orleans, LA.

Cloward, R.A. & L.E. Ohlin (1960). *Delinquency and Opportunity: A Theory of Delinquent Gangs*. New York, NY: The Free Press.

Coelho, G.V., D.A. Hamburg & J.E. Adams (eds.) (1974). *Coping and Adaptation*. New York, NY: Basic Books.

Cohen, A. (1955). *Delinquent Boys: The Culture of the Gang*. Glencoe, IL: The Free Press.

Conly, C.H. (1993). *Street Gangs: Current Knowledge and Strategies*. Washington, DC: National Institute of Justice.

Connors, E.F. (1991). "Violent Street Gangs" [Summary]. In *Attorney General's Summit on Law Enforcement Responses to Violent Crime: Public Safety in the Nineties*, pp. 49-50. Washington, DC: Bureau of Justice Statistics (NCJ 130958).

Cooley, C.H. (1909). *Social Organization*. New York, NY: Scribners.

Covey, H.C., S. Menard & R.J. Franzese (1992). *Juvenile Gangs*. Springfield, IL: Charles C Thomas Publishers.

Criminal Conspiracy Statutes (1993). 13A *Alabama Criminal Code Annotated* 4.3-4.4.

Cummings, S. & D.J. Monti (eds.) (1993a). *Gangs: The Origins and Impact of Contemporary Youth Gangs in the United States*. Albany, NY: State University of New York Press.

_____ (1993b). "Public Policy and Gangs: Social Science and the Urban Underclass." In Cummings & Monti (eds.) *Gangs: The Origins and Impact of Contemporary Youth Gangs in the United States*, pp. 305-320. Albany, NY: State University of New York Press.

Currie, E. (1989). "Confronting Crime: Looking Toward the Twenty-First Century." *Justice Quarterly*, 6:5-25.

_____ (1991). *Dope and Trouble: Portraits of Delinquent Youth*. New York, NY: Parthenon.

Curry, G.D., R.A. Ball & R.J. Fox (1994). *Research in Brief: Gang Crime and Law Enforcement Recordkeeping* (Report No. NCJ Report 148345). Washington, DC: U.S. Department of Justice.

Curry, G.D. & I.A. Spergel (1988). "Gang Homicide, Delinquency and Community." *Criminology*, 26:381-406.

Curry, G.D. & I.A. Spergel (1992). "Gang Involvement and Delinquency Among Hispanic and African-American Adolescent Males." *Journal of Research in Crime & Delinquency*, 27(3):273-291.

Curry, G.D. & R.W. Thomas (1992). "Community Organization and Gang Policy Response." *Journal of Quantitative Criminology,* 8:357-374.

Daniel, S. (1987). "Prison Gangs: Confronting The Threat." *Corrections Today,* (April):66, 126, 162.

Dart, R.W. (1992). "Chicago's 'Flying Squad' Tackles Street Gangs." *Police Chief,* October:96-104.

Dart, R. (1993). "Street Gang Trends Give Little Cause for Optimism." *CJ The Americas,* 5/6:5-6,8.

Delattre, E.J. (1990, May/June). "New Faces of Organized Crime." *The American Enterprise,* 38-45.

Dery, D. (1984). *Problem Definition in Policy Analysis.* Lawrence, KS: University of Kansas Press.

Dery, D. (1990). *Data & Policy Change: The Fragility of Data in the Policy Context.* Boston, MA: Kluwer Academic Publishers.

Disraeli, B. (1845/1926). *Sybil: The Two Nations.* London: Oxford University Press.

Downs, G.W. & P.D. Larkey (1986). *The Search for Government Efficiency: From Hubris to Helplessness.* Philadelphia, PA: Temple University Press.

Dror, Y. (1968). *Public Policymaking Reexamined.* San Francisco, CA: Chandler Publishing Company.

————— (1986). *Policymaking Under Adversity.* New Brunswick, NJ: Transaction Books.

Dull, R.T. (1984). "An Empirical Examination of the Social Bond Theory of Drug Use." *The International Journal of the Addictions,* 19:265-286.

Dumpson, J.R. (1949). "An Approach to Antisocial Street Gangs." *Federal Probation,* 1:22-29.

Dumpson, J.R., E. Piper & M. Moore (1986). "Violent Delinquents and Urban Youths." *Criminology,* 24:439-471.

Edelman, M. (1964). *The Symbolic Uses of Politics.* Urbana, IL: University of Illinois Press.

Elliott, D.S., D. Huizinga & S.S. Ageton (1985). *Explaining Delinquency and Drug Use.* Newbury Park, CA: Sage.

Empey, L. (1982). *American Delinquency: Its Meaning and Construction.* Homewood, IL: Dorsey.

Erickson, M. (1971). "The Group Context of Delinquent Behavior." *Social Problems,* 19:14-29.

Erlanger, H.S. (1979). "Estrangement, Machismo, and Gang Violence." *Social Science Quarterly,* 60:236-247.

Esbensen, F. (1995). "Overview of the National Evaluation of the GREAT Program." Paper presented at the Annual meeting of the Academy of Criminal Justice Sciences, Boston.

Esbensen, F. & D. Huizinga (1993). "Gangs, Drugs, and Delinquency in a Survey of Urban Youth." *Criminology,* 31:565-589.

Esbensen, F., D. Huizinga & A.W. Weiher (1993). "Gang and Non-Gang Youth: Differences in Explanatory Variables." *Journal of Contemporary Criminal Justice,* 9:94-116.

Fagan, J. (1989). "The Social Organization of Drug Use and Drug Dealing Among Urban Gangs." *Criminology,* 27:649-652.

————— (1990). "Social Processes of Delinquency and Drug Use Among Urban Gangs. In C.R. Huff (ed.), *Gangs in America,* pp.183-219. Newbury Park, CA: Sage Publications, Inc.

Federal Bureau of Investigation (1988). *FBI Organized Crime Report—25 Years After Valachi.* Washington, DC: U.S. Department of Justice.

Field, T.M., P.M. McCabe & N. Schneiderman (1985). *Stress and Coping.* Hillsdale, NJ: Lawrence Erlbaum Associates Publishers.

Floyd, N. (1987). "Terrorism in the Schools." *School Safety,* Winter:22-25.

Folkman, S. (1984). "Personal Control and Stress and Coping Processes: A Theoretical Analysis." *Journal of Personality and Social Psychology,* 46:839-852.

Fong, R.S. (1990). "The Organizational Structure of Prison Gangs: A Texas Case Study." *Federal Probation,* LIV(4):36-43.

Fong, R.S. & S. Buentello (1991a). "The Detection of Prison Gang Development: An Empirical Assessment." *Federal Probation,* LV(1):66-69.

————— (1991b). "The Management of Prison Gangs: An Empirical Model." *The Justice Professional,* (Winter)6(1):66-69.

Fong, R.S. & R.E. Vogel (1994). "A Comparative Analysis of Prison Gang Members, Security Threat Group Inmates and General Population Prisoners in The Texas Department of Corrections." *The Journal of Gang Research,* 2(2):(in press).

Fong, R.S., R.E. Vogel & S. Buentello (1992). "Prison Gang Dynamics: A Look Inside The Texas Department of Corrections." In P.J. Benekos & A.V. Merlo (eds.) *Dilemmas and Directions in Corrections*, pp. 57-78. Cincinnati, OH: Anderson Publishing Co.

Forst, M.L. & M.E. Blomquist (1992). "Punishment, Accountability, and the New Juvenile Justice." *Juvenile and Family Court Journal*, 43:1-10.

Friedman, L.M. (1993). *Crime and Punishment in American History*. New York, NY: Basic Books.

Frye, J.R. (1973). *Locked-Out Americans*. New York, NY: Harper and Row.

Furfey, P.H. (1928). *The Gang Age*. New York, NY: Macmillan.

Furfey, P.H., G.L. Mays & T. Vigil-Backstrom (1994). "Youth Gangs and Incarcerated Delinquents: Exploring the Ties Between Gang Membership, Delinquency, and Social Learning Theory." *Justice Quarterly*, 11(2):229-255.

Galipeau, J (1994). Testimony before the U.S. Senate Juvenile Justice Sub-Committee on Gang Violence. Broadcast on C-Span 2 12/19.

Gang Manual (1994). Santa Rosa, CA: National Law Enforcement Institute, Inc.

Gardner, T.J. & T.M. Anderson (1992). *Criminal Law: Principles and Cases*. St. Paul, MN: West Publishing Company.

Gaustad, J. (1991). *Schools Attack the Roots of Violence*. Office of Educational Research and Improvement. Washington, DC.

Genelin, M. (1991). Violent Street Gangs [Summary]. In Attorney General's *Summit on Law Enforcement Responses to Violent Crime: Public Safety in the Nineties*, pp. 49-51. Washington, DC: Bureau of Justice Statistics (NCJ 130958).

Glueck, S. & E. Glueck (1950). *Unraveling Juvenile Delinquency*. New York, NY: Commonwealth Fund.

Gold, M. (1970). *Delinquent Behavior in an American City*. Palo Alto, CA: Stanford University Press.

Goldstein, A. (1991). *Delinquent Gangs: A Psychological Perspective*. Champaign, IL: Research Press.

——————— (1995). *The Prosocial Gang: Implementing Aggression Training*. Newbury Park, CA: Sage.

Goldstein, A. & C.R. Huff (eds.) (1993). *The Gang Intervention Handbook*. Champaign, IL: Research Press.

Goldstein, H. (1990). *Problem-Oriented Policing*. New York, NY: McGraw-Hill.

Gottfredson, G. & D. Daiger (1979). *Disruption in Six Hundred Schools: The Social Ecology of Personal Victimization in the Nation's Public Schools.* Baltimore, MD: Johns Hopkins University Press.

Gottfredson, M.R. & T. Hirschi (1990). *A General Theory of Crime.* Stanford, CA: Stanford University Press.

Graubard, S.R. (1992). *Mr. Bush's War: Adventures in the Politics of Illusion.* New York, NY: Hill and Wang.

Hagan, J. (1993). "Structural and Cultural Disinvestment and the New Ethnographies of Poverty and Crime." *Contemporary Sociology,* 327-332.

_____ (1994). *Crime and Disrepute.* Thousand Oaks, CA: Pine Forge Press.

Hagedorn, J.M. (1988). *People and Folks.* Chicago, IL: Lake View Press.

_____ (1990). "Back in the Field Again: Gang Research in the Nineties." In C.R. Huff (ed.) *Gangs in America,* pp. 240-259. Newbury Park, CA: Sage.

_____ (1992). "Gangs, Neighborhoods, and Public Policy." *Social Problems,* 38:529-542.

Hamm, M.S. (1995). "Researching Gangs in the 1990s: Pedagogical Implications of the Literature." In J.M. Miller & J. Rush (eds.) *A Criminal Justice Approach to Gangs: From Explanation to Response.*

_____ (1993). *American Skinheads: The Criminology and Control of Hate Crime.* Westport, CT: Praeger.

Hawkins, J.D. & R.F. Catalano (1993). Communities that Care: Risk-Focused Prevention Using the Social Developmental Model. Seattle, WA: Developmental Research and Programs, Inc.

Hearings Before the Government Information, Justice, and Agricultural Subcommittee of the Committee on Government Operations House of Representatives (1990). Oversight of Federal Law Enforcement Assistance Programs Administered by the Department of Justice.

Hellman, D. & S. Beaton (1986). "The Pattern of Violence in Urban Schools: The Influence of School and Community. *Journal of Research in Crime & Delinquency,* 23:102-127.

Hilsman, R. (1992). *George Bush vs. Saddam Hussein: Military Success! Political Failure?* Novato, CA: Lyford Books.

Hindelang, M.J., T. Hirschi & J.G. Weiss (1981). *Measuring Delinquency.* Beverly Hills, CA: Sage.

Hirschi, T. (1969). *Causes of Delinquency.* Berkeley, CA: University of California Press.

Horne, A.M. (1993). "Family-Based Interventions." In A.P. Goldstein & C.R. Huff (eds.) *The Gang Intervention Handbook*. Champaign, IL: Research Press.

Horowitz, R. (1983). *Honor and the American Dream: Culture and Identity in a Chicano Community*. New Brunswick, NJ: Rutgers University Press.

————— (1990). "Sociological Perspectives on Gangs: Conflicting Definitions and Concepts." In C.R. Huff (ed.) *Gangs in America*. Newbury Park, CA: Sage.

Houston, J.G. (1994a). "Gang Migration: Impact on a Small Rural Community in the Midwest." Paper presented at the Annual meeting of the Academy of Criminal Justice Sciences, Chicago.

Huff, C.R. (1989). "Youth Gangs and Public Policy." *Crime & Delinquency*, 34:524-537.

————— (ed.) (1990a). *Gangs in America*. Newbury Park, CA: Sage Publications.

————— (1990b). "Denial, Overreaction, and Misidentification: A Postscript on Public Policy." In C.R. Huff (ed.) *Gangs in America*. Newbury Park, CA: Sage Publications.

Huff, C.R. & W.D. McBride (1993). "Gangs and the Police." In A.P. Goldstein & C.R. Huff (eds.) *The Gang Intervention Handbook*, pp. 401-416. Champaign, IL: Research Press.

Huizinga, D., R. Loeber & T.P. Thornberry (1992, 1994). *Urban Delinquency and Substance Abuse: Technical Report*. Washington DC: U.S. Department of Justice.

Humphrey, K.R. & P.R. Baker (1994). "The GREAT Program: Gang Resistance Education and Training." *FBI Law Enforcement Bulletin*, September:1-4.

Hunt, G., S. Riegel, T. Morales & D. Waldorf (1993). "Changes in Prison Culture: Prison Gangs and The Case of the 'Pepsi Generation'." *Social Problems*, 40(3):398-409.

Jackson, P. (1989). "Theories & Findings About Youth Gangs." *Criminal Justice Abstracts*, June:310-329.

Jackson, P. & W.D. McBride (1987). *Understanding Street Gangs*. Placerville, MA: Custom.

Jackson, P. & C. Rudman (1993). "Moral Panic and the Response to Gangs in California." In Cummings & Monti (1993a) (eds.), pp. 257-275.

Jacobs, J. (1974). *Stateville*. Chicago, IL: University of Chicago Press.

Janis, I.L. (1983). *Groupthink: Psychological Studies of Policy Decisions and Fiascoes*. Boston, MA: Houghton Mifflin Company.

Jankowski, M.S. (1991). *Islands in the Street: Gangs and American Urban Society*. Berkeley, CA: University of California Press.

Jensen, G.F. (1972). "Parents, Peers and Delinquent Action: An Empirical Test of the Differential Association Perspective." *American Journal of Sociology,* 78:63-72.

Kandel, D.B., D. Treiman, R. Faust & E. Single (1976). "Adolescent Involvement in Legal and Illegal Drug Use: A Multiple Classification Analysis." *Social Forces,* 55:438-458.

Kappeler, V.E., M. Blumberg & G.W. Potter (1993). *The Mythology of Crime and Criminal Justice.* Prospect Heights, IL: Waveland Press, Inc.

Kasadra, J.D. (1985). "Urban Change and Minority Involvement." In P.E. Peterson (ed.) *The New Urban Reality.* Washington, DC: Brookings Institute.

Keene, L.L. (1987, September). *Oriental Organized Crime.* Washington, DC: Federal Bureau of Investigation (Limited Distribution).

Keiser, R.L. (1969). *The Vice Lords: Warriors of the Streets.* New York, NY: Holt.

Kelley, B.T. (1994). "A Comprehensive Strategy to Address America's Gang Problem." Washington, DC: U.S. Department of Justice.

Kitsuse, J. & D.C. Dietrick (1959). "Delinquent Boys: A Critique." *American Sociological Review,* 24:208-15.

Klein, M.W. (1971). *Street Gangs and Street Workers.* Englewood Cliffs, NJ: Prentice-Hall.

_____ (1992). "The New Street Gang . . . Or Is It?" *Contemporary Sociology,* 21:80-82.

Klein, M.W., C.L. Maxon & L.C. Cunningham (1991). "Crack, Street Gangs, and Violence." *Criminology,* 29:623-650.

Knox, G.W. (1991). *An Introduction to Gangs.* Berrien Springs, MI: Vande Vere Publishing Ltd.

_____ (1994). "Addressing and Testing the Gang Migration Issue: A Summary of Recent Findings." Paper presented at the Annual meeting of the Academy of Criminal Justice Sciences, Chicago, IL.

_____ (1994). *Gangs and Guns: A Task Force Report.* Chicago, IL: National Gang Crime Research Center, November.

_____ (1994). "Gangs and Guns in the Heartland." Paper presented at the Annual meeting of the American Society of Criminology, Miami, FL.

Knox, G.W., T.F. McCurrie, J.G. Houston, E.D. Tromhanauser & J.L. Laskey (1994). *Results of the 1994 Illinois Law Enforcement Survey: A Preliminary Report on Gang Migration and Other Gang Problems in Illinois Today.* Chicago, IL: National Gang Crime Research Center, March 31.

Knox, G.W. & E.D. Tromhanauser (1991). "Gangs and Their Control in Adult Correctional Institutions." *The Prison Journal*, LXXI(2):15-22.

Kornhouser, R.R. (1978). *Social Sources of Delinquency*. Chicago, IL: University of Chicago Press.

Kramer, L.C. (1986). *How Will Changes in the Asian Population Impact Street Gang-Related Crime in California?* Sacramento, CA: California Commission on Peace Officer Standards and Training.

Krohn, M.D., R.L. Akers, M.J. Radosevich & L. Lanza-Kaduce (1982). "Norm Qualities and Adolescent Drinking and Drug Behavior: The Effect of Norm Quality and Reference Group on Using and Abusing Alcohol and Marijuana." *Journal of Drug Issues*, 4:343-359.

Larsen, D. & B. Abu-Laban (1968). "Norm Qualities and Deviant Drinking Behavior." *Social Problems*, 15:441-450.

Laskey, J.L. (1994). "Gang Migration by Parental Good Intentions: Moving to New Neighborhoods Within a Metropolitan Area." Paper presented at the Annual meeting of the Academy of Criminal Justice Sciences, Chicago, IL.

Lasley, J.R. (1992). "Age, Social Context, and Street Gang Membership: Are 'Youth' Gangs Becoming 'Adult' Gangs?" *Youth and Society*, 23:434-451.

Levine, R.A. (1972). *Public Planning: Failure and Redirection*. New York, NY: Basic Books, Inc.

Liebow, E. (1967). *Tally's Corner*. Boston, MA: Little, Brown and Company.

Lilly, J. R., F.T. Cullen & R.A. Ball (1989). *Criminological Theory: Context and Consequences*. Newbury Park, CA: Sage.

Lindblom, C. (1965). *The Intelligence of Democracy: Decision-Making Through Mutual Adjustment*. New York, NY: The Free Press.

Lo, C.N. (1991). "A Social Model of Gang-Related Violence." *Free Inquiry in Creative Sociology*, 19:37-44.

Lozano, A.R., G.L. Mays & L.T. Winfree, Jr. (1990). "Diagnosing Delinquents: The Purposes of a Youth Diagnostic Center." *Juvenile and Family Court Journal*, 41:25-39.

Lukas, J.A. (1985). *Common Ground: A Turbulent Decade in the Lives of Three American Families*. New York, NY: Random House.

Lyon, J.M., S. Henggeler & J.A. Hall (1992). "The Family Relations, Peer Relations, and Criminal Activities of Caucasian and Hispanic-American Gang Members." *Journal of Abnormal Psychology*, 20:439-449.

MacLeod, J. (1987). *Ain't No Makin' It: Leveled Aspirations in a Low-Income Neighborhood.* Boulder, CO: Westview.

Majors, R. & J.M. Billson (1992). *Cool Pose: The Dilemmas of Black Manhood in America.* New York, NY: Lexington Books.

Mann, C.R. (1993). *Unequal Justice: A Question of Color.* Bloomington, IN: Indiana University Press.

Martin, R., R.J. Mutchnick & W.T. Austin (1990). *Criminological Thought: Pioneers Past and Present.* New York, NY: Macmillan.

Matsueda, R.L. & K. Heimer (1987). "Race, Family Structure, and Delinquency: A Test of Differential Association and Social Control Theories." *American Sociological Review,* 52:826-840.

Maxson, C.L. (1993). "Investigating Gang Migration: Contextual Issues," *The Gang Journal,* 2:1-8.

Maxson, C.L. & M. Klein (1994). "Gang Structures and Crime Patterns in U.S. Cities." Presented at the Annual meeting of the American Society of Criminology, Miami, FL.

McBride, Sergeant W. (1990). Speech given at Gulf Shores, Alabama, September.

McConnell, E.H. (1993). "Gangs, School Safety, and Violence." Paper presented to the Southern Criminal Justice Association, Charleston, SC, October 9.

———— (1994). *Texas Youth Gangs: Final Report to FYSB/DHHS,* Washington, DC: Department of Health and Human Services.

McDermott, J. (1983). "Crime in the School and in the Community: Offenders, Victims, and Fearful Youth." *Crime & Delinquency,* 29:270-282.

McKinney, K.C. (1988). *Juvenile Gangs: Crime and Drug Trafficking.* Washington, DC: U.S. Department of Justice, Office of Juvenile Justice and Delinquency Prevention.

Menacker, J., W. Weldon & E. Hurwitz (1982). *Crime by Youth Gangs and Groups in the United States.* Washington DC: National Institute of Juvenile Justice and Delinquency Prevention, U.S. Department of Justice.

———— (1990). "Community Influence on School Crime and Violence." *Urban Education,* 25:68-80.

Merton, R.K. (1938). "Social Structure and Anomie." *American Sociological Review* 3:672-682.

Messner, S.F. & R.R. Rosenfeld (1994). *Crime and the American Dream.* Belmont, CA: Wadsworth Publishing Company.

Mieczkowski, T. (1986). "Geeking Up and Throwing Down: Heroin Street Life in Detroit." *Criminology*, 24:645-666.

———— (1988). "Crack Distribution in Detroit." Presented at the annual meeting of the American Society of Criminology, Chicago.

Miller, W.B. (1958). "Lower-Class Culture as a Generating Milieu of Gang Delinquency." *Journal of Social Issues*, 14:5-19.

———— (1962). "The Impact of a 'Total Community' Delinquency Control Project." *Social Problems*, 10:168-191.

———— (1974). "American Youth Gangs: Past and Present." In A. Blumberg (ed.) *Current Perspectives on Criminal Behavior*. New York, NY: Knopf.

———— (1990). "Why the United States Has Failed to Solve Its Youth Gang Problem." In C.R. Huff (ed.) *Gangs in America*, pp. 263-287. Newbury Park, CA: Sage.

Mills, C.W. (1959). *The Sociological Imagination*. New York, NY: Oxford University Press.

Moles, O. (1987). "Trends in Student Misconduct: The 70s and the 80s." Paper presented at the annual meeting of the American Educational Research Association, Washington, DC.

Moore, J. (1978). *Homeboys: Gangs, Drugs, and Prisons in the Barrios of Los Angeles*. Philadelphia, PA: Temple University Press.

———— (1983). "Residence and Territoriality in Chicano Gangs." *Social Problems*, 31:182-94.

———— (1985). "Isolation and Stigmatization in the Development of an Underclass: The Case of Chicano Gangs in East Los Angeles." *Social Problems*, 33:1-10.

———— (1988). "Changing Chicano Gangs: Acculturation, Generational Change, Evolution of Deviance or Emerging Underclass?" In J.H. Johnson, Jr. & M.L. Oliver (eds.) *Proceedings of the Conference on Comparative Ethnicity*. Los Angeles, CA: Institute for Social Science Research, UCLA.

Moos, R.H. & J.A. Schaefer (1986). "Life Transitions and Crises: A Conceptual Overview. In Moos in collaboration with Schaefer (eds.) *Coping with Life Crises: An Integrated Approach*, pp. 3-28. New York, NY: Plenum Press.

Morash, M. (1983). "Gangs, Groups, and Delinquency." *British Journal of Criminology*, 23:309-335.

Moriarty, A. & T. Fleming (1990). "Youth Gangs Aren't Just a Big-City Problem Anymore. *Executive Educator*, 12:13-16.

Moynihan, D.P. (1975). *Coping: On the Practice of Government.* New York, NY: Vintage Books.

National School Safety Center (1986). School Safety Programs, Office of Juvenile Justice and Delinquency Prevention. Washington, DC.

_____ (1988). *Gangs in School: Breaking Up is Hard to Do.* Office of Juvenile Justice and Delinquency Prevention. Washington, DC: U.S.Government Printing Office.

Needle J.A. & W.V. Stapleton (1983). *Police Handling of Youth Gangs.* Washington DC: National Institute of Justice.

Nichols, D. (1991). "Preparing for School Crises." *FBI Law Enforcement Bulletin,* 60:20-24.

Nichols, Sergeant M. (1994). Testimony Before the U.S. Senate Juvenile Justice Sub-Committee on Gang Violence. Broadcast on C-Span 2 12/19.

Nielson, S. (1992) "The Emergence of Gang Activity: One Junior High School's Response." *NASSP Bulletin,* 76:61-67.

Office of Juvenile Justice and Delinquency Prevention (1993). *Comprehensive Strategy for Serious, Violent, and Chronic Juvenile Offenders: Program Summary.* (Report No. NCJ 143453). Washington, DC: U.S. Department of Justice.

Okaty, G. (1991). "Kids at School/Kids at Risk." *Police Chief,* 58:39-41.

Orcutt, J.D. (1983). *Analyzing Deviance.* Chicago, IL: The Dorsey Press.

Organized Crime Statutes (1995). 11 *Texas Penal Code Sections* 71.01-71.05.

Osgood, D.W., P.M. O'Malley, J.G. Bachman & L.D. Johnston (1989). "Time Trends and Age Trends in Arrests and Self-Reported Illegal Behavior." *Criminology,* 27:389-417.

Owens, R.P. & D.K. Wells (1993). "One City's Response to Gangs." *Police Chief,* 58:25-27.

Pace, D.F. (1991). *Concepts of Vice, Narcotics, and Organized Crime* (3rd ed.). Englewood Cliffs, NJ: Prentice-Hall.

Padilla, F.M. (1992). *The Gang as an American Enterprise.* New Brunswick, NJ: Rutgers University Press.

Palumbo, D.J., R. Eskay & M. Hallet (1992). "Do Gang Prevention Strategies Actually Reduce Crime?" *The Gang Journal,* 1:1-10.

Pearson, F. & J. Toby (1991). "Fear of School-Related Predatory Crime." *Sociology and Social Research,* 75:117-125.

Pfohl, S. (1992). *Death at the Parasite Cafe: Social Science Fiction and the Postmodern.* New York, NY: St. Martin's Press.

Philippians (1953). *The Holy Bible.* Revised standard version. New York, NY: Thomas Nelson and Sons.

Piller, C. (1991). *The Fail-Safe Society: Community Defiance and the End of Technological Optimism.* New York, NY: Basic Books.

Pink, W. (1984). "Schools, Youth, and Justice." *Crime & Delinquency,* 30:3.

President's Commission on Organized Crime (1986). *The Impact: Organized Crime Today* (Report No. 1986 0-168-556:QL3). Washington, DC: U.S. Government Printing Office.

Prophet, M. (1990). "Safe Schools in Portland." *American School Board Journal,* 177:28-30.

Prothrow-Stith, D. with M. Weissman (1991). *Deadly Consequences.* New York, NY: Harper Collins Publishers.

Puffer, J.A. (1912). *The Boy and His Gang.* Boston, MA: Houghton, Mifflin.

Quade, E.S. & G.M. Carter (1989). *Analysis for Public Decisions.* New York, NY: North Holland.

Quinn, J.F., P.M. Tobolowsky & W.T. Downs (1994). "The Gang Problem in Large and Small Cities: An Analysis of Police Perceptions in Nine States." *Journal of Gang Research,* 2:13-23.

Racketeer Influences and Corrupt Organizations (1970). 18 U.S.C. Sections 1961-1968.

Ralph, P.H. & J.W. Marquart (1991). "Gang Violence in Texas Prisons." *The Prison Journal,* LXXI(2):38-49.

Rattay, K. & J. Lewis (1990). "Gangs and the School: A Plan for Action." *Thrust,* 19:17-22.

Reid, S.T. (1990). *Crime and Criminology.* Fort Worth, TX: Holt, Rinehart, and Winston, Inc.

Reum, E. (1992). "Student Activity Programs Enhance Education Experience for Nation's Youth." *NASSP Bulletin,* 76:60-65.

Reuter, P. (1989). "Youth Gangs and Drug Distribution: A Preliminary Study." Paper prepared for the Office of Juvenile Justice and Delinquency Prevention. Washington, DC: RAND Corporation.

Rogers, J.W. (1977). *Why Are You Not a Criminal?* Englewood Cliffs, NJ: Prentice-Hall.

Sanders, W.B. (1994). *Gangbangs and Drivebys: Grounded Culture and Juvenile Gang Violence*. New York, NY: Aldine de Gruyter.

SchSeingold, S.A. (1991). *The Politics of Street Crime: Criminal Process and Cultural Obsession*. Philadelphia, PA: Temple University Press.

Schur, E.M. (1973). *Radical Nonintervention: Rethinking the Delinquency Problem*. Englewood Cliffs, NJ: Prentice-Hall.

Schwartz, A. (1989). "Middle-Class Educational Values Among Latino Gang Members in East Los Angeles County High Schools." *Urban Education*, 24:323-342.

Sellers, C.S., L.T. Winfree, Jr. & C.T. Griffiths (1993). "Legal Attitudes, Permissive Norm Qualities and Substance Use: A Comparison of American Indian and Non-Indian Youths." *Journal of Drug Issues*, 23:493-513.

Sellers, C.S. & L.T. Winfree, Jr. (1990). "Differential Associations and Definitions: A Panel Study of Youthful Drinking Behavior." *The International Journal of the Addictions*, 25:753-769.

Shaw, C.R. (1930). *The Jack Roller: A Delinquent Boy's Own Story*. Chicago, IL: University of Chicago Press.

Shaw, CR. & H.D. McKay (1942). *Juvenile Delinquency in Urban Areas*. Chicago, IL: University of Chicago Press.

Shaw, J. (1989). "Dealing Effectively With Gangs." *Thrust*, 18:12-13.

Sheley, J.F. & J.D. Wright (1993). *Research in Brief: Gun Acquisition and Possession in Selected Juvenile Samples* (Report No. NCJ 145326). Washington, DC: U.S. Department of Justice.

Shelley, L.I. (1981). *Crime and Modernization*. Carbondale, IL: Southern Illinois University Press.

Shoemaker, D.J. (1984). *Theories of Delinquency: An Examination of Explanations of Delinquent Behavior*. New York, NY: Oxford University Press.

Short, J.F. (1963). "Foreword." In F.M. Thrasher *The Gang*. Chicago, IL: University of Chicago Press.

_____ (1989). "Exploring Integration of Theoretical Levels of Explanation: Notes on Gang Delinquency." In S.F. Messner, MD. Krohn & A.E. Liske (eds.) *Theoretical Integration in the Study of Deviance and Crime: Problems and Prospects*. Albany, NY: SUNY Press.

_____ (1990). "Gangs, Neighborhoods and Youth Crime," *Criminal Justice Research Bulletin*, 4:1-11.

Short, J.F. & F.I. Nye (1958). "Extent of Incarcerated Juvenile Delinquency." *Journal of Criminal Law, Criminology, and Police Science,* 49:296-302.

Short, J.F. & F. Stodtbeck (1965). *Group Process and Gang Delinquency.* Chicago, IL: University of Chicago Press.

Siegel, L.J. & J.J. Senna (1981). *Juvenile Delinquency: Theory, Practice & Law.* St. Paul, MN: West Publishing Co.

Silwa C. (1987). Speech given at Birmingham, Alabama, October.

Simon, H. (1976). *Administrative Behavior.* New York, NY: Free Press.

Skolnick, J. (1988). The Social Structure of Street Drug Dealing—BCS Forum. Bureau of Criminal Statistics. Sacramento, CA: Office of the Attorney General.

————— (1990). *Gang Organization and Migration.* Sacramento, CA: Office of the Attorney General of the State of California.

Skolnick, J.H., R. Blumenthal & T. Correl (1990). "Gang Organization and Migration." Berkeley, CA: Center for the Study of Law and Society, Feb. 18, 1990.

Speirs, V. (1988). Safer Schools, Better Schools, Office of Juvenile Justice and Delinquency Prevention, Washington, DC.

Spergel, I.A. (1964). *Racketville Slumtown Haulberg.* Chicago, IL: University of Chicago Press.

————— (1966). *Street Gang Work: Theory and Practice.* Reading, MA: Addison-Wesley.

————— (1984). "Violent Gangs in Chicago: In Search of Social Policy." *Social Service Review,* 58:199-226.

————— (1986). "The Violent Gang in Chicago: A Local Community Approach." *Social Science Review,* 60:94-131.

————— (1989). "Youth Gangs: Continuity and Change." In N. Morris & M. Tonry (eds.) *Crime and Justice: An Annual Review of Research* (Vol. 12). Chicago, IL: Chicago University Press.

————— (1994). Testimony before the U.S. Senate Juvenile Justice Subcommittee on Gang Violence. Broadcast on C-Span 2, 12/19.

Spergel, I. & G.D. Curry (1990). "Strategies and Perceived Agency Effectiveness in Dealing With the Youth Gang Problem." In C.R. Huff (ed.) *Gangs in America,* pp. 288-309. Newbury Park, CA: Sage.

Stockman, D.A. (1987). *The Triumph of Politics: The Inside Story of the Reagan Revolution.* New York, NY: Avon.

Stone, D.A. (1988). *Policy Paradox and Political Reason*. Glenview, IL: Scott, Foresman and Little, Brown.

Stover, D. (1986). "A New Breed of Youth Gang is on the Prowl and a Bigger Threat Than Ever." *American School Board Journal*, 173(8):19-25.

Sullivan, C. (1991). "Prison Gangs: A Look At The Deadly Gangs That Receive Little Publicity." *Police*, (November):38-40, 91-92.

Sullivan, M.L. (1989). *Getting Paid: Youth Crime and Work in the Inner City*. Ithaca, NY: Cornell University Press.

Summers, Colonel H.G., Jr. (Ret.) (1992). *On Strategy II: A Critical Analysis of the Gulf War*. New York, NY: Dell Publishing.

Sutherland, E. (1947). *Principles of Criminology*. Philadelphia, PA: J.B. Lippincott.

Sutherland, E., T. Vigil-Blackstrom & G.L. Mays (1994). "Social Learning Theory, Self-Reported Delinquency, and Youth Gangs: A New Twist on a General Theory of Crime and Delinquency." *Youth and Society*, 26(2):147-177.

Tannenbaum, F. (1938). *Crime and the Community*. New York, NY: Columbia University Press.

Tapp, J.T. (1985). *Multisystems Holistic Model of Health, Stress and Coping*. In Field et al. pp. 285-304.

Taylor, C.S. (1990). *Dangerous Society*. East Lansing, MI: Michigan State University Press.

Taylor, C.S. (1990). "Gang Imperialism." In C.R. Huff (ed.) *Gangs in America*, pp. 103-115. Newbury Park, CA: Sage Publications, Inc.

Thompson, D.W. & L.A. Jason (1988). "Street Gangs and Preventive Interventions." *Criminal Justice and Behavior*, 15(3):323-333.

Thornberry, T.P. (1987). "Toward and Interactional Theory of Delinquency." *Criminology*, 25:863-891.

Thornberry, T., M. Moore & R. Christenson (1985). "The Effect of Dropping Out of High School on Subsequent Criminal Behavior." *Criminology*, 23:3-18.

Thornberry, T.P., M. Krohn, A. Lizotte & D. Chard-Wierschem (1993). "The Role of Juvenile Gangs in Facilitating Delinquent Behavior." *Journal of Research in Crime and Delinquency*, 30:55-87.

Thrasher, F.M. (1927). *The Gang; A Study of 1,313 Gangs in Chicago*. Chicago, IL: The University of Chicago Press.

Toby, J. (1983). *Violence in Schools: A Research Brief*. National Institute of Justice, Washington, DC.

Topping, R. (1943). "Treatment of the Pseudo-Social Boy." *American Journal of Orthopsychiatry,* 1:313-360.

Tromhanauser, E.D. (1994). "A Statewide Analysis of Gang Migration: Illinois Law Enforcement Data." Paper presented at the Annual meeting of the Academy of Criminal Justice Sciences, Chicago, IL.

U.S. Department of Justice (1993). *Crime in the United States 1992: Uniform Crime Reports.* Washington, DC: U.S. Department of Justice.

U.S. Senate Judiciary Committee (1975). School Violence and Vandalism. Hearings before Subcommittee to Investigate Juvenile Delinquency. Washington, DC.

Vetter, H.J. & I.J. Silverman (1980). *The Nature of Crime.* Philadelphia, PA: W.B. Saunders Company.

Vickers, G. (1970). *Value Systems and Social Process.* Harmondsworth. Middlesex, England: Penguin Books.

Vigil, J.D. (1988). *Barrio Gangs: Street Life and Identity in Southern California.* Austin, TX: University of Texas Press.

_____ (1990). "Cholos and Gangs: Culture Change and Street Youth in Los Angeles." In C.R. Huff (ed.) *Gangs in America.* Newbury Park, CA: Sage.

Vigil, J.D. & J.M. Long (1990). "Emic and Etic Perspectives on Gang Culture: The Chicano Case." In C.R. Huff (ed.) *Gangs in America,* Newbury Park, CA: Sage.

Vold, G.B. & T.J. Bernard (1986). *Theoretical Criminology* (3rd Edition). New York, NY: Oxford University Press.

Waldorf, D. (1993). "When The Crips Invaded San Francisco—Gang Migration." *The Gang Journal,* 4:11-16.

Weiner, J.A. (1993). "Priority Prosecution of Juveniles in Philadelphia. *National Institute of Justice Journal,* 11:29-31.

Weldon, B.A. (1990). *Guide for the Identification of Street Gangs.* Birmingham, AL: Birmingham Police Department (Limited Distribution).

Werthman, C. (1967). "The Function of Social Definitions in the Development of Delinquent Careers." In P.G. Garabedian & DC. Gibbons (eds.) *Becoming Delinquent: Young Offenders and the Correctional Process.* Chicago, IL: Aldine.

Werthman, C. & I. Piliavin (1967). "Gang Members and the Police." In D. Bodura (ed.) *The Police: Six Sociological Essays.* New York, NY: Wiley.

Weston, J. (1993). "Community Policing: An Approach to Youth Gangs in a Medium-Sized City." *Police Chief,* August:80-84.

Wetzel, J. (1988). "Kids and Crime." *School Safety*, Spring:4-7.

Whyte, W.F. (1943). *Street Corner Society; The Social Structure of an Italian Slum*. Chicago, IL: The University of Chicago Press.

Wildavsky, A. (1964-1993). *The Politics of the Budgetary Process* (several editions). Boston, MA: Little Brown.

Wildavsky, A. (1979). *Speaking Truth to Power: The Art and Craft of Policy Analysis*. Boston, MA: Little, Brown.

Williams, L.E., L. Clinton, L.T. Winfree, Jr. & R.E. Clark (1992). "Family Ties, Parental Discipline, and Delinquency: A Study of Youthful Misbehavior by Parochial High School Students." *Sociological Spectrum*, 12:381-401.

Wilson, J. (1977). *Crime in the Schools, Violence in Schools: Perspectives, Programs and Positions*. Lexington, MA: Heath.

Wilson, J.Q. (1990). "Drugs and Crime." In M. Tonry & J.Q. Wilson (eds.) *Drugs and Crime*. Chicago, IL: University of Chicago Press.

Wilson, J.Q. & R.J. Herrnstein (1985). *Crime and Human Nature*. New York, NY: Simon and Schuster.

Wilson, W.J. (1987). *The Truly Disadvantaged: The Inner City, the Underclass, and Public Policy*. Chicago, IL: University of Chicago Press.

Winfree, L.T., Jr. (1985). "Peers, Parents, and Adolescent Drug Use in a Rural Community: A Two-Wave Panel Study." *Journal of Youth and Adolescence*, 14(6):499-512.

Winfree, L.T., T. Vigil & G.L. Mays (1994). "Social Learning Theory and Youth Gangs: A New Twist on a General Theory of Crime and Delinquency." *Youth and Society*, 26:147-177.

_____ & C.T. Griffiths (1985). "Trends in Drug Orientations and Behavior: Changes in a Rural Community, 1975-1982." *International Journal of the Addictions*, 20:1503-1516.

Wolfgang, M.E. & F. Ferracuti (1967). *The Subculture of Violence: Towards An Integrated Theory in Criminology*. London: Tavistock.

Yablonsky, L. (1959). "The Gang as a Near-Group." *Social Problems*, 7:108-117.

_____ (1962). *The Violent Gang*. New York, NY: Macmillan.

Zevitz, R. & S. Takata (1992). "Metropolitan Gang Influence and the Emergence of Group Delinquency in a Regional Community." *Journal of Criminal Justice*, 20:93-106.

Subject Index

accessing gangs 17
adaptation 8, 157
agency-based research 22
anti-gang programs 66, 89, 91, 135

casework 26
Chicago School 4
collaborative research model 25
colors 64
conflict perspective 11
control theory 12
coping 157
courage 21
courthouse criminology 5, 149
crisis intervention 63

demagoguery 151
denial 86
DID syndrome 85
differential association 43
drug trafficking 20, 60, 79

economic opportunity 12-13
employment opportunity 6, 13
emulation 72
enterprise theory 97
ethnography 4

familial transplant 74, 159
family control 13, 36
field research 4
firearms 60
franchising 75, 78, 101

gang-related 5
gang control 156
gang culture 15
gang definition 146
gang development 6
gang expansion 110

geographic dispersion 75-76, 132
gun control 60, 155-156
graffiti 64-66

hand signals 40
historical portrayals 3, 131, 143
homicide 96, 98

imperialism 75
intelligence processing 88
interstitial 6
intervention1 34

labeling theory 11, 61

martial arts 19
measurement 147
media portrayals 15, 90, 147
migration 68, 71

near-group 6, 73-76

organized crime groups 94
overlabeling 5, 87

participant observation 18
peer influence 40-43
policy analysis 144
policy recommendations 14, 140, 150
prison field studies 29
prison gang development 107
prison gang expansion 116
prison gang structure 119-120
prison transfers 73
proliferation 72
psychosis 7
public perception 1, 144

race 7, 14
racism 14

181

About the Contributors

Salvador Buentello—the leading gang specialist and vice chairman of the State Classification Committee in the Institution Division of the Texas Department of Criminal Justice. He was a member of the ACA advisory board for the nationwide study of prison gangs. He also serves as a consultant to the National Institute of Corrections on prison gang dynamics. He has been called to testify as an expert witness in many criminal trials involving prison gang members both in federal and state courts.

Albert Cohen—Professor Emeritus, University of Connecticut. A pioneer in cultural deviance theory and a nationally recognized expert in the area of gangs, Professor Cohen is an American Society of Criminology Fellow and a past president of the ASC and the Society for the Study of Social Problems.

Finn-Aage Esbensen—Associate Professor, Department of Criminal Justice, University of Nebraska at Omaha. He has published numerous articles on delinquency and drug use, most recently in *Criminology*, *Journal of Contemporary Criminal Justice* and the *Journal of Criminal Law and Criminology*.

Robert S. Fong—associate professor and chairperson of the Department of Criminal Justice at California State University—Bakersfield. He received his Ph.D. from Sam Houston State University in 1987. Previously he served as an assistant professor at the University of North Carolina—Charlotte and later at East Carolina University. His primary research interest is in the area of prison gangs.

Mark S. Hamm—Professor in the Department of Criminology at Indiana State University. He is a nationally recognized expert on the subject of hate crime and author of *American Skinheads: The Criminology and Control of Hate Crimes*.

James G. Houston—Associate Professor of Criminal Justice at St. Ambrose University. Dr. Houston has recently authored a book on correctional management and has extensive experience with Gang Research Task Forces. His previous research has included a census of incarcerated gang members in the midwest.

George W. Knox—Director of the Gang Research Center, Chicago State University and Editor-in-Chief of *The Gang Journal: An Interdisciplinary Research Quarterly*. He is the author of numerous articles, chapters and books on gangs, including *An Introduction to Gangs* (1991), which has recently been expanded for a 2nd edition (1993).

John A. Laskey—Instructor of Criminal Justice at Morton College in Cicero, IL and sergeant in a major midwestern police department.

G. Larry Mays—Professor of Criminal Justice at New Mexico State University. Dr. Mays served as a police officer in Knoxville, Tennessee and has been a faculty member at East Tennessee State University and Appalachian State University. He has published in numerous regional and national jails and has coauthored two texts.

Elizabeth McConnell—Assistant Professor of Criminal Justice at Valdosta State University. Dr. McConnell has published on gangs in various journals and serves on the Board of Directors of the Southern Criminal Justice Association.

Thomas F. McCurrie—Managing editor of *The Gang Journal* and a former chief investigator for Cook County, IL. Professor McCurrie has co-authored a variety of publications on gangs and is involved extensively in providing gang training to police and in public service through the production of cable television shows about gang problems.

J. Mitchell Miller—Ph.D. candidate in the Department of Sociology at the University of Tennessee. He authored the 1993 ACJS/Anderson Outstanding Paper Award and the 1993 SCJA Outstanding Graduate Student Paper Award. A former research associate for the Society for the Study of Social Problems and an American Sociological Association Honors Program selection, he has recently published in *Justice Quarterly*, *American Journal of Criminal Justice*, and the *Journal of Crime and Justice*.

Gregory Orvis—Assistant Professor of Criminal Justice at the University of Texas at Tyler. He received his J.D. from Tulane and his Ph.D. from the University of Houston.

Jeffrey P. Rush—Assistant Professor of Criminal Justice in the College of Criminal Justice at Jacksonville State University. He received his Doctor of Public Administration degree from the University of Alabama. His interests include juvenile justice policy, practice, and law; gangs and cults; and law enforcement. He is a Reviewing Editor of *The Gang Journal* and immediate Past President of the Southern Criminal Justice Association.

Ira Sharkansky—Wolfson Professor of Public Administration at the Hebrew University. His research on policymaking in several contexts enjoys international regard.

Edward Tromanhauser—Professor and Chair of the Department of Criminal Justice at Chicago State University. He co-authored *Schools Under Siege* (1992) with George Knox and David Laske, a research-based book on gang violence in schools today. Dr. Tromanhauser's expertise on violence in the schools and social intervention programs is well known.

Ronald E. Vogel is currently a professor and chairperson of the Department of Criminal Justice at California State University—Long Beach. He received his Ed.D. from the University of Massachusetts—Amherst in 1978. After receiving his degree, he taught one year at West Georgia College and twelve years at the University of North Carolina—Charlotte where he was chairperson for three years before relocating to California.

L. Thomas Winfree—Professor of Criminal Justice at New Mexico State University. He has published widely on gangs in several journals and textbooks.